More Praise for *Joyful Reading*

"I have never seen so many students reading with this level of enjoyment before! In the SEM-R, every child is engaged in challenging and interesting reading."

—**Dr. Willard White, program planner, Palm Beach County Schools, Florida**

"This important book, *Joyful Reading,* presents strategies for helping all students become independent, engaged, and motivated readers. The SEM-R is unique in that it is both evidence based and also extremely practical and teacher friendly."

—**Michael D. Coyne, associate professor, Department of Educational Psychology, Special Education Program, Center for Behavioral Education and Research, University of Connecticut**

"In classrooms using SEM-R I have seen a new relationship between the teachers and their students. They share their interests, passions, and insights through sharing books, conferencing, and journaling."

—**Melanie Crawford, literacy coach, Capitol Hill School, St. Paul Public Schools, Minnesota**

Jossey-Bass Teacher

Jossey-Bass Teacher provides educators with practical knowledge and tools to create a positive and lifelong impact on student learning. We offer classroom-tested and research-based teaching resources for a variety of grade levels and subject areas. Whether you are an aspiring, new, or veteran teacher, we want to help you make every teaching day your best.

From ready-to-use classroom activities to the latest teaching framework, our value-packed books provide insightful, practical, and comprehensive materials on the topics that matter most to K–12 teachers. We hope to become your trusted source for the best ideas from the most experienced and respected experts in the field.

Joyful Reading
Differentiation and Enrichment for Successful Literacy Learning, Grades K–8

Sally M. Reis

with

Rebecca D. Eckert
Elizabeth A. Fogarty
Catherine A. Little
Angela M. Housand
Sheelah M. Sweeny
Brian C. Housand
Lisa M. Muller
Erin E. Sullivan

JOSSEY-BASS
A Wiley Imprint
www.josseybass.com

Published by Jossey-Bass
A Wiley Imprint
989 Market Street, San Francisco, CA 94103-1741—www.josseybass.com

Jossey-Bass books and products are available through most bookstores. To contact Jossey-Bass directly call our Customer Care Department within the U.S. at 800-956-7739, outside the U.S. at 317-572-3986, or fax 317-572-4002.

Jossey-Bass also publishes its books in a variety of electronic formats. Some content that appears in print may not be available in electronic books.

Library of Congress Cataloging-in-Publication Data

Reis, Sally M.
    Joyful reading: differentiation and enrichment for successful literacy learning / Sally M. Reis.
        p.   cm.
    "Grades K–8."
    Includes bibliographical references and index.
        ISBN 978-0-470-22881-4 (pbk.)
        1. Reading (Elementary)   2. Reading (Middle school)   3. Individualized instruction.   I. Eckert, Rebecca D.   II. Title.
    LB1573.R43 2009
    372.41'7—dc22   2008050159

Printed in the United States of America
FIRST EDITION
PB Printing   10 9 8 7 6 5 4 3 2

Contents

About This Book   ix

About the Authors   xiii

Part One: Toward Joyful Reading   1

**1.   The Schoolwide Enrichment Model for
Reading   3**

Why Now?   5

Case Studies of Children Who Have Benefited from
SEM-R Programs   6

Introduction to The Schoolwide Enrichment Model for
Reading   8

Goals of the SEM-R   9

Background on the SEM-R   13

Research on the SEM-R   17

Teachers' Perceptions of Their Success with
SEM-R Programs   18

Summary   20

2.   Why Differentiate Reading Instruction?   21

Changing Classroom Demographics and Types of Reading
Programs   21

Declining Reading for All Students   22

Children Learn Differently   24

Self-Regulation and Study Skills   31
Differentiation and the Use of Differentiated Teaching Strategies
to Teach Reading   35
What We Have Learned About Using Differentiated Instruction
in a SEM-R Program   41
Summary   44

3.   **Reading Instruction Essentials   45**
What Is Reading and How Should It Be Taught?   46
Developmentally Appropriate Practices for
Teaching Reading   47
Reading Comprehension Strategies   52
Summary   61

Part Two: The SEM-R Program Phases   63

4.   **Hooking Kids on Reading: Phase One   65**
Home and School Connections: Children with Literacy
Advantages   66
Exciting Phase One Book Hooks   68
Bookmarks with Embedded Reading Strategies   80
Resources to Help You Find the Best Books for Your
Book Hooks   82
Phase One: Indicators of High-Quality Book Hooks   84
Summary   88

5.   **Supporting Independent Reading: Phase Two   89**
Book Match: Finding Appropriately Challenging
Reading Material   91
Reading Conferences: Differentiating Instruction to Meet the
Needs of All Readers   95
Self-Regulation and Supported Independent Reading   102
Assessing Phase Two of a SEM-R Program   112
Phase Two: Indicators of High Quality in Supported
Independent Reading   113
Summary   113

6.   **Facilitating Interest and Choice: Phase Three   115**
The Rationale for Phase Three   115
Implementing Phase Three: Stories from Two Classrooms   117
Getting Started with Phase Three   119
A Continuum of Services   119
Student-Selected Activities   121

Teacher-Directed Creativity Activities   123
Independent Student Activities   124
Phase Three: Indicators of High-Quality Facilitation of Independent Student Work   130
Summary   131

Part Three: Succeeding with the SEM-R   133

7.   Library and Classroom Management Strategies   135
Creating and Organizing Your Classroom Library   135
Organizing Your Library for Optimal Matches in Reading   137
Physical Setup of the Classroom   142
Managing Conferences   144
Helping with Transitions Between Phases in a SEM-R Program   147
Incorporating the SEM-R in an Elementary Reading Classroom   150
Adapting the SEM-R for Use in a Middle School   150
Summary   152

8.   Differentiated Practices to Challenge All Readers   153
A Rich Mix of Students   154
Reading Stages of Development   155
Matching Readers to Texts   157
Talented Readers   161
Strategies to Support Students with Reading Difficulties   167
Summary   172

9.   The Role of the SEM-R Coach   173
Role of a Coach   174
Coaching During All SEM-R Phases   178
Ongoing Professional Development and Classroom Support   181
Coaching in Action: Sample Situations   184
Summary   190

10.   The SEM-R Program in After-School and Other Settings   193
The SEM-R Program After School   193
Expanding the Vision   198

Appendix A: Sample SEM-R Bookmarks   199
Appendix B: Reading Interest-a-Lyzer   205

Appendix C: Books for Young, Talented Readers   209

Appendix D: Template for Sun/Cloud Card   213

Appendix E: Chart for Recording Growth in Reading Time   215

Appendix F: Teacher Log: Sample and Template   217

Appendix G: Student Log: Sample and Template   227

References   235

Index   241

About the DVD: Joyful Reading for All Children   253

How to Use the DVD   255

About This Book

My dream about the enrichment approach to reading that you will read about in this book is that if you decide to use it in your classroom, you will do so to give your students the gift of loving to read. Nothing has saddened me more during the last few decades than watching the declining student interest and joy in reading that has become widespread in our schools. Good books give children the gift of imagination and creativity; they enable children to see beyond their lives and experiences and dream of a future that is ripe with ideas and possibilities. Books teach children about character, courage, and other ways of living their lives. Books enable children to feel braver, safer, and less lonely. Books teach children that they are not alone and that others have felt happy and sad like them, been scared like them, and survived!

As a young girl, the oldest in a busy family of six children, I still remember the elation I felt when I entered the school library and realized that I could have access to the books there, as well as the sadness I felt when I learned I was limited to checking out only two books each week. I also remember my first heady days at college and the thrill I felt when I could give myself an entire rainy Saturday to read, without interruption, a Jane Austen novel in a corner of my beautiful old college library. The bliss of moments such as those are with me today. Books have been my lifelong friends, and they are the impetus for the development of the Schoolwide Enrichment Model for Reading (SEM-R), a program that gives children both the chance to learn to love reading and the time within school to read.

This book introduces the SEM-R program, an approach that is designed to enhance traditional reading instruction and that can be used as part of a language arts program or as an additional literacy program in grades K–8. This innovative approach to reading has been developed over ten years of research on how to increase enjoyment in the process of learning while simultaneously focusing on differentiated instruction and engaging reading enrichment experiences.

In Phase One of a SEM-R program, teachers do planned read-alouds of wonderful segments of literature for students, called *book hooks,* interspersed with higher-order questioning and thinking skills instruction. In Phase Two of a SEM-R program, teachers develop students' self-regulation skills in order to prepare them to read challenging self-selected books. In this phase, students have individualized, differentiated reading conferences with their teacher. In Phase Three, students choose reading enrichment activities such as discussion groups, creative writing, buddy reading, creativity training, investigation centers, interest-based projects, continuation of self-selected reading, and book discussion groups. All of these experiences enhance the basic theme of the SEM-R, which is that reading should be a joyful experience, one that children want to do both in school and at home!

The SEM-R is the result of a decade of work by a dedicated group of researchers and educators with whom it has been my privilege to work. Members of this group include the coauthors of this book, as well as others who worked with me in earlier years such as Joan Jacobs, Ric Schreiber, Christine Briggs, and others. We are especially grateful to the administrators and teachers in the many schools and districts that have implemented the SEM-R as part of our research on this approach to foster joyful reading, including educators in Hartford, Manchester, Windsor Locks, and Willimantic in Connecticut, as well as West Palm Beach, Florida; Baltimore, Maryland; St. Paul, Minnesota; Dublin, Ohio; Bayboro, North Carolina; and all of the districts that are participating in our current research in states such as New York, California, Illinois, and Colorado.

We are particularly proud that the research that has been conducted on the SEM-R has documented that it supports teaching all state standards, is practical and easy to implement, and that it works! Rigorous scientific research on the SEM-R conducted over the last several years and published in high-level educational journals has proven that this practical, student-centered approach to literacy results in higher reading fluency and comprehension and is implemented with ease by most teachers. Students who have the opportunity to participate in SEM-R programs have higher reading scores and enjoy reading more than those who do not.

This book offers both practical guidance and the tools you will need to implement the SEM-R, including Phase One book hooks that excite children about reading, Phase Two differentiated supported independent reading, and Phase Three opportunities for independent choice of reading work and projects. We have learned from our many years of experience in implementing the SEM-R that our original hopes have been realized: teachers who have used it describe it as

- Helping children enjoy reading more
- Easy-to-use differentiation
- Supported independent reading

- A tool that emphasizes self-regulation
- Easy to implement
- Differentiated reading strategies
- Helpful classroom management
- Collegial coaching
- Flexible implementation during and after school
- A way to help children understand that reading is a doorway to creativity and exploration of interests

We dedicate *Joyful Reading* to all of the teachers, administrators, and students who have worked with us over the last decade to teach differentiated and enriched reading skills and strategies in a way that respects students' interests, helps them to learn to enjoy reading more, and helps them to become more self-regulated readers.

This book was developed by the Schoolwide Enrichment Model Reading Project (SEM-R). The SEM-R Project was funded by the Jacob K. Javits Gifted and Talented Students Education Program (Grant No. S206A040094) as administered by the Office of Elementary and Secondary Education, U.S. Department of Education. This product does not necessarily represent positions or policies of the Government, and no official endorsement should be inferred.

About the Authors

Sally M. Reis is a Board of Trustees Distinguished Professor of educational psychology at the University of Connecticut, where she also serves as principal investigator of The National Research Center on the Gifted and Talented. She was a teacher for fifteen years, eleven of which were spent working with gifted students at elementary, junior high, and high school levels. She has authored more than two hundred publications and has traveled extensively across the country to conduct workshops and provide professional development on enrichment programs and gender equity programs for school districts. She is coauthor of *The Schoolwide Enrichment Model, The Secondary Triad Model, Dilemmas in Talent Development in the Middle Years,* and *Work Left Undone: Choices and Compromises of Talented Females.* Sally serves on the editorial board of *Gifted Child Quarterly* and is a past president of the National Association for Gifted Children. She is also a fellow of the American Psychological Association.

Rebecca D. Eckert is a professor in the Neag School of Education at the University of Connecticut, where she works with college students as they prepare to become teachers. In her former role as the gifted resource specialist for the National Association for Gifted Children, Becky co-edited the book *Designing Services and Programs for High-Ability Learners* with Jeanne Purcell. Her previous work at The National Research Center on the Gifted and Talented included participation on the research team that developed and implemented the Schoolwide Enrichment Model for Reading. Her research interests include talented readers, recruitment and preparation of new teachers, arts in the schools, and public policy and gifted education. She is a former middle school teacher with experience in geography, history, and theater arts.

Elizabeth A. Fogarty graduated with a Ph.D. in reading and gifted education from the University of Connecticut in May 2006 and moved to North Carolina, where she now teaches at East Carolina University. She teaches classes in literacy and elementary education, is the author of several articles, and travels often to facilitate staff development with teachers in schools throughout the country. Her research interests include talented readers, differentiation, and teacher effectiveness.

Catherine A. Little is assistant professor in educational psychology in the Neag School of Education at the University of Connecticut. She teaches courses in gifted and talented education and in the education honors program, and she serves as program advisor to UConn Mentor Connection. Catherine received her Ph.D. in educational policy, planning, and leadership with an emphasis in gifted education administration from the College of William and Mary. Her research interests include professional development, talent development in teachers, curriculum differentiation, and perfectionism in gifted students. She presents regularly at state and national conferences and in local school districts, and she has written or co-written several curriculum units as well as book chapters and journal articles related to curriculum implementation and other issues in gifted education.

Angela M. Housand, a research associate with the Neag Center for Gifted Education and Talent Development and assistant professor at the University of North Carolina–Wilmington, has a doctorate in educational psychology with an emphasis in talent development and gifted education and educational psychology. A former teacher and a published author, Angela works as an instructor and as a presenter and leader of workshops on self-regulation, meeting the needs of talented readers, theories of cognitive development, program planning, creativity, and curriculum differentiation.

Sheelah M. Sweeny recently graduated from the University of Connecticut with a doctorate in curriculum and instruction, focusing on literacy instruction and a concentration in educational psychology in the area of gifted and talented education. She is assistant professor of reading at Rhode Island College and is interested in reading instruction for all students, including high-ability readers; instruction in comprehension strategies; and integration of new literacies throughout the curriculum. Her dissertation research focused on instructional reading conferences within the Schoolwide Enrichment Model for Reading.

Brian C. Housand recently completed his doctorate at the University of Connecticut with an emphasis in gifted education and instructional technology and is assistant professor in curriculum and instruction at East Carolina University. Brian is author of the column "Technology Untangled," which appears in the

National Association for Gifted Children's newsletter *Teaching for High Potential*. His research interests include instructional technology, new literacies, and selective underachievement of gifted students. Brian is currently exploring what it means to be creative in a digital age.

Lisa M. Muller graduated from American International College with a master's degree in forensic psychology. She has been working as a program specialist at the Neag Center for Gifted Education and Talent Development since 1999.

Erin E. Sullivan is completing her doctoral work in school psychology, counseling psychology, and gifted education at the University of Connecticut. Erin's research interests include social-emotional issues in gifted youth, underachievement, behavioral interventions, and gifted girls and women.

Toward Joyful Reading

The Schoolwide Enrichment Model for Reading

The Schoolwide Enrichment Model for Reading (SEM-R) is an enrichment-based approach to teaching reading that encourages young children to read for pleasure for long periods of time both during and after the school day. Our motto during the decade we have been working on the SEM-R has been that reading should be a joyful experience for students, and in implementing the SEM-R, we have achieved that goal. Over the last several years, we have worked with classroom teachers and administrators from across the country to implement the SEM-R (Reis and others, 2005) as part of their reading or language arts programs in diverse classrooms, resulting in very positive effects. We have found that the SEM-R can be used to teach state standards within an enrichment approach to reading instruction. The SEM-R is not a complete language arts program; rather, it is intended to enrich and replace the grouped reading instruction that teachers carry out each day in their language arts block. The research summarized in this book proves that this easily implemented approach to joyful reading and differentiated instruction works, producing either similar or, in many cases, higher scores in reading fluency and comprehension than when teachers use a more traditional method of instruction. The SEM-R, when implemented for an hour each day over a period of five or six months, has resulted in improved reading comprehension and fluency and more positive attitudes toward reading.

In this chapter, you will learn about the background and the goals of the SEM-R, as well as receive an overview of how this enrichment approach to reading works. You will also learn about the research conducted on the SEM-R and gain an understanding of how teachers in elementary, middle, and high schools have implemented this balanced literacy approach to reading. They report feeling inspired as they watch students gain self-confidence and self-regulation as readers after using this approach for only a few months. Teachers also tell us about the sense of elation they feel when reluctant or even resistant readers become engaged with books in which they have developed an interest. Such increased interest and engagement, we believe, can be fostered through the use of this differentiated reading approach.

The SEM-R is based on the Schoolwide Enrichment Model (SEM) (Renzulli, 1977; Renzulli & Reis, 1997), a widely used approach to providing enrichment and talent development opportunities for all students. During the last several years, we have helped educators implement this enrichment approach to reading with very positive results. Why consider an enrichment approach to reading? The simple reason is that despite all of our efforts and the billions of dollars spent on remedial reading practices and direct instruction, students' reading fluency and achievement have failed to increase in our country (National Assessment of Education Progress, 2002; National Center for Education Statistics, 2007). Indeed, despite increased attention to remedial instruction and practice in reading, scores have plummeted and fewer young people are reading than ever before.

The SEM-R focuses on enrichment for all students through engagement in challenging, self-selected reading that is accompanied by instruction in high-level thinking and reading strategy skills. A second core focus of the SEM-R is differentiation of reading content and strategies, coupled with more challenging reading experiences and advanced opportunities for metacognition and self-regulated reading. In other words, a SEM-R program challenges and prepares all students, from those who need remediation in reading to those who are extremely talented in reading, to begin reading in school and to continue this reading at home. The goals of this approach are simple and straightforward: to encourage children to begin to enjoy the reading process by giving them access to high-interest, self-selected books that they can read for periods of time at school and at home; to develop independence and self-regulation in reading through the selection of these books as well as the opportunity to have individualized reading instruction; and, finally, to enable all students to improve in reading fluency and comprehension through the use of reading comprehension strategies.

Joseph Renzulli (1977) has been encouraging educators to focus on increasing engagement in learning for more than three decades. Current research in reading suggests that increased engagement in reading can occur when students are matched with texts in which they are interested. For example, Guthrie (2004), a leading reading researcher, has explained that engagement in reading occurs across several dimensions. According to Guthrie, one part of engagement is simply the amount of time that readers spend on task. A second way to define engagement refers to the strategic cognitive behaviors that enable children as readers to create meaning from text. Still another indicator of engagement explained by Guthrie relates to affect and the need to consider qualities such as liking of, enthusiasm for, and enjoyment of reading. Our work on the SEM-R has shown that children and young adults become engaged in reading when they read for pleasure, read to satisfy an initial curiosity or interest, or read to understand topics in which they already have some interest. Students become regular readers when they have the opportunity to read for enjoyment—a key component of the SEM-R—and when they have the skills they need to understand and connect with the text.

Why Now?

Why are increased engagement and interest in reading so crucial? Wigfield (1997) reported that across the elementary school years, students' interest in reading declines. McKenna, Kear, and Ellsworth (1995) reported that on average, students' attitudes toward both recreational and academic reading begin positively but decline by the end of elementary school. These studies of elementary school readers are corroborated by other studies that show a continuation of the trend; for example, Greenberg, Gilbert, and Fredrick (2006) found relatively low levels of interest in reading among middle school students, along with limited engagement in reading behaviors. Our research on the SEM-R shows that over the course of a school year, students in control groups who used basal readers have shown declining attitudes toward reading while students who participate in a SEM-R program have shown more positive attitudes. Such findings suggest that perhaps we educators should be focusing on ways to ensure that reading is a more pleasurable experience for children and young adults.

The SEM-R encourages enjoyment of the reading and learning process through a focus on the development of self-regulation in readers, the use of planned enrichment experiences, and emphasis on differentiated instruction and individual attention. In some schools, the SEM-R is integrated into regular reading instruction as a part of a language arts program or implemented as an additional literacy block in addition to a regular language arts program; it may also be added as an after-school extension of literacy programming. The model lends itself to implementation in a variety of contexts and configurations, depending on the schedules and needs of schools and students. Our experiences suggest that with minimal professional development and by using the information included in this book, which describes all aspects of the approach, teachers can learn to use the SEM-R to differentiate instruction and integrate higher-order thinking skills in order to challenge and engage students at all levels of reading achievement. Even assessment has proven easy with the SEM-R. Teachers become very comfortable with using more authentic assessment strategies based on student conferences, students' book choices, and students' written and oral responses to instruction in literacy strategies. The three phases of the SEM-R expose students to good literature, encourage readers to become more self-directed and self-regulated, and allow learners to apply high-level thinking skills to their reading while they learn to enjoy reading and pursue their interests through books.

Case Studies of Children Who Have Benefited from SEM-R Programs

Brad was a fourth-grade student who read at a sixth-grade level but rarely read anything that challenged him. Brad loved joke books and comic books, but refused to read anything that appeared to require effort on his part. Brad's Reading Interest-a-Lyzer suggested that he might enjoy science fiction and initially, he was encouraged to read novels geared toward students at his independent reading level of sixth grade. His teacher recommended several appropriately challenging books at this level for him in his interest areas of science and science fiction in the beginning of the SEM-R program and Brad began to read some books with some interest. Typically, however, he would begin to fidget after just one page and said he did not like the challenging names used for the science fiction characters. When Brad selected books on his own, without the suggestions of his teacher, he gravitated toward simple books that he found humorous. One book entitled *Sideways Stories from Wayside School* by Louis Sachar was well below his reading ability, but he showed great enthusiasm for the content. Another selection, a 166-page book by Patricia McKissack entitled a *The Dark-Thirty: Southern Tales of the Supernatural* that appeared to be in his interest area did not appeal to Brad, who explained that he was daunted by the size of the book.

During Phase One read-alouds, Brad was often inattentive and frequently said to his teacher, "What if I don't want to listen or read?" During Phase Two, he would often smile as he refused to read the books she offered to him and would initially gravitate toward books he had already read or were very easy for him. His classroom teachers reported regular instances in which Brad avoided reading at appropriate challenge levels. Brad seemed uncomfortable with the challenge of new material despite the fact that the books suggested to him were well within his reading level. When offered high-interest, appropriately challenging content, Brad said he wanted to read a book about the brain and how it operated the body. When a book about this content area was found for him, he skimmed through the book and appeared to merely look at the pictures.

Brad's efforts to read occurred intermittently and were varied in the first few weeks of the SEM-R program. By the end of the program, however, Brad displayed more interest in reading on a more consistent basis, and even asked to read the graphic version of *Moby Dick* by Herman Melville. He seemed to enjoy the text and gravitated toward other similar books. By the end of the second month, Brad was consistently reading more challenging books in his interest area. His teacher was delighted with Brad's progress and reported that he continued to increase his stamina for and interest in reading as the program continued during the semester.

Joe was an eight-year-old third grader who did not like to read. Although he reads slightly above grade level, Joe explained that he never reads at home, despite being encouraged by his parents to do so. Joe was an energetic student who had difficulty with being still for any extended period of time. Although he could be quite focused when reading, Joe fidgeted often and his classroom teacher explained that he was often distracted and lacked focus. Unfortunately, although he was capable of reading on a fifth-grade level and despite being encouraged to read at a higher level, Joe's choices of books to read in school were always from the Goosebumps series, which was well below his challenge level. When his teacher started to use the SEM-R with him, Joe liked some of the challenging books suggested to him, including biographies of baseball stars, but would discontinue reading if he perceived that he could not finish the book in a certain period of time, such as a half hour or forty-five minutes. He could, for example, read one Goosebumps book in forty-five minutes and initially seemed to need the extrinsic praise that he had been consistently given if he finished a book in that time period.

When he completed his Reading Interest-a-Lyzer, Joe indicated that he liked science, fantasy, and comics. Joe also explained that he liked reading about spiders and frogs and that he often read children's science books he found in the library and in the classroom. During the course of the SEM-R intervention, Joe began reading many novels that were suggested to him because of the match of interest and challenge level but stopped reading shortly after he began almost every novel. The amount of time he could read silently and independently, even when he read less challenging books, increased each week during the hour each day that his teacher set aside for the SEM-R program. His oral reading fluency increased dramatically as the weeks turned into months, and he was able to read much more challenging books at the end of a few months.

Maria, a ten-year-old girl of Latino descent, was a third grader who read above her chronological grade level and had been identified as academically gifted. She read in both English and Spanish and spoke both languages fluently due to her home language experiences. Maria enjoyed poetry and was interested in creative writing, but her teachers were concerned because her school records showed that her reading level had not increased over the time she had been in school. That is, she had entered first grade reading at a fourth-grade level and three years later was still reading at a fourth-grade level. During the first week of the SEM-R program, Maria brought in poems she had written about colors and ice cream, using precise language and rhyme.

Maria showed consistent enthusiasm for reading, but despite her enthusiasm, when given a choice of books to read, Maria consistently selected picture books that were well below her reading ability for her supported independent reading time. Maria also had difficulty maintaining her focus and concentration for more than ten minutes during independent reading sessions, despite the focus on increasing minutes at each session. Several strategies were suggested to Maria during her SEM-R time, to enable Maria her to read for longer periods of time. Maria needed to have space from the other readers in the group and was easily distracted. She consistently claimed to be bored with longer, more appropriately challenging chapter books. When asked why, she replied that she did not know, but that they were "just too long." By trying several different strategies, her teachers found that Maria could focus longer when she applied different approaches to reading. When she was encouraged to remove herself from other distractions, she was able to focus for slightly longer periods of time. She also enjoyed reading with a partner, but was still easily distracted. Soon, she was reading for twenty minutes, and within a month, she was reading a lengthy biography about Martin Luther King Jr. who was familiar to her, and her interest in him seemed to help her discern the meaning of the words.

Because Maria enjoyed poetry so much, one strategy that her teachers used was to pair her with another advanced reader, Sarah, who also loved poetry. They read *Joyful Noise: Poetry for Two Voices* by Paul Fleischman aloud together during Phase Three of the SEM-R program. In the second month of the SEM-R program, Maria became excited about reading *Esperanza Rising,* a young adult novel by Pam Munoz Ryan, in Spanish. Maria wrote short, insightful responses about the opening scene of *Esperanza Rising* in her writing prompt during the first week she spent reading this book. Her time reading more challenging content increased, and she began to be able to spend twenty-five to thirty minutes a day in reading appropriately challenging content during the SEM-R block. During the year, she alternated reading in Spanish and English during her SEM-R time, and by the end of the year, she had increased her oral reading fluency and comprehension and was reading two years above the level at which she had entered third grade.

Introduction to The Schoolwide Enrichment Model for Reading

The SEM-R is an enrichment-based reading program that has resulted in increased reading fluency and achievement as well as more positive attitudes toward reading (Reis & Fogarty, 2006; Reis and others, 2004). The instructional framework leading to these results employs high-interest books—which students select for themselves at levels slightly above their current proficiency—as the basis for stimulating interest and joy in reading. We have found that after just a few weeks of participating in a SEM-R program, students begin to read more challenging material on a regular basis and, more important, demonstrate a willingness to do so. The SEM-R is not intended to constitute a complete language arts program; it primarily focuses on reading, increasing reading comprehension and fluency, and increasing self-regulation in reading. While students are encouraged to complete written reflections each week in their student log, the SEM-R program is intended to be the reading component of a more comprehensive language arts program. Most teachers who have used this approach have coupled the SEM-R with other instruction in vocabulary development, spelling, language mechanics, and writing. They have found the creative use of books suggested in the SEM-R to be a welcome enhancement of a direct instruction program or a more teacher-directed whole-class or group basal program. In this chapter, each phase of the SEM-R program is explained briefly as an introduction to subsequent chapters that focus on implementation and practical suggestions for incorporating the SEM-R into your school or classroom. Figure 1.1 depicts the three phases of the SEM-R, keyed to the related components of the Enrichment Triad.

Goals of the SEM-R

The SEM-R has three distinct goals: increasing enjoyment of and positive attitudes toward reading, encouraging students to pursue independent reading at appropriately challenging levels, and improving reading fluency and comprehension. The SEM-R includes three general categories of reading instruction that are dynamic in nature and designed to enable some flexibility of implementation and content in response to both teachers' and students' needs (see Figure 1.2). In the SEM-R, each of the three general categories is referred to as a *phase* of instruction. Phase One focuses on

FIGURE 1.1. COMPONENTS OF THE SCHOOLWIDE ENRICHMENT MODEL FOR READING.

Phase One Exposure	Phase Two Training & Self-Selected Reading	Phase Three Interest & Choice Components

• High-interest books to read aloud
 	
   ❦ Picture Books
   ❦ Novels/Fiction
   ❦ Nonfiction
   ❦ Poetry
 	
• Higher-order thinking probing questions
 	
• Bookmarks for teachers with questions regarding Bloom's Taxonomy, biography, character, illustrations, and other topics relevant to the study of literature
	• Training and discussions on Supported Independent Reading
	
	• Supported Independent Reading
	
	• One-on-one teacher conferences on reading strategies and instruction
	
	• Bookmarks for students posing higher-order questions regarding character, plot, setting, considering the story, and other useful topics
		Increasing degree of student selection ↓ • Introducing creative thinking
		• Genre studies
		• Library exploration
		• Responding to books
		• Investigation centers
		   ❦ Creative thinking
		   ❦ Exploring the Internet
		   ❦ Reading non-fiction
		   ❦ Focus on biographies
		
		• Buddy reading
		• Books on tape
		• Literature circles
		• Creative or expository writing
		• Type III investigation

Type I Activities	**Type II Activities**	**Type II & Type III Investigations**

FIGURE 1.2. THE ENRICHMENT TRIAD MODEL.

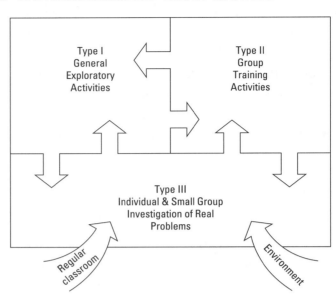

listening comprehension through the use of advanced, high-interest books, coupled with strategy and process training; the key emphasis of this phase is exposure to a variety of genres, levels of reading challenge, and interests. Phase Two of the SEM-R emphasizes development of students' capacity to engage in independent reading, for extended blocks of time, of self-selected books that are slightly above their independent reading level. Phase Three encourages students to move from teacher-directed work to self-chosen reading-related activities in areas such as student-directed projects, enrichment activities involving technology, literature circles, advanced questioning and thinking skills, and creativity training as applied to reading.

Phase One: Hooking Kids on Literature with Teacher Read-Alouds

In Phase One of a SEM-R program, teachers select diverse literature across a variety of genres to read aloud to students and intersperse these readings with higher-order questioning, lessons on the use of specific reading strategies, and thinking skills instruction. These sessions, called *book hooks,* usually begin with ten to fifteen minutes during which the teacher reads excerpts aloud from high-interest, challenging books designed to hook children on reading. The read-alouds are accompanied by brief discussions or instructional moments in which teachers encourage discussion, share a personal connection to the book, or teach reading strategies; in total, Phase One sessions usually last ten to twenty-five minutes at the beginning of SEM-R implementation. Over time, the length of sessions gradually decreases as students begin to spend more time reading independently in Phase Two.

Phase One of a SEM-R program includes listening comprehension and process training skills within the context of exposing students to a range of literary works, authors, and genres. Through the use of challenging, high-interest books as focal points for student listening skills, teachers read aloud from high-quality, exciting literature, following up with higher-order questioning and instruction in thinking skills. Each day, the teacher shares a short excerpt or *snippet* from one or more books to hook students on reading and expand learners' reading horizons. The SEM-R emphasizes enjoyment of the process of reading, so selections for book hooks are made based on student engagement with content, reactions to previous book hook selections, and a desire to promote interest and subsequent engagement in independent reading. Moreover, in Phase One, teachers use bookmarks with higher-order questions to help differentiate instruction and pose questions on reading strategies, literary terms, and higher-order thinking skills to all students. A sampling of the comprehensive collection of these bookmarks is available in Appendix A.

The approximate time of this phase of a SEM-R program varies, but it averages about ten to twenty-five minutes daily; the goal is to decrease the time spent on Phase One over a period of weeks. As students' ability to maintain their focus for longer periods of time increases, along with their self-regulation in Phase Two independent reading, Phase One time is shortened to enable more independent reading time. Details of how to implement Phase One of a SEM-R program are explained in Chapter Four.

Phase Two: Supported Independent Reading and Differentiated Conferences

Phase Two of a SEM-R program is designed to increase students' engagement and self-direction in independent reading of self-selected books, supported by individualized, differentiated reading conferences with their teacher. During this supported independent reading (SIR), teachers encourage students to select books that are slightly above their current reading level to promote continual growth in reading skills and use of reading strategies. Teachers meet regularly with students, usually in biweekly conferences, to assess whether books are appropriately matched. Our experiences with the SEM-R have demonstrated that initially, the majority of students select books that are too easy for them. Within the SEM-R context, students are instructed to take these easier books home to read; they are told that during school it is their job to select books that are more challenging for them while still appropriate to their areas of interest. Teachers also work to help students understand that appropriately challenging books will include some words that students do not know and some ideas that are new to them. In other words, teachers urge students to engage in reading in an area of personal interest that is slightly above their current independent reading level. Another observation that we have made in our many years of implementing the SEM-R is that another group of children, those who read well below grade level, often select books that are too difficult for them. During the individualized interactions in Phase Two, teachers must also treat students in this group with dignity and respect, helping them to find books that more appropriately meet their needs and working over time to enable them to read books at increasingly higher levels.

Phase Two incorporates differentiated instruction within individualized conferences; the focus of this instruction is on reading strategies that will allow students to modify their reading processes to facilitate greater fluency and comprehension in the challenging books they are reading. During conferences, teachers and students discuss and consider critical thinking questions that focus on synthesis, making inferences, and determining importance. Such questions provide open-ended opportunities to children of all reading levels for reflection on and discussion of their books. Teachers also are able to provide scaffolding, as necessary, to enable readers of all ability levels to think critically about text. In our SEM-R studies, the majority of elementary students initially could read independently for only five to ten minutes a day without losing concentration or focus, and most displayed little self-regulation in reading. Teachers subsequently worked to add a minute or two during each day of reading time, eventually extending the time that students read to thirty to forty-five minutes daily. This extended Phase Two SIR time enables teachers to circulate around the room conducting short (four- to five-minute) conferences in order to provide individualized support and differentiated instruction for several students each day. The types and levels of reading strategies as well as higher-order thinking skills that are exercised within conferences help increase students' skills and self-regulation in reading. Suggestions on strategies to use to increase self-regulation in reading are also provided in subsequent chapters.

Informal and formal methods are used to identify and develop students' interests and to encourage students to pursue these interests through their reading. Students can complete the Reading Interest-a-Lyzer (Appendix B), an adapted version of a general interest assessment (the Interest-a-Lyzer) (Renzulli, 1977), to assist teachers both in helping identify students' interests in reading and in guiding students as they select challenging and interesting books. More information on implementing Phase Two of a SEM-R program is available in Chapter Five, and sample forms and pages from student and teacher logs are included in the Appendixes.

Phase Three: Interest and Choice Activities

The ultimate goal in Phase Three of a SEM-R program is to help students progress from teacher-directed opportunities to independent, self-chosen activities over the course of a few months. The experiences available in Phase Three provide opportunities for students to engage in areas of personal interest and to continue to develop enjoyment of reading. Student-chosen activities can include experiences in exploring technology and reading online (for example, e-books, children's authors' Web pages); writing activities; creativity training in language arts; investigation centers on topics in which students have an interest; interest-based projects; continuation of self-selected reading; reading with a friend; book chats in literature circles; or independent or small-group studies, as shown in Type III of the Enrichment Triad Model (see Figure 1.2). These experiences enable students to develop and explore their interests and apply creative and critical thinking skills to self-selected, literature-based explorations. Phase Three enables students to learn to read critically, synthesize what they have read and apply it in a new context, and locate other enjoyable and stimulating reading materials, especially high-quality, challenging literature.

Teachers usually begin Phase Three by allowing students to choose one activity out of three or four teacher-determined options to participate in for fifteen minutes each day or during a weekly one-hour block of reading or language arts. Within this structure, teachers can provide the parameters and scaffolding necessary to help students develop both the cognitive and affective skills needed to become self-directed, independent learners. As students become more comfortable with independent work, Phase Three activity choices expand to involve more student-directed opportunities, while the teacher's role shifts from instructor to facilitator. Like Phases One and Two, this component of the SEM-R was developed to help students enjoy reading, increase their reading skills by using individual differentiated reading strategies, and apply instruction in higher-order thinking and reading strategies while reading books in areas of personal interest. Additional information about creative ways in which teachers can implement Phase Three is introduced in Chapter Six.

Background on the SEM-R

The conceptual background of the SEM-R is Joseph Renzulli's Enrichment Triad Model (Renzulli, 1977) and the subsequent thirty years of field-testing and research (Renzulli & Reis, 1994) related to the Schoolwide Enrichment Model, which address some fundamental questions about both how we can develop the potential of all children and how we can provide differentiated instruction and curriculum. The Schoolwide Enrichment Model (SEM) was developed to encourage and develop interests, engagement, and creativity in young people. To lay the groundwork for understanding the SEM-R, in the following section we introduce a brief overview of the SEM, describe the original Enrichment Triad Model, and summarize pertinent research highlights.

The Schoolwide Enrichment Model

The Schoolwide Enrichment Model promotes engagement through the use of three types of enrichment experiences that are enjoyable, challenging, and interest-based. This model provides a broad range of structured enrichment experiences for all students and follow-up advanced learning opportunities for students with high levels of achievement and interest. Separate studies on the SEM have demonstrated its effectiveness in schools with widely differing socioeconomic levels and program organization patterns (Olenchak, 1988; Olenchak & Renzulli, 1989). The SEM used Renzulli's Enrichment Triad Model as its core (Renzulli, 1977; Renzulli & Reis, 1985, 1997) and has been implemented in more than two thousand schools across the country (Burns, 1998); interest in this approach has continued to expand nationally and internationally. The effectiveness of the SEM has been studied in more than thirty years of research and field tests, which suggest that the model is effective at serving high-ability students and providing enrichment for all students in a variety of educational settings, including schools serving culturally diverse and economically disadvantaged populations. Research on the SEM is summarized online at www.gifted.uconn.edu/sem/semresearch.html.

The Enrichment Triad Model, the learning approach at the heart of the SEM, encourages enjoyment of learning and gives students the opportunity to pursue creative work through exposure to various topics, areas of interest, and fields of study. The Enrichment Triad Model also incorporates detailed attention to the practices of various disciplines and further enables students to learn how to apply advanced content and methodological training to self-selected areas of interest (Renzulli, 1977). Three types of enrichment are included in the Enrichment Triad Model (see Figure 1.2); as we will see, these three types also provide a basis for the key components of the SEM-R.

Type I enrichment is designed to expose students to a wide variety of topics, issues, and activities not ordinarily covered in the regular curriculum. In a SEM-R program, Type I enrichment occurs when teachers expose their students to exciting read-alouds from books and stories that are purposefully selected to develop and stimulate student interests. Excerpts from interesting and enjoyable selections of literature representing various genres (nonfiction, poetry, or historical fiction, for example) are read aloud to promote enjoyment of reading and listening. In a SEM-R program, students are exposed to this literature on a daily basis, stimulating an interest in and an enjoyment of reading.

Type II enrichment involves teaching students to use methods that are designed to promote the development of thinking processes—for example, creative thinking, problem solving, and communication skills. In addition to these skills, Type II enrichment involves supporting students in developing critical thinking; affective processes such as character development, self-efficacy, and empathy; skills needed for the appropriate use of advanced-level reference materials; and skills in written, oral, and visual communication. In a SEM-R program, Type II enrichment occurs as students develop the skills to choose appropriately challenging, high-interest books; to discuss high-level questions about literature; to employ increasingly advanced and complex reading strategies; and during conferences when teachers provide method training (on how to do certain things), using individualized instruction.

Type III enrichment, in the Enrichment Triad Model, enables students who become interested in particular topics to pursue self-selected areas of study for more intensive individual or small-group involvement. Type III studies provide opportunities to apply interests, knowledge, creative ideas, and task commitment to a self-selected problem or area of study. These opportunities allow students to acquire advanced-level understanding of the knowledge (content) and methodology (process) used within particular disciplines. In a SEM-R program, Type III enrichment occurs through various literacy-based activities and options that build on the interests that students show in selecting books, extends these interests into further independent or small-group explorations, provides opportunities to develop advanced skills, promotes projects based on books read, and encourages general sharing and engagement in a community of readers.

Differentiated Curriculum, Instruction, and Challenge

Another central dimension in the conceptual background of the SEM-R is the idea of differentiated instruction and the ways in which we should be challenging students at their own level of need in reading. Individual differences in ability and experience translate, over time, into an ever-widening range of reading levels in any given classroom; some students are highly capable readers who may be craving new challenges and independence, while others may begin at a disadvantage and fall further and further behind as the years pass. In order to accommodate the needs of students across so many different levels of academic achievement in every area, many teachers have adopted a variety of classroom strategies collectively referred to as *differentiated instruction*. Differentiation is an attempt to address the variation of learners in the classroom through multiple approaches that modify instruction and curriculum to match the individual needs of students, including individual differences in readiness, interests, and other aspects of the learning profile (Tomlinson, 2000). Tomlinson (1995) emphasized that when teachers differentiate curriculum, they stop acting as dispensers of knowledge and, instead, serve as organizers of learning opportunities. Differentiation of instruction and curriculum often involves providing students with materials and work of varied levels of difficulty with scaffolding, diverse opportunities for flexible grouping, and different time schedules (Tomlinson, 2000).

Renzulli (1977, 1988; Renzulli & Reis, 1997) defined differentiation as encompassing five dimensions: content, process, products, classroom organization and management, and the teacher's own commitment to change himself or herself into a learner as well as a teacher. The differentiation of *content* involves adding more depth to the curriculum by focusing on structures of knowledge, basic principles, functional concepts, and methods of inquiry in particular disciplines. The differentiation of *process* incorporates the use of various instructional strategies and materials to develop and motivate students with varied learning styles. The differentiation of *products* enhances students' communication skills by encouraging them to express themselves and demonstrate their learning in a variety of ways. To differentiate *classroom management,* teachers can change the physical environment and grouping patterns they use in class and vary the allocation of time and resources for both groups and individuals. Classroom differentiation strategies can also be greatly enhanced by using the Internet in a variety of creative ways. Teachers can differentiate *themselves* by teaching different children differently and by regarding the role of a teacher as a facilitator instead of a front-of-the-classroom lecturer. Teachers can model the roles of athletic or drama coach, stage or production manager, promotional agent, or academic advisor. All these roles differ qualitatively from the teacher-as-instructor role. Teachers can also "inject" themselves into the material they teach through a process called *artistic modification* (Renzulli, 1988). This process guides teachers in sharing direct, indirect, and vicarious experiences related to personal interests, travel experiences, collections, hobbies, and teachers' extracurricular involvements that can enhance content. Differentiation is included in every phase of a SEM-R program and will be discussed throughout this book as a critical component in meeting the needs of all students in reading.

The differences among students in terms of their readiness, experiences, and individual learning needs suggest that different levels of challenge are appropriate for different children, and differentiated instruction responds to this principle. Learning occurs when there is an appropriate match between the experience and the learner's readiness. Vygotsky (1962), a Russian psychologist, described individual development as relying on the critical role of the interaction of the person with the social environment in the *zone of proximal development,* defined as the distance between what a student can do independently and what a student can do with assistance provided by more capable peers or by the student's teachers. As a consequence, students' learning and development must be studied in light of what a teacher can do to challenge children and then increase the level of challenge that they encounter (Vygotsky, 1962).

Two central tasks for teachers involve identifying the correct levels of academic difficulty for each student and finding ways to know whether texts are appropriately challenging. Chall and Conard (1991) described an optimal text as one that is slightly above a student's reading level, thus requiring the student to make an effort to read the text and, occasionally, to ask for assistance. To achieve optimal challenge, a reader must encounter new concepts and language—as suggested by Vygotsky's (1962) theory of the zone of proximal development of language. Thus, knowledge can be seen as socially influenced and constructed. In a model for instruction based on this idea, a zone established as a proximal level of difficulty would allow students to work with adult assistance in a format that includes guided practice. In the SEM-R, teachers attempt to find the zone of proximal development for each child. That is, children are assisted by adult evaluation of independent performance and are encouraged to read at levels that are slightly above their current level of independent reading in order to create a level of challenge; adult assistance is provided through individualized conferences in which teachers guide students in developing strategies for managing and understanding these more advanced texts. Vygotsky believed that studying challenging material in this way enabled students to learn more complex material than they could understand without support. In other words, there must be a supported struggle, and that supported struggle is a major goal for students, accompanied by teachers, as they implement the SEM-R.

Research on the SEM-R

With the aid of external grant funding, the SEM-R has been studied in elementary schools for more than seven years. Rigorous experimental designs have been used to compare the performance of treatment and control groups of students. Data sources have included pre- and post-assessments of reading achievement and attitudes, including the Iowa Test of Basic Skills (ITBS) Reading Comprehension Subtests, oral reading fluency tests, and the twenty-item Elementary Reading Attitude Survey (McKenna & Kear, 1990).

SEM-R programs were first implemented in two high-poverty urban schools (90 percent culturally and linguistically diverse students and all students on free or reduced-price lunch) using a cluster-randomized experimental design during a daily fifty-minute afternoon literacy block for fourteen weeks between February and May. At the conclusion of the initial intervention, 90 percent of SEM-R students had achieved thirty to forty-five minutes of sustained reading, a major achievement for the majority of students who previously could not read for more than five minutes at one sitting. Significant differences favoring the treatment group were found in comprehension, reading fluency, and attitudes toward reading. Results have shown that talented readers, as well as average and below-average readers, benefited from the SEM-R intervention (Reis and others, 2005; Reis and others, 2007).

A second study (Reis, Eckert, McCoach, Jacobs, & Coyne, 2008) examined the effects of implementing a SEM-R program during one hour of a two-hour language arts block at the elementary level for thirteen weeks in a suburban school and an urban school. Using a rigorous cluster-randomized experimental design, similar findings emerged at the end of the intervention: 90 percent of students in all the SEM-R classrooms achieved forty to forty-five minutes of sustained reading. Significant differences favoring the treatment group were found in reading fluency gains.

Over the last few years, we have scaled up SEM-R programs to more than a dozen schools across six states, and our results have continued to demonstrate that students in the treatment group perform similarly to or better than students in the control group, with the strongest results emerging from high-need schools in urban areas (Reis, Muller, and others, 2008). These results are encouraging in regard to the SEM-R's usefulness as a powerful model for supporting student achievement, and they are an important demonstration of the influence of differentiated instruction.

In summary, SEM-R programs have improved student achievement in the following ways: increased reading fluency and achievement test scores in reading; an increase in total hours spent reading and number of books read; positive change in students' attitudes about and enjoyment of reading; positive change in students' motivation to read; and increases in student confidence when responding to higher-order thinking questions. And teachers and students love the SEM-R!

Teachers' Perceptions of Their Success with SEM-R Programs

As part of the many studies we conducted on implementation of SEM-R programs, we interviewed teachers who had used this approach during an academic year, in order to learn about their perspectives on what worked best. Interviews were conducted with teachers before, during, and after each year of SEM-R implementation, and findings consistently show that teachers believe that using the SEM-R results in more enjoyment and increased self-regulation in reading on the part of their students and that the SEM-R allows teachers to match students to more appropriately challenging texts. They also believe that using the SEM-R challenges students at all levels of achievement and enables teachers to provide more effective and differentiated instruction.

The themes that emerged from teacher interviews and logs are threefold: first, teachers admit that they had not realized how much middle-of-the-road reading instruction they did and how few of their students they really challenged before using SEM-R; second, they acknowledged that the differentiated individual conferences resulted in their average to above-average or gifted readers' moving well beyond what the teacher ever thought they could do in independent reading, advanced thinking skills, and questioning skills ("At first, I just wanted them to finish a book. Then I became more confident and would say, 'Come on now, that is just too easy for you.' They would smile, because they knew I was right"); and third, teachers and students both enjoyed the freedom to try new reading opportunities in both their teaching and their learning. One teacher's comments were representative of many others relating to this theme: "The individualized reading was so enjoyable. I found the basal program brutally boring! The same activities each day followed by the same kinds of questions." Many teachers offered similar comments that aptly summarized one of our most important goals for the SEM-R, explaining, "I don't think I had one student who wasn't excited about reading."

Teachers described their most frequent successes in implementing SEM-R programs in the following ways:

> I like to look at the kids who came in and did not like to read. I have students who had never read before who now have piles of books that they want to read. In the beginning, I had a boy who had no reading skills and all he would speak about was getting help.

After using SEM-R, he gained reading strategies and took ownership of his skills and can discuss visualizing, monitoring, summarizing, and making connections.

I did really well in differentiating instruction in reading. With my higher-achieving kids, I used more analysis or synthesis skills, but I also used these strategies with lower kids.

My success has been the extent to which the kids read without complaining and students who did not like to read who are now reading regularly. Parents have even told me great stories about their children and how often they are reading at home.

My biggest success is that kids see themselves as readers now. Most of my students in this class are lower readers, and at the beginning of the year, they were so resistant to read any book. I had kids that were reading one page over a twenty-minute time period. Now, with their practice during SIR, kids are able to read for long periods. I have students now who read independently who never would.

My biggest success in implementing the SEM-R was having my weakest readers actually sit and read nonstop for thirty minutes day after day. This was an outstanding outcome for my kids!

My success was my use of less direct instruction and much less whole-group instruction. I actually have never done so little whole-group teaching, and it was such a relief not to have to drag kids through books that they did not like. I loved having kids come up to me during SIR to share something that they read in a book. This was so exciting to me.

Getting some of the lowest readers in the class to be excited about reading was my greatest success. My most resistant readers were the most likely to read, and some of my lowest readers have been reading at home. Parents are calling me to tell me kids are reading at home!

Every teacher also shared individual success stories about one or several children in their class:

Hannah was a struggling reader with very low scores, but her initiative and excitement increased a thousandfold after using SEM-R. Her writing also improved when I used the book hook writing prompts in her student log.

One particular student, Christopher, reads on a high school level and had some issues in the beginning of the year. He is so bright, but he is kind of lazy. When I let him read during Phase Two, he is incredible. What he reads in my class amazes me, as does the knowledge he brings to class. He reads biographies on John F. Kennedy, history books about World War II, and his journal is amazing.

I also think Arman has really improved. His teachers fought last year for him to be retained, and his parents disagreed. He was labeled special education, and he failed summer school. At the beginning of the year, his reading was dismal. This program, I am telling you, changed him completely! He has read every single book by Walter Dean Myers, and he is using the dictionary. He is reading independently. He has done amazingly well; for example, after my book hook on it, he actually finished *Role of Thunder*. He never used to read, and he is a new kid now. He asks to go to the school library, and his parents take him to Borders for books. He has developed a love for reading.

Richard, a gifted reader, read *Of Mice and Men* and other classics and gained so much. My high kids all have a chance to go beyond now. If we stayed in the regular program, they would have read only three books all year. But now, the more talented readers can go so far beyond. Some of them have read a dozen books in one semester! My lower readers have also been stretched by SEM-R in wonderful ways.

Consistently, when asked which students benefited most from SEM-R programs, teachers explained that all of their students benefited, as indicated, for example, in these comments:

My highest-achieving students had the time to read, and they would go beyond. But all of my students, even my low students, benefited. All tried hard to read, and some of my lowest kids really went beyond. In the past, my lowest students read well below the level they did this year.

All kids have benefited somewhat from SEM-R. All of my kids have gotten better. When I do conferences, my kids are more confident and they do not mind reading to me. They have begun to choose harder books without my suggestions.

Oh my gosh, the student who benefited the most in my class was Pat, who is identified as special education and read on a second-grade level (in fifth grade) has really improved.

Summary

Unlike many other reading programs, the most important goal of the SEM-R is to increase students' enjoyment of reading. All too often, teachers are expected to create student achievement without student motivation and interest. At times, students may be willing to expend the time and energy to achieve, but without a personal interest, they are unlikely to sustain enough energy to increase their reading achievement. In a SEM-R program, students are asked to expend time and energy to read more, but they are also encouraged to read books in an interest area of choice.

Developing students into lifelong readers cannot be accomplished simply by giving multiple-choice tests to measure comprehension each time they finish a book. If adult book clubs were conducted in the same manner, no one would join! Students should be given the chance to interact with literature in the same way that adults do—through reading and discussion. Adults do not read to score well on a test of their comprehension of the elements of a story; rather, adults read to appreciate life, to find happiness, to escape reality, or to better understand their place in the world.

In the next chapter, we discuss the reasons that differentiated instruction, the cornerstone of the SEM-R, is so necessary for students, as well as the differentiated reading strategies that are embedded in the SEM-R.

Why Differentiate Reading Instruction?

Why must we differentiate in reading? Simply put, reading instruction in the United States has failed to engage students; caused declining interest in reading in many, if not most of our students; failed to address changing demographics; caused reading scores to plummet; and resulted in inequalities among different groups of students, including those who live in poverty, those who speak English as a second language, those who read well above grade level, and those who have special needs.

The success of reading instruction for all children depends on the degree to which teachers can adapt and differentiate instruction to address the many ways that individual children learn to read. The last two decades of research in reading and differentiation demonstrate that there is no single best way to teach reading because different students learn to read differently. Both phonics and whole-language methods provide fundamental training in the different ways that children acquire reading skills, and differentiated instruction that attends to variations in reading development can help students learn to understand and apply specific skills that enable them to use and comprehend written language. Because children learn differently, various instructional strategies in reading must be explored in order to enable each child to learn to read. In other words, a one-size-fits-all approach will only result in a failure of some young children to learn effective reading skills. Differentiation in reading instruction occurs when teachers can and do assess individual students' abilities, interests, and profile in reading and then use their knowledge to match their students with appropriately challenging reading content and individual reading and strategy instruction. This chapter suggests specific strategies for differentiation in reading instruction that are a part of the SEM-R.

Changing Classroom Demographics and Types of Reading Programs

Changes in student demographics and increasing academic expectations for all children to make progress in school require that teachers differentiate classroom instruction in order to provide students with an education that allows each individual to progress academically in accordance with his or her needs and strengths. In research on the use of differentiation strategies in regular classrooms, we found that teachers had difficulty implementing differentiated instructional strategies across all content areas and that differentiation in reading instruction happens rarely (Reis and others, 2004).

As classroom composition grows increasingly more diverse, the need for more differentiation would appear obvious, yet our own research suggests that during the years since the No Child Left Behind (NCLB) legislation was enacted, educators are emphasizing instruction for students who struggle academically, to the detriment of more advanced learners. The reading needs of students at risk for not achieving state mastery in reading have been championed, while the needs of advanced readers have been left behind. Instead, we must attempt to teach reading in a way that challenges and engages all students.

At the same time that classrooms are becoming more diverse, the reading curriculum is becoming more rigid and one-dimensional, with more group instructional time and, often, more review of previously taught reading concepts. Since the inception of NCLB, nearly two-thirds of U.S. schools have increased the amount of time spent on teaching reading, language arts, and mathematics but scores remain flat, especially for older students (Wyner, Bridgeland, & DiIulio, 2007). The types of reading instruction that are used in schools range on a continuum from programmed instruction such as Success for All (SFA), developed by Slavin and Madden (1999), in which teachers follow a skills-based script and all students read the same materials, to an eclectic approach that is characterized by a more balanced approach that stresses strategy instruction and literature-based reading. The results of programmed instruction such as SFA have been mixed, particularly in regard to the effectiveness of its teaching of comprehension strategies. Our review of the research suggests that literature-rich classes in which children have extensive opportunities to read produce students who read more and, subsequently, perform better on some reading achievement measures.

Declining Reading for All Students

In a recent study, the ACT college-entrance test scores of 1.2 million high school students were reviewed, and results showed that only 51 percent of high school graduates who took the exam had the reading skills necessary to succeed in college or job training programs (ACT, Inc., 2006). These results represented the lowest proportion in more than a decade. Of particular significance in this study was the high percentage of culturally and linguistically diverse and low-income students who were unprepared for college-level reading, including 79 percent of African American students, 67 percent of Latino students, and 33 percent of students from families with annual incomes below $30,000. Research by the Education Trust (2006b) found that reading achievement among Latino students increased during the 1970s and 1980s but declined precipitously in the 1990s. A recent National Assessment of Educational Progress (2002) determined that only 14 percent of fourth-grade Latino students read at a proficient or advanced level, while 57 percent could not read at even a basic level. Similarly, only 12 percent of fourth-grade African American students read at a proficient or advanced level, and 61 percent read below basic level (ACT, Inc., 2006). In addition, research on elementary children who live in poverty demonstrates that even when these students benefited from well-regarded reading interventions, they usually fell behind again in the middle grades (Forman, Francis, Fletcher, Schatschneider, & Mehta, 1998; Hiebert, 1994). A 2007 study funded by the Jack Kent Cooke Foundation discovered a deficit in lower-income high achievers in the first grade: only 28 percent of students in the top quarter of their first-grade class were from lower-income families, while 72 percent were from higher-income families. The same report found that nearly half of the lower-income students in the top 25 percent of their class in reading fell out of this rank by fifth grade (Wyner, Bridgeland, & DiIulio, 2007).

Each decade, the National Endowment for the Arts (NEA) issues a report about reading in America. The most recent report, entitled *Reading at Risk: A Survey of Literary Reading in America* (National Endowment for the Arts, 2004), found that literary reading of any kind is declining faster than ever before. The findings in the report show a steady drop in the percentage of Americans who read; only 56.6 percent of respondents reported reading any type of book in 2002, a decline of 7 percent from the previous decade. Fewer than half of Americans, according to this report, read literature of any type. The change in reading practices has been particularly striking among those aged eighteen to twenty-four. The report finds that over the past two decades, the share of the adult population engaged in literary reading declined by 14 points, from 56.9 percent in 1982 to 43 percent in 2002. For the eighteen-to-twenty-four cohort, the drop has been faster, sinking from 59.8 percent to 32.8 percent, a decline of 27 percent. A new report released by the National Endowment for the Arts (2007), entitled *To Read or Not to Read,* makes a convincing argument about the correlations between the decline in reading and income disparity, lack of exercise, and voting. The report states that readers exercise more, watch less television, and vote more often, and that poor readers are more likely to be unemployed, have lower wages, less advancement in work, and even end up in prison. Indeed, the introduction written by NEA chair Dana Gioia states that poor reading skills correlate with lack of employment and lower wages. The same report tells us that Americans spent less for books in 2005 than they did ten years ago.

According to reports released by the U.S. Department of Education, approximately 2.9 million children aged six to twenty-one were identified with specific learning disabilities in a recent academic school year. This figure is 14.2 percent higher than a decade ago. Research reported in 2001 by the National Institute of Child Health and Human Development (NICH) and cited in a position statement of the Learning Disabilities Association of America (2001) indicates that 20 percent of elementary school students are at-risk for reading failure and of that number, 5 to 10 percent continue to have difficulty learning to read despite reading instruction that is successful for most students.

Current figures suggest that one in five students (20 percent of all children in school) have some form of reading disability (National Institute of Child Health and Human Development, 2000). These figures should be an alarming cause for concern. Fewer children are reading today, and more are being identified as having reading disabilities. Report after report has found that older students' proficiency in reading has declined over the last decade (NEA, 2007; National Institute of Child Health and Human Development, 2000). What does all of this suggest? As a nation, we are reading less both in school and at home.

Children Learn Differently

Over the last thirty years of research and practice in differentiated curriculum and instruction across all content areas, teachers have started to understand more fully the many ways that children vary in their ways of learning. The intensity of these learning differences and the ways in which they are manifested in school affect both the speed and the efficiency with which children learn.

How and why do children vary in how they learn, and what are the implications for the classroom? The following summary of learning differences helps to demonstrate why teachers should provide differentiated reading instruction instead of focusing solely on group teaching (whether the group is small or large) of reading skills and strategies.

Aptitudes and Abilities

Students' levels of potential in both verbal and nonverbal areas affect how quickly and efficiently they learn to read. Children begin to read at different ages; some are already reading fluently when they begin kindergarten or even preschool, while others focus their first years of school on learning to read. Still other children may struggle throughout their school experience to develop fluency in reading. Even children with similar ability levels in verbal areas will follow different patterns in learning to read.

For example, two children, Sara and Yvonne, have very similar high verbal IQ scores but completely different reading skills. Sara has a significant learning disability and a very low performance score, while Yvonne has a very high performance score in addition to her high verbal score and no reported learning disability. Yvonne taught herself to read independently at age four and read at an advanced level throughout her school career. Sara, although she had a similar verbal aptitude, did not read independently until she was in third grade, and she continued to struggle with reading throughout elementary and middle school. These reading difficulties were most likely due to her nonverbal spatial disability. Reading is a code, and most children begin to learn to read when they begin to break the code.

All children have the potential to learn, and all children should have opportunities to develop their abilities and talents in school. Special talents in reading or writing might mean that children understand challenging texts or write thoughtful and original stories. Talents at home might be demonstrated in hobbies such as writing songs, building complex designs using blocks, or programming computers. Students may have talents in artistic areas such as writing, drawing, or painting. Special talents can be demonstrated in school subjects or in athletics, computer science, leadership, or other areas. Having the choice to read in areas of interest can help students to identify their talents and aptitudes or their potential in these areas.

Achievement

High potential is not always associated with high achievement, for achievement is influenced by many variables. Children with very high aptitude and ability can begin to underachieve due to factors such as motivation, affect, interest, and effort. As children with learning disabilities or low motivation to read grow older, their achievement in reading and their reading levels may falter. In our reading research, we have found that in some schools with a large population of low-achieving students, some children who enter first grade reading at a fourth-grade level leave fourth grade still reading at a fourth-grade level. This fact indicates that the educational opportunities available to these students, who show great potential, do not match their needs or abilities. In a recent report on children who live in poverty, for example, shocking statistics show that the total percentage of urban students test below the level of "at proficiency" on the National Assessment of Educational Progress (NAEP) (2002). High percentages of African American students tested below the level of proficiency in reading in each of the following cities: Atlanta, 91 percent; Austin, 90 percent; Boston, 86 percent; Charlotte, 87 percent; Chicago, 90 percent; Cleveland, 92 percent; District of Columbia, 91 percent; Houston, 89 percent; Los Angeles, 91 percent; New York, 90 percent; and San Diego, 88 percent (Lewis, James, Hancock, & Hill-Jackson, 2008). In the same study, the percentage of African American students scoring at the advanced level on the NAEP was appalling, with 0 percent in Atlanta, Austin, Chicago, Cleveland, District of Columbia, Houston, Los Angeles, New York City, and San Diego. In a similar study, Reardon (2008) analyzed data in math and reading from seven thousand students, using the federal Early Childhood Longitudinal Study of Kindergarten Cohort, and found that from kindergarten to grade 5, the brightest African American students fall behind fastest. The achievement gaps grew twice as fast among those who scored above the mean compared with those who scored below. Our research on the SEM-R has demonstrated strong positive results with urban students and those who are culturally and linguistically diverse, suggesting that an enriched reading program may be one way to help to reduce this achievement gap and that the use of different types of books at different reading levels enhances reading fluency and achievement for students who read at such different levels.

Academic Background

Poor preparation and limited exposure also make a difference in how and why children learn and most likely contribute to the statistics reviewed in this chapter. When students with strong potential for learning do not have an appropriate academic background, they fail to learn at the same level as their peers who do. For example, students who have limited exposure to books, few experiences with hearing books read aloud, or poor literacy environments at home or school will fail to make similar levels of progress as compared to better prepared peers. An example of this scenario is chronicled in Ron Suskind's moving book *A Hope in the Unseen* (Suskind, 1995), the story of Cedric Jennings, a student from Washington, D.C., who attended a low-achieving, urban high school. Susskind's tale of Cedric's life provides a lesson about what happens to children of high potential when they do not receive adequate content exposure or levels of challenge to enable them to compete at challenging universities. When Cedric Jennings arrives, against all odds, at Brown University as a freshman, he wanders through the bookstore, looking at books written by and about people he has never heard of, such as Sylvia Plath. He encounters biographies of eminent persons he knows he should recognize, such as Winston Churchill. He struggles academically during his first few semesters at Brown because he does not have the background content knowledge and the exposure to books of all types that most of his fellow students arrived with. Academically talented students like Cedric deserve the right to succeed at Ivy League universities and colleges. Teachers must continue to ask why some young people with high potential do not get the opportunities or challenges they deserve in school. We also must realize what young children like Cedric can contribute to our society in character, intelligence, resilience, commitment, and grace!

The SEM-R reading program is designed to differentiate and individualize reading instruction for all students. Students like Cedric, who deserve to make continual progress in reading and to be exposed to literature that will provide challenge, benefit from the SEM-R. The program also is designed for students with potential who have not begun to read at grade level but who, with encouragement and support, can make progress, especially when they are able to read books that they select themselves in their own areas of interest.

Cultural Differences

A few years ago, a professor and colleague who was born and raised in Puerto Rico helped us to learn valuable lessons about the cultural aspects of reading and second language acquisition. Two of those lessons are relevant to this discussion. The first occurred after she had participated in a panel discussion in front of our faculty. Upon leaving the stage, Eva burst into tears when she was congratulated on a stellar presentation.

"I can't reason quickly and understand well," she explained, "when I have to mentally translate and consider what others are saying. If I could have participated in the panel in Spanish, I would have been so much better able to contribute, and I am frustrated at being able to answer so less well in English as opposed to Spanish. I spoke with less authority and less competence and could only contribute a fraction of what I might have been able to give in my own language."

The second lesson related to the cultural connotations of reading. Eva explained that reading her own books and studying was never considered something that would be more important than spending time with her family or with dear friends. Her family came first, she explained, and time for her own reading and studying always came second. Reading, a solitary activity, took her away from her family and so it was discouraged by her parents during her childhood.

In the research that we have conducted on the SEM-R, we have worked with students from all cultural, racial, and socioeconomic groups and noticed differences in reading practices both at school and at home. Some students come to school with reading habits already embedded in their self-regulated practice—due to parental training and monitoring at home—while others do not. Some have many opportunities to read at home, while others do not. It is our belief that despite these cultural differences, we must expose all students to rich, exciting reading experiences and enable them to gain reading practices and strategies that we hope they will adopt and use as students and continue to develop as they enter adolescence and adulthood.

Affect

It is easy to teach a child who is enthusiastic and wants to learn; it is much more challenging to work with children who have little enthusiasm for learning. Children who are shy or show little emotion or excitement about learning are more difficult to reach and teach, and thus they may be differentially affected by their teachers' subtle or not-so-subtle preferences for working with children who demonstrate more enthusiasm for learning to read. It is necessary, therefore, for teachers to learn as much as they can about each student, especially about his or her literacy experiences, in order to find a way to spark interest in reading in all of their students.

Effort and Ability

Del Siegle and Sally Reis (1998) conducted research about the interaction between effort and ability in students who are above grade level in reading. Because they often are not challenged as they should be, these students may coast through school without having to expend much effort; consequently, they associate high levels of ability with minimum levels of effort. Many average and above-average readers spend a great deal of their time reading content that is too easy for them. When they do encounter a challenge, however, these students may experience a loss of confidence in their ability or a loss of interest. Conversely, children who are below average in reading often fail to comprehend the connection between effort and outcome—that is, increased effort leads to improved outcome. In any area, from athletics to music to academics, effort expended makes a difference; luckily for students who are used to coasting, effort can be learned over time, with practice and with an understanding of its benefits and outcomes. The SEM-R can help students better understand the relationship between effort expended and improvement in reading skills, fluency, and comprehension.

Interests

Every child has special interests, abilities, and talents or the potential to develop them in a specific area in school or in activities that they do at home or out of school; however, many children haven't been shown how, been given the chance, or put forth the effort to develop their interests. For these children in particular, reading is one way to begin the journey of interest development. Use of the SEM-R enables children to spend time pursuing their interests by choosing the books they want to read.

It is important for children to have an increasing awareness of their special talents, interests, and abilities. Too often, the focus in school is on what children do not do well. Using the SEM-R helps children consider what they already like, what they think they may like, and what they may want to learn more about. Learning more about their interests can help children find opportunities through reading to develop these interests and, ultimately, their talents. One major goal of the SEM-R is to help students better understand their interests and talents as well as the ways they like to learn. Enriching and challenging reading opportunities can help students to identify their interests and talents in some of the following areas:

Performing arts: Students may enjoy music, dance, pantomime, or drama; they may enjoy performing in front of an audience or working behind the scenes—directing, managing, or creating sets.

Writing and journalism: Students may enjoy writing fictional stories, prose, or poetry or recording news events.

Mathematics: Students may enjoy working with numbers, problems, patterns, or logic (for example, in using computers or solving logic puzzles or word problems).

History: Students may have an interest in studying the past—wars, famous historical figures, antiques, or old photographs. They may enjoy oral histories (talking to people about their past experiences).

Fine arts: Students who have an interest in fine arts may like to work with color or texture or to design products such as fabrics, jewelry, costumes, sets, or furniture. These students also may be interested in photography or graphic design.

Sciences: Students who like science usually enjoy activities related to learning about biology, chemistry, environmental protection, or geology and doing something with this knowledge, like experimenting, conducting a science fair project, or even collecting specimens such as leaves or arrowheads.

Athletics or sports: If students are interested in athletics or sports, they usually like physical activity or are interested in learning about sports figures, diet, nutrition, physical therapy, or sports medicine.

Photography or videography: Students may enjoy the process of producing photographic images or making a motion picture or a music video.

Social action: Students may show a concern for legal, moral, or philosophical issues (for example, women's rights, AIDS issues, animal rights, or environmental issues). These students may want to change a law or do something to make the world a better place.

Business: Students may show an interest in making money, organizing or starting a business, or being in a leadership role in dealing with people—for example, being the director of a play or editor of the yearbook.

Technology: Students may like activities that involve computers, multimedia equipment, or communication.

Teachers can learn more about students' interests or potential interests by having students complete the SEM-R Reading Interest-a-Lyzer (Appendix B).

Learning Styles

Learning styles—the ways in which students learn and the modes they prefer for learning—affect their ability to learn efficiently. If attention is never or rarely paid to the ways in which students learn, there is less opportunity for them to learn in a way that will both challenge and engage them. Both informal and formal methods can be used to identify students' learning styles and encourage students to further develop and pursue learning in styles and modes that they enjoy and in which they can excel academically. Our work on learning styles has focused on the preferences that students demonstrate for varying modes of learning—for example, learning through doing projects, independent study, learning games, simulations, peer teaching, programmed instruction, lecture, drill and recitation, and discussion. We recommend that this information, which focuses on strengths rather than deficits, be used to make decisions about reading opportunities. The term *learning styles* can also refer to a more global preferred style of how students learn—for example, visual (through observing), auditory (by listening), concrete (by participating in real or simulated experiences), or hands-on or tactile (by doing something with their hands or creating and building a model, for example). Some learning styles assessments primarily evaluate sensory learning styles, summarizing them into auditory, hands-on, and visual styles.

When students with preferences for auditory learning begin to learn to read, several learning strategies can help them to be better readers (Corbo, 1984). For example, auditory readers often remember what they hear, talk while they read, and like to read aloud. Auditory readers benefit from discussions of the materials they read. Auditory learners can be asked to read the material aloud and then to explain what they have read. They benefit from the oral discussions and conferences that are a part of Phase Two in the SEM-R. Auditory readers also benefit from listening to books on CD or tape and being encouraged to explain what they have listened to with you or with a reading buddy or partner. Auditory readers do well in a group in which they read to others and are read to, so pairing such students with a reading partner is a good strategy to encourage them to read more often. Students who are auditory learners should be encouraged to write down questions and ideas while they are reading and then be allowed to discuss them; this process could, for example, help such students better understand the sequence of events in a story.

Visual learners often excel in reading, but some strategies can enhance their preferred visual style. When they read, children who are visual learners remember what they see more than what they hear. These learners should be encouraged to visualize the scenes, settings, plots, characters, and events that they read about and to discuss the metaphors they read about in visual terms. They also can be encouraged to use diagrams and illustrations to create a visual picture of what they are reading. Visual learners might benefit from the use of color-coding, highlighting, and visual cues to remember what they have read. They often think in terms of pictures, have a vivid imagination, and remember illustrations.

Hands-on or tactile learners may not catch on as quickly to traditional reading and may benefit from reading practices that enable them to use their hands, such as reading books online and scrolling while they are reading. They also benefit from dramatic read-alouds and from gestures that teachers use as they read aloud to students in order to make reading come alive. Hands-on learners can be encouraged to make models to help them remember settings and places or to make diagrams or flash cards to help them remember sequences, events, or even a complicated list of characters. Flash cards with different events of a story or book can be given to a student who can then try to organize the events in the plot in correct order to help students remember the plot or events in a story or book. Tactile learners should be encouraged to make lists, use technology, use CDs or tapes, or even move as they read.

Product Styles

Students also have preferences about the ways they like to express themselves. Joseph Renzulli calls these preferences *expression styles;* in this book, we refer to them as *product styles.* Students may use different expressive techniques such as writing, oral debates, stage performance, sculpture, dance, or a host of others; similarly, students have preferences for different product styles, which can include written, oral, hands-on, artistic, audiovisual, dramatic, service, technological, musical, and commercial products. In the SEM-R, we provide opportunities for students to express themselves during Phase Three, when they choose their work and products. If they prefer writing, they may choose to write stories or newspaper articles. If they prefer expressing themselves orally, they may choose to participate in a discussion of a book or an oral project, such as recording a favorite book on tape or a computer. If they are artistic, they may choose to draw or paint book jackets or illustrate a favorite scene from a book. If they like technology and computers, they may want to design a Web site or a multimedia computer game for a favorite book. If they like audiovisual products, they may want to film and edit a video or a brief movie or select photographs and music for a presentation. If they are interested in business or commercial work, they may want to start a small business, market a product, or try to sell an idea. If they are interested in service, they may help in the community by working to make a difference by, for example, collecting food or clothing for persons in need of help. If they are interested in drama, they may want to act in a play, act out an event or story, or role-play a favorite character in a book. If they like hands-on or manipulative work, they may want to assemble a working model or a project from a kit or build a creation or invention. If they are musical, they may want to play a musical instrument or compose and perform music.

Self-Regulation and Study Skills

Self-regulation in students is defined as the behaviors they learn to enhance their own learning. Students' acquisition of self-regulation strategies vary greatly. Our research has shown that self-regulation in reading can increase with practice and support during the time students spend reading in the SEM-R. Students face different types of challenges in learning how to meet their parents' and teachers' expectations while they also learn to develop their own strengths and talents and a set of behaviors that constitutes their own self-regulation; research suggests that they benefit from learning to assume responsibility for their own learning (Zimmerman, 1989, 1990). In effect, students may need to develop better self-regulation skills to become more successful in school. When students are self-regulated, they develop a set of constructive behaviors that can positively affect their learning. In order to be responsible for decisions about their own learning and performance, students need to learn some specific skills.

Barry Zimmerman (1989) has demonstrated that there are both a common set of self-regulation strategies and an *individual* set of skills that each child can develop to be successful in school and in life. These skills include methods of organization for the time and place in which academic work is completed, the types of regular patterns of homework completion and test preparation one learns to use, and emerging self-control. Research by Zimmerman and others strongly suggests that self-regulation skills can be taught, learned, and controlled, and, in our experience over the last three decades, absence of these self-regulation skills can have an extremely detrimental impact on student learning.

Self-regulation strategies used by successful students can be divided into three categories: personal, behavioral, and environmental.

Personal strategies involve how a child classifies and interprets information and include

- **Organizing and transforming information.** Strategies such as outlining, summarizing, highlighting, using flash cards or index cards, and drawing pictures, diagrams, or charts enable children to become much more efficient at learning. Even some of our brightest students do not always understand how to study well or efficiently.

- **Goal setting and planning.** These strategies include identifying goals or standards for children that they will eventually adopt as their own. Other self-regulation strategies in this category include sequencing, timing, time management, pacing, and thinking about how one can accomplish one's best work. For example, parents might help their children learn to complete homework before they watch television or play video games and to limit the time they spend on entertainment to a certain number of hours each night. Teachers should provide strategies and practices to help students increase their self-regulation in reading, a major goal of Phase Two in the SEM-R.

- **Keeping records and monitoring.** The goal of this type of strategy is to help children learn to be in charge of understanding their strengths and weaknesses and to identify areas in need of improvement. They need to take the time to assess why they do well on some kinds of assignments and tasks and not as well on others. These strategies include note taking, listing their own errors, keeping drafts of assignments, considering their own improvements, and maintaining a portfolio of their most special work.

- **Written or verbal rehearsing and memorizing.** These strategies help children learn to memorize more efficiently and learn how to improve their written and verbal language. Examples include using mnemonics to remember important information (for example, by remembering the first initials of each word in a list), using imagery to remember diagrams or visualize concepts, and using repetition (for example, repeatedly reciting material orally or mentally, teaching someone else the material, or making sample questions).

Behavioral strategies occur when students learn to check their own progress or quality of work by examining the actions they take during the learning process. Children must learn to evaluate their actions and understand the consequences of those actions. In this type of self-evaluation, children analyze the learning task to determine what their teacher expects and whether they want to put forth the time and effort necessary to do the task. They also learn to reflect on their self-instructions, attentiveness, and teacher feedback. When they have learned to think about the consequences of their actions, they may think about what will happen if they do not learn to read challenging material for twenty to twenty-five minutes each day or if they play a video game instead of studying for a spelling test.

Children also can learn how to provide their own rewards to motivate themselves to meet their own goals in reading. They can learn to reinforce their own positive actions and to delay gratification until they have achieved their goal. For example, Jonna can learn to say to herself, "I really want to watch that DVD. If I finish twenty-five minutes of reading for my social studies assignment, I will watch a half hour of the movie and then go back to studying if I need more time." Our experiences with the SEM-R and research conducted by Barry Zimmerman (1989, 1990) suggest that the most successful students in reading use self-regulation strategies regularly.

Environmental strategies for self-regulated learning involve adaptation of a student's environment and the use of external resources—for example, seeking information from sources such as the library and the Internet; seeking assistance from peers, teachers, or other adults; emulating exemplary models; reviewing notes and textbooks; and rewriting notes from class and independent reading. Structuring their study environment for optimal results can also help children become more self-regulated; such strategies include selecting or arranging the physical setting; isolating, eliminating, or minimizing distractions; and breaking up study periods and spreading them over time—also known as *chunking* assignments. In a SEM-R program, environmental self-regulation strategies might lead students to find a place in the classroom where they will be less inclined to be distracted, sit next to another student who is a positive role model, try to focus on increasing their independent reading time by a few minutes each day, or achieve personal goals by reflecting on what has worked best for them in reading.

Teachers can encourage self-regulation by helping students acquire specific strategies that enable them to increase their control over their own behavior and environment. Teachers can also help by modeling these behaviors and discussing how they themselves learned to focus on reading and how they set goals for personal, pleasurable reading as well as for challenging reading. Researchers who study self-regulated learning believe that self-regulation is enhanced when someone carefully observes and considers his or her own behaviors and acts on what has been learned. The goal is to have children learn to decrease negative behaviors and increase positive behaviors in reading. Self-regulated students learn to ask themselves, "Does this reading strategy work for me in this situation?" For example, students who struggle with reading or writing will have to plan for ample time to complete written work and long reading assignments.

In order to improve students' self-regulation skills, teachers can encourage them to carefully consider their own goals and the work patterns they use to achieve their goals instead of comparing their performance with that of their peers. Self-regulated behaviors can help to decrease the discrepancy between a student's current and desired levels of performance in school and ability to attain goals. Students should learn that there are different ways to attain goals and how to select the best way to complete a specific task at home or in school. In many classrooms, teachers assume most of the responsibility for the learning process, and students may begin to depend on this model of learning. It is critical that when teachers use the SEM-R, they encourage and support students in taking control of their own reading. Teachers can accomplish this goal by modeling good reading strategies in Phase One, providing time for quiet, self-directed reading in Phase Two, and creating a supportive environment in which students can take risks.

Harold Stevenson and others (1990) conducted several cross-cultural studies of school achievement, investigating and comparing the achievement of American children with those from other cultures. Their work focused on achievement in both mathematics and reading and the identification of characteristics associated with the high performance of some students who consistently surpass other students in achievement. One fascinating part of Stevenson's research explored how many parents in other cultures support the high achievement of their children by having a quiet time every evening when everyone in the family works and reads together. During this quiet study time, parents and children read and do their own work in the same room, so parents are available to help or guide their children if necessary.

When parents of high-potential, underachieving students contact us, they often explain that they cannot understand why their smart children are not doing well in school. Sometimes the same parents insist that their children spend hours on homework each night. When asked where their children do their homework, often these parents respond that their children do their homework in their bedroom. When we ask whether distractions might be present in their child's bedroom, these parents explain that their children have access to computers and instant messaging, telephones, music, and often television. Children who have many temptations and distractions may not learn to fully develop their own unique set of self-regulation skills; thus, the parental monitoring of homework and study skills that Stevenson and his colleagues have found in other cultures might be necessary for some U.S. students. Because so many parents fail to instill these self-regulated learning strategies for reading, it becomes the task of teachers to help in this process.

Some students are better self-regulators than their peers, and some talented students have done very well in school without self-regulation strategies due to the combination of their high abilities and an unchallenging curriculum. If learning is relatively easy for someone, effort, organization, and other self-regulated activities are often limited or nonexistent. Some social conditions or personal issues such as distractibility, behavior issues, or lack of support at home can also prevent students from developing self-regulated learning strategies. Such issues may prevent some students who have already gained some of these strategies from using them regularly, and they may need to be helped and encouraged to do so. Many students find it difficult to learn self-regulation when it is not taught, modeled, or rewarded by the adults or teachers in their home and school.

Even if students interact regularly with adults who demonstrate self-regulation, some still fail to use the skills and strategies their parents or teachers regularly employ at home or school. Using the SEM-R gives these students a second chance to learn these strategies, a task that is considered essential for one compelling reason: compared with low-achieving students, high achievers set more specific learning goals, use a variety of learning strategies, self-monitor more often, and adapt their efforts more systematically. The quality and quantity of self-regulation processes are crucial. Any particular self-regulation strategy will not work for all students, and the same few strategies will not work optimally for each person on every task. It is important that students learn to differentiate their own use of self-regulatory learning skills instead of using a single strategy. They also must learn that their goals and their choice of self-regulation strategies need to be continually adjusted. Teachers should help students focus on understanding content and academic material and persisting when they are challenged.

Differentiation and the Use of Differentiated Teaching Strategies to Teach Reading

Differentiation of curriculum and instruction attempts to address differences in students and the ways they learn. Multiple approaches enrich, modify, adapt, and differentiate instruction and curriculum to match students' individual needs (Renzulli, 1977, 1988; Tomlinson, 1995). Tomlinson (1995) emphasized that in differentiating the curriculum, teachers are not dispensers of knowledge; rather, they are organizers of learning opportunities. Differentiation of instruction and curriculum enables teachers to address differences in student learning through materials and work of varying levels of difficulty and through scaffolding, enrichment, acceleration, diverse kinds of grouping, and different time schedules (Tomlinson, 1995). Renzulli (1988) has discussed differentiation on five dimensions: content, processes and teaching practices, classroom organization and management, student product choices, and the personal choices that teachers make about how to begin and enact the process.

Specific strategies for differentiating curriculum and instruction in reading can be used to help ensure both that every child can make continual progress and that all students, whether they are on, at, or below grade level in reading, are reasonably challenged and engaged. Many principals and superintendents urge classroom teachers to use differentiated curriculum and instructional strategies across all grade levels to ensure sufficient challenge for all students. Some of these strategies are introduced in this chapter, and most are integrated into the SEM-R.

Grouping Students for Instruction

Many forms of grouping are used in schools. Students can be grouped by achievement or instructional level or grouped by interests or learning styles. They can be grouped heterogeneously, as they are in most schools, or they can be grouped by reading or instructional level within or across classrooms. In some schools, cluster grouping is used to enable students who are academically advanced in a certain content area, such as reading, to be grouped in one classroom with other students who are talented in the same area. When cluster grouping is used, one fifth-grade teacher may have a group of six advanced reading students clustered in a classroom instead of having them purposely distributed among four different classrooms. This arrangement enables more in-depth and complex differentiated learning opportunities to be offered by a teacher with advanced training to meet the needs of these students.

Researchers have found that cluster grouping and other forms of instructional grouping, when coupled with differentiated instruction and content, benefits gifted and talented students and also helps to challenge other students across *all* levels of achievement. For example, grouping by instructional levels allows differentiated content to be more easily used as the range of achievement levels in classrooms is reduced; as different books are used to challenge and engage students of different reading levels, understanding and enjoyment of literature increases. In general, grouping students by achievement and instructional level has been found to produce positive achievement outcomes when the curriculum provided to students in different groups is appropriately changed so that it meets the needs of the students (Gentry, 1999; Kulik & Kulik, 1991). In other words, it is the differentiated instruction that occurs within groups that makes grouping an appropriate instructional strategy, not simply the fact that students are grouped (Kulik & Kulik, 1991; Rogers, 1991).

Many forms of instructional grouping can be used for reading. Cluster grouping is just one option for grouping both high-potential and low-potential students in reading. Research on grouping (Gentry, 1999; Kulik & Kulik, 1991) suggests benefits for all students in some forms of grouping, while emphasizing the important point that grouping alone has a very small effect on academic gain and other outcomes. In order for cluster grouping for reading instruction to work, it is necessary to use different instructional methods and content that has been adapted and differentiated for the needs of the students in the group. Marcia Gentry's (1999) research on cluster grouping has proven that this practice, coupled with differentiated curriculum and instructional methods that meet the educational needs of students, raises achievement and promotes opportunities for growth for all students.

Acceleration and Curriculum Compacting

Various forms of acceleration can be used in reading instruction; the most commonly used types are content-level acceleration (enabling students who are advanced in reading to work at an advanced level that is commensurate with their reading comprehension level) and curriculum compacting. A report entitled *A Nation Deceived* provides research support for the many types of acceleration that have been used with students for decades (Colangelo, Assouline, & Gross, 2004). Since this report, some districts have adopted policies that enable acceleration to be more widely used in schools.

Curriculum compacting is a differentiation strategy that has been very successfully used in reading instruction (Reis, Burns, & Renzulli, 1992). In this process, the teacher (1) defines the goals and outcomes of a particular unit or segment of instruction, (2) uses assessment procedures to determine and document which students have already mastered most or all of a specified set of learning outcomes, and (3) provides replacement strategies for material already mastered through the use of instructional options, some based on student interests, that enable a more challenging, engaging, and productive use of the student's time.

When teachers compact curriculum and instruction in reading, they often list the objectives for a particular reading skill or unit and follow these with data on students' proficiency in those objectives, which can include test scores, behavioral profiles, and past academic records. Teachers can subsequently select assessment tools or procedures that document strengths in reading. The pretest instruments can be formal measures, such as pencil-and-paper tests, or informal measures, such as performance assessments based on observations of class participation and written assignments.

The procedures that are used to carry out curriculum differentiation include the introduction of greater depth into regular curricular material (Renzulli, 1988; Reis and others, 1993). Teachers who are using curriculum compacting in reading instruction should replace the regular reading material that has been eliminated with more appropriately matched trade books or other materials such as those suggested for Phase Two of the SEM-R. Alternate books should be accelerated or enriched options in reading based on students' individual strengths, interests, and learning styles. Teachers should never simply replace compacted regular reading work with more material or more advanced material that is solely determined by the teacher; instead, students' interests should be considered. For example, if a student loves reading biographies, that option can be used to replace easier reading material from the regular curriculum. Teachers should also be careful to help monitor the challenge level of the material that is being substituted. Students need to understand the nature of effort and challenge, and teachers should ensure that students are not simply replacing the compacted material with basic reading or work that is not advanced or of personal interest to the student.

Curriculum compacting enables teachers to (1) adjust levels of required learning so that all students are challenged, (2) increase the number of in-depth learning experiences that they can offer, and (3) introduce various types of enrichment into regular curricular experiences. Teachers who use compacting in reading can compact reading content as well as instruction with one student or with a group of students with similar curricular strengths. In the SEM-R, compacting can be used to eliminate grouped instruction, to individually determine what instruction should be provided during Phase Two reading conferences, and to determine the choice of books and activities in both Phase Two and Three activities.

In a national study (Reis and others, 1993), curriculum compacting was used to differentiate curriculum to accommodate the specific strengths of academically talented students. After teachers eliminated 40–50 percent of regular reading curricular content for the 440 gifted and talented students identified in their classrooms, no differences between treatment and control groups were found in posttest achievement scores in reading comprehension. These teachers were able to assess the areas of the curriculum that could be compacted, but some struggled with replacing the reading curriculum they eliminated because there were so few challenging and appropriate texts in the classroom.

Tiered Reading Instruction

Differentiated instruction and content can be used by teachers to engage and challenge students at all reading levels. When teachers tier reading instruction, they provide different levels (easy or below grade level, intermediate or at grade level, and challenging or well above grade level) of opportunities for students. They may tier the goals they have for a lesson as well as their level of instruction, class activities, resources, products, or homework, leaving some open-ended choices to enable flexibility for students. Tiering assignments enables teachers to give students choice and opportunities to respond to appropriately challenging questioning skills in the classroom and for easier or more complex assigned reading and writing. Tiering can also enable independent choice of these reading and writing assignments in class and should not be used to predetermine which students will work at which tier all the time. Tiering reading assignments is an essential strategy in the SEM-R, in which teachers encourage students to select books at appropriate levels of challenge and provide differentiated instruction for individual students.

Choice

Choice contributes to engagement, motivation, and interest in reading. In the SEM-R, we recommend independent choice in reading and writing activities, as well as choice of project and independent study options in Phase Three. Choice is a core component of our work and has been a major factor, we believe, in the success of the SEM-R with students of all socioeconomic and cultural groups. Independent reading choices enable children to pursue books in areas of interest and to continue reading in these areas over the course of the time they spend in a SEM-R program. Choice also enables students to continue with independent study opportunities in Phase Three, during which they can create independent project choices based on their interests. Interest assessment and interest-based reading opportunities can enable choice to occur easily, and in our experience, in a few short days, most children become accustomed to choosing books in which they have an interest and then learn to self-regulate their reading as they begin to receive individual, differentiated instruction that applies to these books.

Differentiation in reading benefits all students, but it perhaps is more important for students at either end of the reading spectrum—those who are well above and those who are well below grade level. It is interesting that in any textbook on reading, one finds multiple suggestions for how to help struggling or below-average readers but little or no focus on what should be done to engage and challenge talented readers. The universal finding that has emerged from our research on differentiated instructional practices is that regular reading instruction is often too easy for talented readers and too challenging for below-average readers. Regular reading textbooks may provide little or no challenge for advanced readers and too much challenge for lower readers, so differentiated practices are important for providing appropriate levels of instruction for these groups.

Most teachers understand what happens to students for whom reading instruction is too difficult; they see the embarrassment faced by students who cannot read aloud or cannot read the same level of texts as their chronological peers. In one study of college students with learning disabilities, for example, recalling their reading experiences brought tears to participants' eyes as they recounted stories of being humiliated when they could not work at the same level of challenge as their peers due to dyslexia. In our research on the SEM-R, we have found that students who read at the lowest level of challenge are often the ones who choose books that are much too challenging for them because they are embarrassed to have their friends see the low-level books from which they should be reading.

The appropriate match between a learner's abilities and the difficulty of the instructional work occurs when instruction is slightly above the learner's current level of functioning; this has been called the *optimal match*. Chall and Conard (1991) state that when the match is optimal, learning is enhanced; if, however, "the match is not optimal, learning is less efficient and development may be halted" (p. 19). Using textbooks and reading books that are several years below students' reading level may result in halted development as well as subsequent motivational problems for talented readers who regard reading as an effortless process. A longitudinal study

(Reis, Hébert, Díaz, Maxfield, & Ratley, 1995) of academically talented students who either achieved in school earning grades of B or better or underachieved in a large urban high school, earning grades of C or lower found that the underachieving students consistently acknowledged that the easy curriculum they had encountered in elementary and middle school had failed to prepare them for the rigors of challenging classes in high school, and most mentioned a lack of challenge in reading. They consistently reported that their classes and academic tasks had been "too easy," and discussed "breezing" through elementary school. The optimal match in cases like these (as in all cases) would have involved some level of supported struggle, a concept that will be discussed in subsequent chapters.

The nature and type of differentiation strategies used with students will vary based on the factors discussed earlier in this chapter in the section "Children Learn Differently." For example, to meet the needs of some advanced readers, teachers must accelerate students' reading by helping them to find material that is above their current grade level and having them read at a rate that challenges them. Advanced readers may also benefit from reading programs that stress the development of creative and critical thinking skills, that present the opportunity to discuss controversial issues, or that offer the opportunity for advanced reading discussions. These opportunities are available within the SEM-R because it is a differentiated program in which curriculum compacting automatically occurs. Using the SEM-R does require personal effort by teachers to find appropriately challenging books in multiple areas of interest and will require some classroom changes, such as finding space for students to read individually, for conferences between teacher and students, for storing more reading materials, and for work completed during the independent and creative Phase Three. All students should have opportunities to participate in appropriate learning experiences, and differentiated instruction provided in a SEM-R program can be used to ensure that all learners experience continual progress and increase their performance in reading.

The SEM-R represents a shift in thinking about how to teach reading from instruction that is the same for a whole class to an approach in which instruction is delivered to individual students during reading conferences. These conferences provide teachers with opportunities to differentiate the types of reading strategies they teach and discuss according to the needs of individual students. All students need to have a large repertoire of strategies that they can access when they encounter problems while reading. Successful readers use multiple strategies simultaneously while reading (Duke & Pearson, 2002; Pressley and others, 1992). By explicitly showing students how and why to use individual strategies, teachers make those strategies visible and understandable to students (Afflerbach, Pearson, & Paris, 2007, 2008; Harvey & Goudvis, 2000; Keene & Zimmermann, 1997; National Reading Panel, 2000; Paris & Jacobs, 1984; Pressley and others, 1992). Teachers often fall into a pattern in which they teach struggling readers only low-level strategies such as decoding or paying attention to punctuation when reading aloud and teach talented readers high-level strategies that involve inference and evaluation (Sweeny, 2008). The SEM-R bookmarks (Appendix A), along with the most common reading strategies discussed in the next chapter, will help teachers provide differentiated strategy instruction that is responsive to the needs of individual readers. An important goal of the SEM-R is to provide all students with high-level strategy instruction. More information about reading strategies, including how to use the SEM-R bookmarks to support strategy instruction and student use of these reading strategies, will be discussed in upcoming chapters.

What We Have Learned About Using Differentiated Instruction in a SEM-R Program

Differentiated instruction is appropriate; explicitly encouraged by advocates for students with learning disabilities (Council for Exceptional Children, 2004) and for gifted and talented students (National Association for Gifted Children, 1994); and included in the literacy standards of the International Reading Association (2004) and the National Council of Teachers of English (2004; International Reading Association & National Council of Teachers of English, 1996). These organizations support the use of differentiation in order to encourage teachers to consider students' strengths as well as their weaknesses when planning instruction.

Effective differentiated instruction requires thoughtful planning. Different methods for providing differentiation involve content, control, grouping, pacing, processes, instruction, and products. The ways in which these differentiation strategies fit within the SEM-R are summarized in this section.

Content

Content focuses on what is being taught and learned. Teachers who differentiate content vary the level of complexity of content according to their students' developmental and interest levels. A student who is passionate about a particular subject may be capable of learning more advanced content than would be typical for someone her age. The materials used to differentiate content may include books of different reading levels, books that have different balances of text and photographs or illustrations, audio books, or online materials that demonstrate advanced concepts through animation. Consider these options when you are providing literacy materials for your students during SEM-R reading times.

Control

When we speak about control, we are considering the degree to which the teacher directs learning and the level of independence that the teacher allows students to develop. A classroom that features differentiated control is a collaborative environ-ment in which the teacher is comfortable in relinquishing some control over the topics studied in order to capitalize on students' interests and to encourage student autonomy in learning. Student choice in reading materials, development of self-regulated reading behaviors, and freedom to pursue creative extensions of literacy activities during Phase Three of the SEM-R are some ways that teachers can turn over some control to students.

Grouping

Teachers can create optimal learning environments by varying the groupings of stu-dents. One consideration in creating groups might be students' preferred learning styles. Phase One is best facilitated as a whole-class experience. Teachers have dif-ferentiated Phase Two time by having most students read on their own, but some students have needed other accommodations such as reading for part of the time with a partner, buddy reading the same book with another student, or alternat-ing between reading a book independently and listening to it in audio form. Phase Three time allows the most flexibility in grouping: some students may want to work in a collaborative group of three to five friends; others may want to work with a partner who shares their passion for a particular topic; and still other students may want to pursue an individual interest during this time. Teachers can also use Phase Three time to pull together small groups of students in order to provide specific skill instruction such as creativity training exercises or an introduction to a compu-ter program or a group of Web sites.

Pacing

Every teacher feels pressure to cover curriculum content within the constraints of the school year, and the pace of instruction is typically governed by this timeline. Yet students need different amounts of time to fully grasp the concepts and content presented. Teachers should attend to the amount of time it takes a student to read a specific book. If it is taking the student a very long time to read the book, the book may be too difficult for her. If the student is reading books very quickly, this is an opportunity for the teacher to determine whether the student understands what she is reading, and if so, to encourage her to read more difficult books.

Processes

Processes are the ways in which teachers support student learning and work, as well as the ways in which teachers provide instruction. There should be a balance between teacher-directed instruction and student-initiated learning and input. For example, during Phase One, teachers can create an interactive climate in which stu-dents are encouraged to share their thoughts and opinions about the books being presented. Many teachers have provided their students with training in what makes a good book hook and have reserved time for student book hooks. During Phase Two conferences, rather than having all teacher-directed questions, students can be asked to contribute their own questions, thoughts, and opinions about the book they are reading and about their own progress in reading. During Phase Three, teachers might consider creating different options that support different learning processes. For example, a mystery book club might need instruction on inductive thinking, while a pair of students who are interested in creating a graphic novel based on a literary classic might need to learn how to condense or summarize information.

Instruction

Different students need instruction in different reading strategies—and to different degrees. Phase One is the optimal time to introduce and model how reading strategies are used. Phase Two is the time when you can follow up on that strategy instruction as needed or provide different strategy instruction. It is important to note that *all* students need strategy instruction. All readers need to engage in high-level conversations about books, even struggling readers. It is tempting for teachers to focus only on low-level strategies such as decoding or fluency instruction with poor readers, but all students need to have more challenging conversations about topics such as a character's motivation or issues that require students to use evaluation and synthesis. Some teachers assume that talented readers are always successful and therefore don't need strategy instruction, but if these readers are reading challenging books, they need support as they tackle the advanced style or content. Teachers can support all readers by asking challenging questions, telling them the name of the reading strategy they are being asked to use, modeling how it is used, giving students multiple opportunities to practice the strategy, and then providing feedback on their use of the strategy. This is an effective, research-based method for improving reading comprehension (Afflerbach, Pearson, & Paris, 2007, 2008).

Products

Products are evidence of student learning and can be differentiated by their type, complexity, and length. When we think about the many ways that students can demonstrate their learning, we consider written, oral, and physical products such as short stories, class presentations, models, multimedia presentations, and demonstrations. Within a SEM-R program, students can demonstrate their learning in many different ways. During Phase Two conferences, teachers can gauge students' use of strategies during questioning about the text or assess students' fluency while listening to them read aloud from a book. Students' written responses or reflections about a book can provide additional insight into their comprehension and application of strategies.

Summary

This chapter has discussed the many ways that children learn and how teachers, by using the SEM-R, can provide students with ideas for different types of products, thereby encouraging use of reading strategies, creativity, and choice so that students have the opportunity to demonstrate their learning in a way that aligns with their learning styles and preferences. In the next chapter we discuss how children learn to read, review some recent reading research, and discuss how we integrate reading instruction and strategy use into the SEM-R.

Reading Instruction Essentials

3

In this chapter, we briefly discuss the ways children learn to read, how the SEM-R aligns with research and best practices in reading instruction, and how it supports fluency and comprehension development. The various differentiated reading strategies that we discuss in this chapter are embedded across all three phases of the SEM-R.

Being able to read well is the most important factor that determines children's success in school, and all students deserve both challenging reading instruction and materials and books that will foster continual progress in reading. Differentiated instruction is integral to this continual process for students of all abilities and instructional levels. Reading is a learned skill, and the ability to read is acquired differently and in different time sequences by different children. When students begin to read fluently, they move beyond the process of *learning to read* to achieve the goal of *reading to learn.* Increasing fluency (how efficiently and easily children read) and comprehension (how well they understand what they read) is necessary in order to make reading more enjoyable. Proficient readers read with automaticity, devoting less effort to decoding and comprehending text. Less able readers, on the other hand, usually read because they have to, not because they want to. Research over the last few decades has demonstrated that talented readers typically enjoy reading (Halsted, 1990; Kaplan, 1999; Reis and others, 2004); perhaps this is because they read with ease. Although a full discussion of the philosophical and practical nuances of the differences in how children learn to read and how most teachers teach reading is beyond the scope of this book, it should be noted that several schools of thought address these complicated processes. Some research suggests that students must have the phonics base to unlock the reading "code" and must be able to decode before comprehension can occur. An alternate view contends that comprehension can be developed together with decoding and that the development of one enhances the other. Research by Snow, Burns, and Griffin (1998), for example, found that most kindergarten students conclude the school year with the ability to read some sight words and that by the conclusion of first grade, they should have a sight word reading vocabulary of three hundred to five hundred words.

In traditional reading classrooms, comprehension skills are primarily applied to workbook pages, activity sheets, and basal stories as opposed to real books and literature because teachers primarily rely on basal readers and a certain prescribed sequence of instruction. In the SEM-R approach, students apply comprehension skills to authentic literature, while in basal reading programs, children view reading primarily as a set of skills that they practice rather than a set of skills that they apply to their learning. Scott Paris (2001), a leading researcher in literacy and reading comprehension, has found that when children cannot connect reading with real books and authentic texts, they are less likely to believe that reading is either enjoyable or worthwhile.

What Is Reading and How Should It Be Taught?

The National Council of Teachers of English (2004) defines reading as a complex and purposeful process in which readers simultaneously use their knowledge of spoken and written language, their knowledge of the topic of the text, and their knowledge of their culture to construct meaning from text. In a fascinating new book, Maryanne Wolf (2007) asserts that the act of reading is not a natural biological act. Wolf, who studies the biology of reading, believes that we can read solely because of the ways that our brains have evolved over time. Regardless of how difficult it may be to teach children to read, that is our charge, and with it, we assume a responsibility for increased efforts as literacy decreases in our country. What, then, must teachers do to increase literacy? How can we teach children to read and to enjoy the process?

To learn to read, children need to understand the sounds of letters (phonics), the meanings of words (vocabulary), the various word parts (grammatical markers), and how to make meaning from both individual words and groups of words (overall meaning or semantics). In most classrooms, teachers focus on two types of reading instruction, the use of phonics and whole language. Phonics instruction focuses on the sounds of letters and words, and this instruction usually enables children to associate printed letters and combinations of letters with their corresponding sounds. When children are taught phonetically, they learn to sound out new words by using the sounds that letters and combinations of letters make. Dog is made up of three phonemes and sounded out as ddd—ooo—ggg (d/o/g). In our experience in hundreds of classroom observations over the last several years of research, most phonics instruction is delivered to children by using workbooks or worksheets with practice exercises based on letter sounds, matching pictures with spoken words, and practicing identification of letters, words, or combinations of vowels. Students, however, need more in-depth and frequent encounters with words than simple worksheets will provide.

The whole-language approach to reading focuses on reading comprehension and enables students to find meaning in written language based on their past experiences with both the spoken and written word. Teachers who use a whole-language approach teach reading during all content areas as well as a specific "reading time" allotment. These teachers emphasize literature and books and integrate multiple reading and writing opportunities into all learning experiences. These two distinct approaches to teaching reading can be summarized this way: in a phonetic approach, children sound out letters and blend them to form words, while a whole-language approach emphasizes literature and the meaning of words.

The last few decades of reading research suggest that there is no one best way to teach reading skills. A balanced approach to teaching reading combines a foundation in phonics with whole-language methods. Only through multiple, differentiated types of instruction can students gain the skills necessary to recognize and manipulate the sounds of letters and words and, subsequently, to understand what they have read. Because all children learn differently, only a balanced approach to teaching reading can provide many with the skills necessary to read well. Literacy is a gradual process of learning to understand and use language from birth throughout the early school years. Children learn to use oral forms of language first as they learn to both listen and speak and, later, to use other forms of language in reading and writing experiences. Reading instruction in the SEM-R incorporates a combination of both methods, as individual student reading conferences enable teachers to apply direct phonics instruction if students need it within a rich literacy approach to reading based on individual choice of high interest books.

Developmentally Appropriate Practices for Teaching Reading

When teachers consider their students' interests and abilities as part of the process of teaching them to read, they draw on their prior teaching experiences and knowledge. Teachers' beliefs about students' abilities and reading instructional levels, coupled with their expectations about the challenge level of the books that students read, influences their perceptions about reading instruction in their classrooms. Both prior training and experience have taught teachers to implement developmentally appropriate content for a given grade level, and many teachers believe that the activities and curriculum that are suitable for students at one grade level will not be suitable for students at another grade level. In our research on SEM-R, for example, we have encountered many teachers who believe that all students should be reading only books that are at or below their recommended lexile or fluency level. Such beliefs may interfere with teachers' ability to differentiate curriculum and instruction that will challenge each student In the SEM-R, we recommend matching students with high interest books that are slightly above their current fluency and lexile level to challenge and engage them.

Debate and discussion continues in regard to what constitutes developmentally appropriate reading practices for children. Unfortunately, these guidelines usually include recommendations for a particular grade level based on typically developing students rather than atypical students or those who need differentiated instruction. Therefore, developmentally appropriate reading practices that are appropriate for most or many students at a particular grade level may actually be inappropriate for either high-potential students or those who are reading below grade level because they do not take into account their advanced or delayed reading development. For example, while it might be appropriate for most kindergartners to learn to form letters by molding clay, such instruction would not advance the literacy skills of a kindergarten student who began the year reading at a third-grade or even higher level. Teachers must have a strong knowledge of both the characteristics of their students and the multiple methods for teaching reading so that they can match their methods to the individual needs of the children they teach. Accordingly, they must also understand the need for differentiated reading instruction to address children's varied needs and be committed to implementing it.

Throughout this book, you will find that we believe that teachers should consider the personal development and reading needs of each child and provide differentiated reading instruction that takes those characteristics into consideration, regardless of grade, predefined grade expectations or limitations, or broad guidelines about what is developmentally appropriate.

Learning to Read

Reading is a learned skill, and most illiterate people were never taught to read. Reading begins when children understand that letters form words, words convey meaning, and written words are images that have to be decoded. In order to read, children must recognize symbols and patterns of symbols. Early literacy skills are evident when children notice and identify symbols in their environment such as a stop sign or the stylized *M* from the McDonald's logo. They learn that those symbols convey meaning. This recognition progresses to understanding that letters are the symbols we use to form words. After a child has become familiar with symbols, then with letters, then with words, a model is formed in the brain that enables subsequent recognition. This model emerges when children receive reading instruction. Research and experience suggest that most children learn to sound out words phonetically during first, second, and third grade. If a child can't make this connection between the alphabet and sounds, reading will be difficult and delayed. The inability to make this connection might be a sign of a learning problem such as dyslexia, a disability that usually causes children to struggle as they learn to read; however, once they develop some initial decoding skills, some dyslexic children can make progress in reading very quickly. Others will struggle with reading throughout their lives.

Dyslexia or other learning disabilities are not the only reasons why some children have difficulty learning to read. When children begin school, they usually have a larger spoken vocabulary than reading vocabulary, developed from home experiences such as being spoken to, being read to, or watching television and from other life experiences. During kindergarten, most children have naturally developed language skills and knowledge about reading and as they begin to read, their reading vocabulary is usually substantially behind their spoken vocabulary, provided that their home experiences have provided them with spoken language experiences. In a study by Betty Hart and Todd Risley (2003), five-year-old children from impoverished language environments were found to have heard 32 million fewer words than children from middle-class homes. The importance of early exposure to language that is rich, frequent, and characterized by complete sentences cannot be stressed enough. Poverty (and the accompanying struggles faced by poor families) is the number one indicator of poor school performance (RAND Labor and Population, 2005). A child in a welfare family grows up hearing millions fewer words than a child in a professional family, and this deficit has a negative impact on the reading development of poor children.

As children begin to read in school, they encounter vocabulary words that extend beyond their spoken vocabulary and they may experience some frustration as they try to read words that they do not recognize. In the early grades, children begin to sound out words, often without knowing what they mean. Children with smaller vocabularies are often those who remain behind academically (Biemiller, 2003). Children who come to kindergarten in the 25th percentile or below in vocabulary remain behind other children in reading comprehension and vocabulary development. By sixth grade, they are three full grade levels behind the children whose vocabulary development was at or above the 75th percentile. When the work is extended to decoding at early grade levels, the consequences are even more disturbing: Juel (2005) found that children's phoneme awareness in grade 1 could be used to predict 88 percent of the lowest readers in grade 4.

Reading well depends on how well children acquire both appreciation and skills related to literacy such as understanding what the written word means, having an awareness of the alphabet and printed language, understanding that letters make up words, realizing that language involves the use of words, acquiring an awareness of letters and sounds and how they fit together, and understanding the connection between letters, words, and print. These basic skills are the best beginning in learning how to read.

The National Reading Panel Report

The National Reading Panel (NRP) report summarized existing research and identified various approaches to reading instruction such as explicit instruction in phonemic awareness, systematic phonics instruction, methods to improve fluency, and ways to enhance comprehension (National Reading Panel, 2000). The panel's findings include information about phonemic awareness—the awareness that words are made up of smaller parts (sounds) called *phonemes*. When we teach phonemic awareness, we provide children with a basic foundation to help them learn to spell. In its review of research, the National Reading Panel (2000) found that children read better when they have specific instruction in phonemic awareness. The panel found that students show marked benefits from explicit phonics instruction from kindergarten through sixth grade and suggested that phonics instruction both teaches students about the relationship between phonemes and printed letters and demonstrates how to use this knowledge to read and spell.

Other findings from the NRP report (National Reading Panel, 2000) involve the need to foster reading fluency, (being able to read quickly), accuracy (word recognition and knowledge), and expression (putting the right feeling, emotion, or emphasis on the right word or phrase). Teaching fluency includes guided oral reading, in which students read out loud to someone who corrects their mistakes and provides them with feedback, and independent silent reading, in which students read silently. The NRP report indicates that for good reading comprehension, students must recognize vocabulary and understand the words they read; thus, both vocabulary instruction and repetition of words is important. The panel found that reading comprehension skills can be taught, and it identified seven ways of teaching text comprehension (National Reading Panel, 2000).

Reading Fluency

Reading fluency is the ability to read with speed, accuracy, and expression. A common characteristic of skillful readers is the speed and effortlessness with which they read. Reading fluency is closely related to reading comprehension, and research shows a pattern of increased fluency and comprehension when students receive early and individualized support. Prominent theorists who have examined the relationship between fluency and comprehension believe that fluent readers are more efficient with low-level reading skills (for example, word recognition) and therefore their brains are better able to focus on high-level reading skills (for example, comprehension) (Perfetti, 1985; Stanovich, 2000). For the nonfluent reader, "reading becomes a slow, labor-intensive process that only fitfully results in understanding" (National Reading Panel, 2000, p. 3) or, as Wolf (2007) suggests, they have less efficient brains. Because reading fluency reflects the interaction of both low-level and high-level processes, it can be considered a reliable indicator of overall reading proficiency (Fuchs, Fuchs, Hosp, & Jenkins, 2001). The National Reading Panel (2000) found that increasing reading fluency can help improve students' ability to recognize new words; enable them to read with greater speed, accuracy, and expression; and help them to better understand what they read.

Reading Comprehension

Reading comprehension involves the many processes that readers use to understand text. Good readers use a wide range of reading strategies, and they learn how to use them deliberately. So logically, in order to increase reading comprehension, teachers must be able to teach students different reading strategies. Reading strategies are behaviors that children use to make meaning of what they are reading independently without the help of a teacher or a parent. Good reading instruction, then, helps readers acquire different reading comprehension strategies to help them read independently and accurately. The goal of reading instruction is to expose students to enough instruction to allow them to achieve reading automaticity—the point when students can read independently with fluency and confidence by applying the instruction that they have received.

In our work with the SEM-R, it became clear that current research agrees on the need to integrate reading comprehension strategies into reading instruction (Harvey & Goudvis, 2000; Keene & Zimmerman, 1997; Paris, 2004). Reading comprehension strategies are used by students to integrate high-level thinking skills such as questioning, making inferences, making connections, understanding one's own thinking processes, visualizing, determining importance, and synthesizing in order to make meaning of text. In our work with teachers, we are often asked about the differences between reading skills and reading strategies. Teaching certain reading skills, like decoding words, can be fairly straightforward because the skills can be taught by using rules that can be followed. In contrast, teaching students how to be strategic readers can be much more difficult because the strategies are contextually dependent and lack a distinct pattern for their use. Reading comprehension strategies are also more difficult to assess because, unlike an area like word knowledge, which can be measured by administering a vocabulary test, students' ability to use reading strategies in context must be determined by teachers. Early readers can be challenged with reading strategy instruction that is appropriately demanding and that engages and interests them.

Kintsch and Kintsch (2005) describe three separate and hierarchical levels in the process of reading comprehension. The first level, the decoding level, is the process of the printed word transferring to meaning in the minds of readers. This process is different from the word-level decoding in which readers assemble letters into words and sentences. At the decoding level of comprehension, readers replace decoded words with meaning. The next level, a slightly deeper level of comprehension, involves the blending of literal and inferential levels of the text to allow the reader to attend to the most important details of the text. These details are not necessarily those that involve direct recall of small details of the text. The important details usually include the bigger ideas that contribute to the theme and the author's message, thus enabling the reader to have a whole-picture view of the reading. The final level of comprehension involves creation of a situation model when the reader's prior experiences and knowledge interact with the text. This level also incorporates the reader's emotions and visuals pertaining to the text. Reading comprehension should be defined, in the highest sense, as the complex integration of reader with text. The following explanation of the most prevalent reading comprehension strategies, along with examples of how the reading strategy questions found on the SEM-R bookmarks can be used to foster high-level thinking and interaction with texts, demonstrate how teachers can help students progress to the highest level of reading comprehension.

Reading Comprehension Strategies

Several reading and literacy researchers have identified and defined reading strategies and, as Table 3.1 suggests, much agreement exists in the field of reading instruction about a common set of reading strategies, providing our rationale for their inclusion in the SEM-R. These reading strategies are embedded across all phases of the SEM-R, and as teachers begin to plan and develop book hooks for classrooms, we hope that they consider how some of the following strategies can be used to enhance student enjoyment and understanding of the books introduced to students. The strategies can also be embedded in some of the activities that students pursue in Phase Three, depending on their choices and interests.

In our work on the SEM-R, we integrated reading strategies into all phases of our literature-based approach to reading. Reading strategies help students better understand what they are reading and connect their reading experiences to their life

TABLE 3.1. CONNECTING READING STRATEGIES WITH THE SEM-R

Paris's Strategies *(Adapted from Paris, 2004)*	*Mosaic of Thought Strategies* *(Keene & Zimmerman, 1997)*	*Strategies That Work* *(Harvey & Goudvis, 2000)*
Making connections	Making connections	Making connections
Determining importance	Determining importance	Determining importance
Questioning	Questioning	Questioning
Visualizing	Visualizing, sensory images	Visualizing and inferring
Making inferences	Making inferences	
Summarizing	Synthesizing	Synthesizing
Metacognition		

experiences. We define as a reading strategy any instruction that a teacher provides to connect readers with texts in order to improve understanding. Leaders in the field of reading who focus on reading comprehension strategies, including Keene and Zimmerman (1997), Harvey and Goudvis (2000), and Scott Paris (2004) agree on several reading strategies: making connections, determining importance, questioning, visualizing, making inferences, and summarizing and synthesizing. In addition, one that Scott Paris believes is important is metacognition, or thinking about one's own reading practices. These strategies, which are further described in this section, can be applied in all phases of the SEM-R.

Making Connections

This reading strategy enables students to make connections between their own background knowledge or prior experiences and what they are reading. Three types of connections are usually involved in enabling students to relate what they are reading to their own experiences: text-to-self (T-S), text-to-text (T-T), and text-to-world (T-W) connections. The goal when making any connection with a text is for the reader to use the connection to better understand what is happening in the text.

Text-to-Self Connections   In text-to-self connections, children are asked to consider how the book they are reading may connect or relate to their own life. Teachers should ask students to use active reading strategies that compare and contrast their own life experiences with the characters or situations they are reading about in the book. They also may consider what they might do if they were to face circumstances similar to those faced by the characters. This strategy helps struggling readers attend to the story by giving them a familiar context in which to think about the events of the story.

Example: How does this story relate to your own life?

A teacher might use this question to begin a conference with a struggling reader. The conference might sound like this:

> *Teacher:* Good morning, Josh! I see that you're reading *Hoot*. How is the book going so far?
>
> *Josh:* It's going pretty well, and I really like the story because the characters are always having adventures.
>
> *Teacher:* Really? Are any of the adventures that the characters have had similar to those you've had in your own life?
>
> *Josh:* [thinking] Well, the characters in the book are trying to stop a company from killing a bunch of owls, so they're doing all kinds of things to get them to stop the project. One of the things that they did was to put alligators in the porta-potties!

Teacher: Wow! That would be a really big surprise. It sounds like they're trying to do a good thing by protecting some animals. Have you ever tried to protect something?

Josh: Sometimes I have to protect my little sister on the bus. Sometimes she gets picked on by one of the other kids, so I have to think of ways to outsmart the bullies. That's a lot like what happened to Roy, the main character in the book. He was new and was constantly getting picked on by this bully, and he had to stand up to him and also find lots of ways to outsmart him.

Teacher: That was an excellent text-to-self connection you just made. It sounds like you and Roy have some things in common. Let's hear you read a page today. [Josh reads, and the conference continues.]

In this exchange, the teacher tried to get Josh to compare the actions of the characters to his own actions, perhaps as a way to understand the characters' motivations for doing what they do. If Josh could relate to the act of protection, he might better understand why the characters in the story were interested in saving the endangered owls.

Text-to-Text Connections   A second aspect of the strategy of making connections involves text-to-text connections. A text-to-text connection occurs when a reader makes a connection between two texts. A text is defined as anything that is written (for example, a book, a Web page, a poem, or a song). The goal is for students to begin to automatically integrate texts they have already read into their background as they compare them with the book they are currently reading. This action of comparing and contrasting enables students to determine whether there are similar characters, plots, settings, or themes among texts they have experienced. Perhaps one event or one character in a book they are reading will remind them of an earlier book they have enjoyed, and a question like this will enable them to read, reflect, and compare.

Example: How is this book similar to the last one you read?

A reading standard that is common to many state curricula involves having readers compare and contrast different works, and it is important for teachers to explicitly instruct students on the similarity between text-to-text connections and the skill of comparing and contrasting. The ability to make text-to-text connections enables readers to discuss ideas that span literary works, including poetry, prose, and nonfiction pieces. A teacher might begin a conference by asking a student how his current book is similar to or different from the last book he read. A teacher also might ask the student to comment on how his current book differs from other books by the same author. These questions should elicit sophisticated levels of thinking that are much more abstract than, for example, using a Venn diagram to compare the characters or other surface-level facets of the two texts. Teachers can use open-ended exploration of texts to push their students' thinking to higher levels.

Text-to-World Connections   A text-to-world connection occurs when the reader makes a connection between the text and something that has previously happened, is happening currently, or may happen in the future. Of the three types of connections, this may be the most complex because it requires students to have a rich understanding of the world around them in order to make sophisticated connections. For instance, a child reading a book about climate change and pollution may begin to consider how her own actions and conservation efforts might affect the environment now and years into the future.

> **Example: How might your parents or friends react to living in the setting of this story?**

The amount of prior knowledge required to answer this question will vary based on the content of the text. If students are reading the book *The Watsons Go to Birmingham–1963* by Christopher Paul Curtis, for instance, they must be familiar with historical references to the civil rights movement and the controversy that it brought. Many people might prefer not to live in Birmingham during this tumultuous time in history. Alternately, students may be able to make judgments on the preferences of their friends or family based on what they know about the setting's features rather than its historical significance. For instance, a boy reading the book *Anne of Green Gables* by L. M. Montgomery, which is set in the peaceful Canadian countryside, may be able to deduce without ever having traveled to Prince Edward Island that his mother would love to live in the setting of the story because she enjoys the family's yearly vacation to a country cottage. He might make this determination based on his knowledge of current events and the fact that Canada is a very peaceful place to live for Americans because Canada and the United States are allies.

Each of these three ways of making connections enables children to use more active cognitive approaches to reading. Embedding the strategies in instruction by explicitly naming them (for example, "That was an excellent text-to-self connection you just made") increases students' metacognitive awareness of the reading strategies they are using. Students, thus, move from a passive mode of reading to thinking about what they are reading and using reading to learn, consider, reflect, and compare. In all three types of connecting, the reader applies his or her past experiences and knowledge in order to better understand and relate to the text.

Determining Importance

When asked to determine importance, students must evaluate material to decide which parts of a book or story are most meaningful or valuable in their understanding of the text. In doing so, students must consider their own interpretation of the text and their own beliefs about what parts of the plot, setting, or characterization are the most essential. Moreover, discussions about individual beliefs about important aspects of a book help students understand that they should take their own judgments into consideration when they respond to questions. In discussions with both teachers and other students, children should understand that there may not be one correct answer to a question like this.

Example: What were some of the most important parts of the story? Why?

Teachers have long asked students to identify the themes and main ideas of stories. Some readers, however, never have the opportunity to understand the importance of being able to determine the theme because the discussion stops once the theme is revealed. The conversation about why an author chose a particular theme must continue. Students should also be able to relate the big ideas that an author is expressing to their own life.

Questioning

Self-questioning occurs when readers ask themselves questions about the text that they are reading. Questioning may occur before students begin reading, while they are reading, or when they finish reading the book. In many adult books currently on the market, a series of questions aimed at participants in a readers' workshop or book club can be found at the conclusion of the book. Often, these questions help readers reflect on ideas that may not have occurred to them. Teachers can use such questions as a model for questions to use in student conferences. Questioning strategies enable readers to consider one aspect of a book, such as setting or characterization, or there may be an overarching question that requires a synthesis of the entire book. The SEM-R bookmarks (see Appendix A) can be used to encourage students to question what they are reading, enabling them to interact with the text by focusing on what they are curious about and what they want to learn and know. The use of sticky notes or reading journals may also encourage the reflective practice of self-questioning.

Example: What is one big question you still have after reading this book?

In a study of the SEM-R that included more than eighty hours of observation in reading classrooms across grades 3–7, the self-questioning strategy was used least often (Fogarty, 2006). Teachers in both SEM-R and regular classrooms rarely asked students to identify questions that they had while they read or after they read. Most teachers probably believe that their students do this subconsciously, as most good readers do. However, it is important to understand that struggling readers often suppress questioning as they read, believing that it will get in the way of their understanding of the text. Therefore, explicit instruction during a conference is a good way to help students understand the importance of asking themselves questions as they read. Good readers, in contrast to struggling readers, know that asking questions will help them understand the text, and they actively seek answers to the questions that come up as they read; however, they rarely have the opportunity to discuss these questions.

Often, however, books that are not sufficiently challenging for the reader will not cause him or her to develop questions during reading. Low-level texts with controlled vocabulary that are typically used by less proficient readers, for instance, may not require much high-level thinking to understand the text and thus will not require readers to ask themselves many questions. Similarly, when talented readers read unchallenging books, they will tend not to develop and answer questions during reading. Either way, unchallenging text is less likely to promote the strategic reading that we hope to develop in students. Books that challenge and raise questions should also be found for students who read below grade level and subsequent chapters provide several resources to match students of all achievement levels to books that both engage and challenge them.

Visualizing

Visualizing involves making pictures in one's mind of what has happened in a scene or story that is read or heard. Many students, for example, visualize the characters in the stories they read. A very precocious and talented reader in one of our SEM-R classrooms explained that she did not want to see the Harry Potter movies because she had her own visions of the setting and the characters in the novel that she did not want to replace with the images selected by those who directed or produced the movies. Visualizing strategies are important in helping students remember and understand important details or concepts in fiction and nonfiction texts, thereby increasing comprehension.

Example: Which scene would you most like to illustrate? Why?

At first, teaching children the strategy of visualization may be difficult because it requires teachers to demonstrate by making their own thinking transparent. During book hooks in Phase One of a SEM-R program, teachers can model how to visualize the characters and scene of a book based on the language of the text. This process helps students learn to run a mental movie of the story as they are reading in order to better understand the book. A particularly effective way to demonstrate visualization is to listen to students read a section of a book in which the author provides a thick description of a character, a scene, or an event. After the reading, the teacher describes what he saw in his mind as the student read. After modeling this several times, the teacher can ask students for their own descriptions. The students should also identify the part of the text that painted the picture for them.

Ms. Thomas, a fourth-grade teacher, wanted her students to better utilize the visualization strategy. She began each book hook for one week by reading them excerpts of novels that provided thick, rich character descriptions and asked her students to visualize as she read. One day, she read the following excerpt from *The Birchbark House* by Louise Erdrich: "She was named Omakays, or Little Frog, because her first step was a hop. She grew into a nimble young girl of seven winters, a thoughtful girl with shining brown eyes and a wide grin, only missing her two top front teeth. She touched her upper lip. She still wasn't used to those teeth gone, and was impatiently waiting for new, grown-up teeth to complete her smile" (p. 5). Ms. Thomas then asked her students to describe what they saw, and all of the students told her that the girl in the description was small, healthy, and missing her front teeth. Her students were able to speculate about her clothing and her heritage from just a short passage and their own visual image of the story.

Making Inferences

Inferences occur when a reader concludes something from the reading or gets an idea that is not directly stated in the text. Good readers are able to make inferences about why events occur and why characters act in certain ways based on their knowledge of the supporting text. Students who read at high levels can be challenged to make inferences by using questions such as this one:

Example: Why do you think that the author set the book in this location?

Good readers are constantly piecing together details from the story in order to fill in gaps in the author's writing or to use clues to solve little mysteries that the author has created. Struggling readers, on the other hand, do this much less frequently. These students, instead, learn to ignore the gaps or do not see that there are gaps in the information. These readers need to be taught to attend to the gaps in order to fill in the meaning themselves. When talented readers read books that are insufficiently challenging, they exercise the strategy of making inferences less often and may be unable to make inferences when faced with challenging reading material later.

Readers of all ability levels should be asked questions that require them to make inferences. Teachers can model this kind of thinking in book hooks during Phase One of a SEM-R program, as illustrated in the following example from Mr. Ortiz's class. Note his explicit reference to the strategy of making inferences.

Mr. Ortiz: Good morning, students! Today we're going to have the opportunity to meet a brand new character. Some of you may even choose to read more about him. I'm going to begin by reading a bit of the story to you and then asking if you can make some inferences based on what I've read. Remember that readers make inferences when they have some of the information, but not all of it. Readers make inferences in order to fill in the blanks. They use the information from the text and add ideas from their own mind. As they read, they look for more clues to see if their inference was accurate. [Mr. Ortiz proceeds to read a bit of the story aloud, then asks students to tell him what they can deduce about the main character in the story *Bud, Not Buddy* by Christopher Paul Curtis.]

Mr. Ortiz recognized the open-ended nature of making inferences. He provided students with an excerpt of the story and gave a very open-ended prompt to his class. The students were able to make inferences about Bud just from the short excerpt that their teacher read. Effective reading teachers will ask students to substantiate their inferences with information from the text. Asking a student to make inferences and substantiate them is also an excellent way, during a student conference, to check for student understanding of a text you have not had the opportunity to read. Asking students about the details in the text that led them to a particular impression, inference, or conclusion will help them learn to anchor their thinking in the text instead of simply guessing.

Summarizing and Synthesizing

Summarizing and synthesizing, though similar, are not the same. Summarizing involves reading through a good deal of information and then describing or recounting the gist of a story or passage as a recognizable, understandable whole. Students must be able to summarize before they can synthesize, which involves combining information in the text with a new thought, idea, or twist in order to answer a question or solve a problem. Synthesis, for example, occurs when students are asked to briefly explain how a main character may have changed over the course of the book.

> **Example: Compare the main character's personality at the beginning of the story to his or her personality at the end. What does this tell you about the character?**

Initially, teachers may ask their students summary questions in order to assess their general understanding of the text. Once they have ascertained students' general comprehension, however, they can ascend to high-level thinking skills, asking questions that require students to use their ability to summarize in order to create new thinking on a question or topic.

The following example illustrates a conference between a reader of average ability and her teacher. The student has been reading the book *When Zachary Beaver Came to Town* by Kimberly Willis Holt, in which two boys befriend an overweight boy who is part of a traveling sideshow.

> *Teacher:* Have you been enjoying your book, Shannon?
>
> *Shannon:* Yes, sometimes, although sometimes this book is hard to read because you feel so sorry for Zachary.
>
> *Teacher:* What about the main character? Let's talk about him. Do you think that the main character's personality has changed at all from the beginning of the story to the end?
>
> *Shannon:* Oh yes, he has definitely changed. In the beginning of the story, Toby wants to see Zachary and maybe even make fun of him, just like

everyone else. He is also willing to do anything to do it. Later in the story, he doesn't want to just look at Zachary; he wants to try to be friends with him. He also becomes upset when people just stare at him. I think that he's become a more sensitive person throughout the story.

This excerpt from Shannon's conference demonstrates her ability to synthesize. Initially, she had to be able to summarize the story to remember what was happening, but once she had summarized the plot of the story, she was more able to draw out information to synthesize new ideas.

Metacognition

Metacognition involves thinking about your own thinking in order to better understand how you learn. Enhancing metacognition during reading enables readers to consider and pay attention to the processes they are using. Metacognition in reading enables children to analyze what works best for them in their use of specific reading skills and strategies and to consider how they can improve their focus and develop better self-regulation when they read. Some researchers refer to this process as *self-monitoring*. An example of how to encourage students to actively use metacognition is described in the following example.

Example: Has any part of the book confused you?

For many of the students who participated in the SEM-R research studies, metacognition was the most important reading strategy because it was imperative that their teachers help them to develop the behaviors associated with reading so that they could begin to develop the fluency and comprehension aspects of reading. These students needed to learn to attend to their thinking in order to figure out what might be holding them back from reading fluently or comprehending the text. SEM-R teachers might need to begin the process of helping students with metacognition by asking students what they are thinking about as they read. Students might not realize, for example, that they are daydreaming and not thinking about the text as they read. Many struggling readers are able to read with excellent fluency and can read for pages and pages without comprehending the text. These students are reading purely at the most basic level—word-level decoding. To begin to climb the levels of comprehension discussed earlier in this chapter, these readers must begin to translate text into meaning. To do this, they must learn that good readers think about each word and sentence in the text and add them to the previous ones in order to construct meaning.

The SEM-R is an especially effective program for working with *word callers*—readers who are able to decode without creating a strong foundation of comprehension to support the text. Struggling readers are often word callers because they are overwhelmed with decoding the text and cannot expend additional mental energy on comprehension. Talented readers may surprise their teachers with word-calling behavior; they usually do it because decoding—and reading in general—has become so easy that they are able to set their brains on automatic pilot and decode without thinking about what they are reading. Word callers must be engaged in thinking frequently as they read in order to break them of this behavior. They must be constantly reminded through questions like "What did you like about the section you just read?" or "What ideas did you find challenging in the last chapter?" that ask them to focus on the task at hand.

Summary

In this chapter, we briefly discussed how reading should be taught and the different ways that teachers should teach reading. We summarized several reading strategies that are included in the SEM-R and give examples of the ways that these reading strategies can be integrated into SEM-R instruction. In the next chapter, we introduce the first phase of SEM-R, a way to expose students to joyful reading experiences.

The SEM-R Program Phases

Hooking Kids on Reading: Phase One

4

This chapter introduces you to the first phase of the SEM-R, an opportunity for teachers to model and foster enjoyment of reading through high-interest read-alouds, also called *book hooks*. As you read this chapter, you will learn why and how you can use the SEM-R to engage your students by linking differentiated reading strategies to state standards and teaching them appealing strategies that will hook them on reading.

Parents and teachers who read aloud to children expose them to the magic of books. When teachers love to read and read aloud to their students, young people benefit from an exposure to literature they may not otherwise have experienced. With some planning and practice, teachers can bring stories and characters to life by sharing short, dramatic segments from children's literature. In addition, students learn to listen carefully and reflect on literary details and devices when teachers ask them carefully crafted questions about what they are hearing.

Books can take children to faraway times and places; expose them to the joy of travel, other cultures, and other ways of life; inform, entertain, and move them; and enable them to know that they are not alone. By listening to their teacher read books aloud, children increase their knowledge and listening skills, develop their language and vocabulary skills, and increase their interest in reading. When children are read to by teachers or parents, they may have the opportunity to experience comfort and joy or to escape feelings of sadness or boredom. When children listen to stories from teachers whom they trust, they may see a path to a new future or realize that others with similar experiences have not only survived but also developed resilience and excelled in life.

Recently, Jon Scieszka, author of *The Stinky Cheese Man and Other Fairly Stupid Tales* as well as the Time Warp Trio series and other favorites, was named the first National Ambassador for Young People's Literature. One reason for Scieszka's popularity may be the joy children experience when they hear *The Stinky Cheese Man* and his other humorous books read aloud. When children listen to stories and books on a consistent basis, they begin to understand that reading can be joyful. When teachers read picture books and show the corresponding illustrations and photographs to young children, those children begin to understand that pictures give clues. When parents and teachers read stories to children, they help children learn that words are clues to events in a story. Listening to stories read aloud helps children understand that books and stories have a beginning and an end. When teachers ask children questions about the stories they have heard, students' vocabulary and comprehension improve. Regular read-alouds enable children to develop prolonged listening skills and an appreciation for different types of literature. Moreover, reading aloud joins reader and listeners alike in a collective experience of story and language, reflecting ancient traditions of community sharing in common interests. For all of these reasons, classroom read-alouds are valuable learning experiences for students of all ages.

In our years of field-testing the SEM-R, we have learned that the simple daily act of reading aloud increases the potential for children to develop enjoyment of reading. For children who have not had extensive experiences with literature at home, classroom read-alouds provide exposure to the world of books, opening important doors to learning. For children who are used to being read to, read-alouds at school continue to promote strong listening skills and broaden the scope of what children know about books and the world around them. The issues of children's different backgrounds in regard to exposure to books are discussed further in the following section.

In addition, by reading aloud excerpts from selected texts, teachers entice students to consider reading more of those texts themselves, in order to find out what happens next or simply continue to appreciate a book to which they have just been introduced. When discussing this approach with teachers, we ask them to consider a Phase One book hook to be like a film trailer for a book. In the same way that a film trailer is designed to hook, inform, and entice viewers to see a particular movie, a book hook is designed to entice children to read.

Home and School Connections: Children with Literacy Advantages

Why are book hooks in school so important? They can help to address the literacy advantages that some children bring to school. The importance of literacy efforts and the benefits that children receive from prolonged exposure at home cannot be underestimated. Children who are exposed to language earlier in their childhood and who access language skills at the earliest times enter school with a literacy and language advantage (Hart & Risley, 2003). Children with this literacy advantage—who have heard an estimated 32 million more words, as we discussed in the preceding chapter—have more exposure to new words and what those words mean. When a child has heard a word and understands what it means, learning to read that word is easier. If you know what a factory is, after you have decoded the letters to read the word *factory*, you can form a connection with the meaning of the word. If you struggle to decode the word *factory* but then have no understanding of what it means, you will struggle with reading about factories. Over time, the greater exposure that some children have had to language gives them access to a wider variety of books and reading experiences because they are not so limited by vocabulary. Children whose parents expose them to language in their earliest days grow up to be students who have more advanced language and speech skills; again, they have a literacy advantage. The importance of such early reading experiences emphasizes the need for more opportunities for children to listen to stories and books being read aloud, beginning early at home and continuing in school.

During this early, emergent literacy phase, beginning at birth and continuing during the years before children enter kindergarten, children who are exposed to both spoken language and print gain clear advantages. Parents of children who are literacy-advantaged not only read to their children; they also teach them to say, sing, color, scribble, and write the letters of the alphabet and the words that are made from them. Such parents also provide other rich literacy experiences to help their children. They rhyme words, sing songs, point out symbols, and, often, may find their children beginning to read or at least to show evidence of word recognition before kindergarten. Parents who are working to establish a language-rich and literate environment often encourage their children to speak in sentences, use more and different words, and connect the spoken word to the written word through activities that involve reading aloud and speaking aloud. In addition, the mere presence of books in the home and modeling of reading activities are valuable for young children; they learn how to hold and handle books, and they see that their parents gain pleasure from the experience of reading.

Children with these literacy advantages understand language, connect spoken words with print, and use language to communicate ideas and feelings. Early literacy experiences prepare children for successful reading experiences in school and continue to influence their reading experiences. To put it simply, children who have talking and listening experiences with spoken and written language are better prepared to enter school and begin to read. As we noted earlier, children with more limited verbal experiences are more at risk for reading difficulties.

Spoken language connects to early reading in many ways. For example, phonological awareness—the understanding that words are made up of separate sounds—connects strongly to learning to read. When a child connects the letters "c," "a," and "t" with the word *cat,* they are displaying early phonological awareness, an understanding that words come from separate speech sounds. Different kinds of oral language activities, including read-alouds such as those used in Phase One of the SEM-R, help children develop oral language awareness and facility with words and syntax. Particular language activities that help children's phonological awareness include helping them understand alliteration (for example, "the silly song is being sung by Sally in her saucy sailboat"), exposing them to rhyme (for example, through reading the book *The Cat in the Hat* aloud), and helping them identify sounds (for example, teaching them that *bat* begins with a "b"; *cat* begins with a "c"; *rat* begins with an "r"). The more opportunities children have for these types of experiences with sound, the more they can understand how words are made up of different sounds, translate these sounds into printed letters, and then begin to read and write. Research strongly suggests that children who successfully achieve such sound awareness are more successful in reading and writing in subsequent years (National Reading Panel, 2000).

Such experiences with sound awareness remain valuable beyond the early literacy years because children continue to benefit from hearing how practiced authors choose and use their words carefully for precision and effect in sound and meaning. Also, even after children achieve basic fluency in reading, they continue to build their vocabulary through the words that they hear as much as or more than through the words that they read; a teacher or parent who reads with comprehension and expression conveys the meaning of words in context and allows children to develop understanding of new words organically. Furthermore, like parents in the home environment, a teacher in the classroom environment goes a long way toward influencing positive reading attitudes just by demonstrating his own enjoyment and valuing of reading.

When teachers present book hooks as part of a conscious effort to read aloud to students, the books they choose and the enjoyable environments they create help students feel positive and excited about reading. Our experience has shown us that one of the easiest ways to hook kids on books is to ensure the availability of and exposure to a wide range of high-quality, high-interest literature while conveying enthusiasm for these books through a variety of sharing activities. Exposing students to books, modeling reading strategies, and generating enthusiasm about reading are the primary goals of the SEM-R. Phase One book hooks will help you instill a love of reading in your students as you introduce and reinforce strategies for selecting books as well as a variety of thinking and discussion skills.

Exciting Phase One Book Hooks

In Phase One of the SEM-R, teachers introduce students to literature by reading short segments of books as an introduction to a wide range of genres and titles. During this part of the program, you should plan to read snippets of books in order to expose your students purposefully to a variety of styles, genres (for example, poetry, historical fiction, or nonfiction), authors, themes, interest areas, subjects, and domains. This Phase One book hook time will encourage students to develop a wider range of interests and knowledge and to select literature that they may not have selected before. Students will become more engaged in reading when they find topics and areas they want to learn more about; this exposure is what Renzulli (1977) calls *Type I enrichment* in the Enrichment Triad Model. Book hook read-alouds in Phase One also introduce scaffolded instruction in both reading strategies and thinking skills. When, as a teacher, you read a short, exciting part of a book to hook your students on literature and then connect a reading strategy to the book hook or introduce an advanced thinking skill, you are extending instruction in an enjoyable and engaging way. The goal of an exciting Phase One book hook is to have many of your students ask to read the book from which you have just revealed an enticing section. We have worked with many teachers who had to compile a waiting list of students who signed up to read a book that was introduced during an exciting book hook! For an example of a wonderful book hook, be sure to watch the DVD that is included with this book and see the joy and gleeful anticipation on the faces of the children whose teachers are conducting these sessions.

When children in our SEM-R studies change classes on their way to a SEM-R classroom, many of them sigh with happiness as they enter the SEM-R classroom. They look with excitement, trying to catch a glimpse of a book that may be sitting on a table or desk. They ask whether this is the book that their teacher has selected in advance to read. Some children run to their teacher to ask whether he or she would like to use a part of their book for Phase One. Some children even take the time to use a sticky note to mark a section of the book they are reading that they believe will make a perfect book hook for their teacher to read to the rest of the class. Phase One book hooks are joyful reading experiences; joy is critical to the implementation of this approach to reading. Listening to good books is one of the best ways for children to begin to love reading, for they begin to associate feelings of comfort and happiness with the time that they spend listening to and reading aloud with family and teachers. These feelings can eventually translate into similar feelings and attitudes toward books and a realization that books can give them comfort, knowledge, inspiration, and the opportunity to take charge of their own learning.

Ready, Set, Begin

As you begin to implement the SEM-R, taking small steps toward larger goals can help you easily begin your path to what may be a different way to teach reading and to make reading a more joyful experience for your students. It is important to the success of book hooks that they are planned in advance. Starting to use Phase One book hooks daily in your classroom will enhance your students' enjoyment of reading as well as provide instructional opportunities that will translate into students' use of reading strategies in their independent reading in Phase Two. In the remaining sections of this chapter, we will focus on several key parts of Phase One and offer suggestions for implementation.

Creating the Environment for Book Hooks

Where should you conduct your daily book hooks? We have watched hundreds of teachers do book hooks over the last several years, and ideally, you should try to find a place in your classroom where every child can sit and both see the illustrations and hear while you read. The environment you wish to create for book hooks is one that will help foster a sense of community and shared interest in exploring a passion for reading. If your classroom is small, you may need to have students sit at their desks, but book hooks are more special when students can sit together on the floor or on their chairs in a corner of the room where they will be comfortable listening quietly. Try to use this arrangement if it is at all possible, even if it requires a regular routine of moving desks and chairs around.

As you are getting started with your book hooks, you may also want to consider how to organize your classroom library. Phase One, with its emphasis on exposure to books, is followed by Phase Two, in which students will select and read challenging books independently; therefore, part of Phase One should involve demonstrating to students where and how they can browse among books in order to make their selections. Book hooks provide the opportunity to introduce students to new genres, authors, and topics, and the location of these in the classroom library should also be highlighted. Teachers who have used the SEM-R have organized their classroom libraries in several different ways, such as by genre, author, reading level, or even areas of interest. We have seen many types of classroom library organization, but our favorite is one in which students can easily access books in each genre that span different reading levels—that is, when there are books of different levels on the same topic. A well-organized classroom library will enable you to both introduce different genres to your students and model selection criteria for books. A discussion of how to find books that are interesting and challenging is an excellent way to begin to help students identify which books are in their areas of interest *and* are at the appropriate challenge level.

Getting Started with Book Hooks: Choosing Books

Throughout Phase One activities, always keep in mind that their primary purposes are to provide exposure to different types of books and to provide enjoyment. Therefore, selecting books for Phase One is all about variety and conveying enthusiasm. We suggest that you begin by selecting a book that you love in some way for a book hook. When we do a book hook with a new class of students, we try to select a book that was one of our own childhood favorites; this might be a classic, such as *Anne of Green Gables, A Christmas Carol,* or a Nancy Drew book; a book about animals that made one of us cry as a child, such as *Old Yeller;* or a book that made us laugh, such as one of Roald Dahl's books or one of Shel Silverstein's poetry collections. We may choose a book based on beautiful illustrations or a topic or a style of writing that we love. Whatever the reason, we start with a book that we love and share it with students because selecting a favorite book and sharing a fond memory associated with the book (while simultaneously modeling a text-to-self connection) helps students want to read.

Another good guide for selecting books for book hooks is past experience with books, authors, and genres that children have enjoyed. Books with suspenseful moments, effective use of language, and memorable characters are good choices. As we will see later in this chapter, a critical element of planning a book hook is not only selecting the book but also finding a good excerpt of the book to read aloud, so some of these elements and details of books are particularly important to consider. Later sections of this chapter will suggest some resources for finding and selecting books for book hooks.

You can use book hooks to pique your students' existing interests as well as to link to other content areas. Don't be afraid to consider other topics or subjects that your students will encounter during the school day. You can use a book hook to connect to a concept or to introduce a unit in another content area—for example, you can use a biography to enrich a science or social studies unit. Reading an interesting book about tornadoes, for example, would be an excellent way to explore nonfiction texts with students while introducing them to a weather unit. A math poetry book might be used to get students interested in a new mathematical concept. Sharing a book as a follow-up to students' demonstrated interest in science or social studies might also serve as an introduction to a wide range of opportunities for independent study during Phase Three of a SEM-R program. Book hooks can introduce or connect with other content areas, helping to set the background for material that your students may be studying either with you or in another class. Book hooks can also be used to expose your students to emerging interests and potential ideas for projects or other follow-up activities that they will have the time to pursue during Phases Two and Three.

Planning the "Hook" in a Book Hook

The best "book hookers" and most reader-inspiring teachers begin their book hooks with a chat about the book. For example, you might want to tell your students what you like best about the book from which you will be reading. You might discuss the dedication. Is the book dedicated to a family member, a teacher, or, in the case of Wally Lamb, perhaps even a night janitor at a library who offered quiet encouragement to an author? You might want to have students consider what a dedication might tell readers about an author. A colleague who worked on the SEM-R research did a wonderful book hook using the publication information on *Squids Will Be*

Squids by Jon Scieszka and Lane Smith because, like the entire book, it is written with humor.

You may also use the book chat as an opportunity to model and discuss with students how you choose the books you read. You might point out features of the synopsis on the back of the book, the illustrations, or the table of contents that caught your attention or explain that you had previous experience with the author or heard a recommendation of the book from a friend. In general, you should try to introduce each book by briefly explaining a little bit about the author, the illustrator, the title, or the topic. You may also find it helpful to relate the book to some aspect of the children's experience (for example, prior knowledge of the author, the illustrator, or the topic), if that is possible.

All of the attention given to the book chat prepares the students for what they will hear during the read-aloud; or the book chat may follow the read-aloud if you wish to elaborate on what struck you about the particular selection. The heart of a book hook, of course, is the reading from the book itself; it should be a relatively short reading that is carefully selected to invite students into the particular book.

To be able to choose a special part of the book to use as a book hook, it is necessary to select a book in advance of your book hook time. Planning will enable you to select a section of the book that is interesting, entertaining, or intriguing. The big idea of a book hook is to read just a *part* of the book so that students will want to know more and subsequently ask to read the book themselves. The most inviting part of a text may not be the first few pages. In our experience, teachers have decided to read selections from the middle of a book, from the cover, from the ending, or even from the author's notes. Not only does such variation in the part of the book read allow you to choose particularly compelling selections, but it also demonstrates to students that when browsing for a book, they may want to flip through more than just the opening pages. We encourage you to vary your selections to expose your students to different genres, literary elements, and styles of narration and writing. For example, on the DVD that accompanies this book, a masterful teacher reads a book hook from a wonderful mystery that leaves every child in the classroom wanting to read more of this genre. In the same school on the same day that the teachers were being taped, we observed several other genres being introduced to children, ensuring that a wide range of interests were not only being addressed, but possibly sparked as well.

Most important to successful implementation of the SEM-R is that you enjoy book hooks and the process of trying to engage all of your students in enjoyment of reading. In other words, have fun with book hooks. Some teachers who have successfully used the SEM-R consider it a personal challenge to engage all of their students with reading enjoyment during read-alouds. Some teachers are natural performers, and they use a wide range of intonations, speeds, and volumes in their voice as they read aloud. Some teachers can explore the range of characters in a book by using different accents or actions as they read. Others, like one of the teachers in the DVD that accompanies this book, use pauses, humor, and facial expressions to add drama to their read-alouds.

Refining Book Hooks: Making a Match with Students

As you continue to work with the SEM-R and conduct book hooks for your students, strive to match the books you choose to read for book hooks with your students' interests—or to interests you feel they are likely to develop once they are introduced to new topics. How can you find out what your students want to listen to or learn about? We have adapted an interest inventory developed by Joseph Renzulli into a reading inventory called the Reading Interest-a-Lyzer (Appendix B) for your use. You can begin to tap into your students' reading interests after they have completed this inventory. If, for example, you know from their responses that a number of your students are interested in bugs, you can find an exciting selection of books that will help them to learn more about the insect world. Then, after finding and sharing one book on a topic of interest, use the same topic to create connections to other genres of books, to explore the many different ways in which one topic can be introduced across texts. If your students like art, you can read from several types of books about art, from how-to books about working with different art materials to biographies of artists to novels involving art, such as *Chasing Vermeer*. If your students have expressed an interest in mummies, you might share a page or two from Aliki's *Mummies Made in Egypt* and add a little humor with a section from Jon Scieszka and Lane Smith's *Tut, Tut*. Exposing your class to different genres helps a broader group of students become interested in and knowledgeable about different types of literature and reading opportunities; such broad exposure may also initiate or develop new interests for students—for example, a student may learn about a new topic within a genre she already enjoys.

When selecting a book for a book hook, think about exposing students to a wide range of interests by using a wide variety of books over time. Phase One book hooks provide an opportunity to expose students to topics, areas, ideas, and places to visit. If, for example, the book is a mystery, perhaps you can encourage students with an interest in geography to understand that mysteries are set in different states, countries, and locations and that the settings are often integral to both the plot and the eventual outcome. During your book chat, you might draw attention to particular aspects of the book you have chosen that might appeal to particular students who otherwise might be unlikely to choose that book.

Of course, not all students will become interested in all of the books that you introduce during your Phase One book hooks. Some students just aren't interested in a particular topic or issue or even in an entire genre. Inspiring interest in reading is one aspect of this phase of a SEM-R program, but another is simply making sure that your students are exposed to different books and genres. They should understand how historical fiction differs from nonfiction, for example, and they should have some familiarity with some well-known historical fiction titles that are appropriate for their age and reading level. If the book hook you are doing does not interest some or even many of your students at this time, knowing the genre and the title of the book will enable them to come back to this type of book at a later time, should they subsequently become interested. Just understanding different genres and having some familiarity with excellent books in each genre is a starting point for beginning to lead a more educated life. Sadly, too many of today's students know the names of sophisticated video games that they hope to purchase and play on expensive equipment but have no knowledge of the authors or books that are considered an integral part of a well-educated childhood.

If you find that a majority of your students do not have an interest in a genre of literature that you have introduced, you should move on to another book, for the primary focus of book hooks should be to find books that bring enjoyment and pleasure to some (initially) and most (subsequently) of your students. It is important to find a balance between exposing students to new avenues in literature and encouraging them to continue pursuing interests that they are already developing. Consider constructing two lists of upcoming book hooks for yourself: one list representing books that you feel fairly certain will be popular with students based on connections to existing interests, and another list through which you challenge yourself to find selections that just might spark an interest in a less popular genre or topic.

Also, consider how varying the format of your book hooks can provide enjoyment for students and create interest in other ways. Several strategies have been used to achieve this enjoyment by the teachers who have participated in our research. Some, for example, vary their book hooks by having students listen to an excerpt from a book on tape or CD that features an outstanding reader. By playing just a few minutes of one of the *Harry Potter* books on CD or tape read by Jim Dale, for example, you could expose your students to an outstanding storyteller and to the enjoyment of listening to a British accent as well as someone with the talent to use several different voices and intonations to represent different characters. Other audio books allow young readers and writers to be inspired by hearing authors read their own work.

You might also hook some of your students back into reading by using picture books to stimulate interests in places, themes, or ideas. Picture books are an ideal way to encourage students who have been turned off by reading; the pictures allow them to approach literature and conversations about books in a nonthreatening, engaging way. For example, using Barbara Cooney's beautiful picture book *Miss Rumphius* to encourage your students to consider beauty in the world and how each of them might contribute to making the world a more beautiful place is an outstanding use of a book hook. The same book also can be used to introduce students to the idea of an individual's pursuit of a quest in life, a theme that is repeated in many fiction and nonfiction books. Several picture books that have been popular in book hooks for both elementary and middle school students are included in Table 4.1.

TABLE 4.1. PICTURE BOOKS TO ENGAGE STUDENTS IN READING

Picture Books Read Aloud May Springboard to . . .	*Independent Reading Selections*
Squids Will Be Squids by Jon Scieszka & Lane Smith	*Tales from Africa* by Mary Medlicott *Just So Stories* by Rudyard Kipling *Psychology for Kids II: 40 Fun Experiments That Help You Learn About Others* by Jonni Kincher & Pamela Espeland *Guys Write for Guys Read* by Jon Scieszka
Art Fraud Detective by Anna Nilsen	*Chasing Vermeer* by Blue Balliett *From the Mixed-Up Files of Mrs. Basil E. Frankweiler* by E. L. Konigsburg *The Annotated Mona Lisa: A Crash Course in Art History from Prehistoric to Post-Modern* by Carol Strickland
The Librarian of Basra: A True Story from Iraq by Jeanette Winter	*Iraq: Enchantment of the World Series* by Byron Augustin *Making It Home: Real-Life Stories from Children Forced to Flee* by Beverly Naidoo *Breadwinner* by Deborah Ellis *The Ballad of Lucy Whipple* by Karen Cushman *Goin' Someplace Special* by Jerry Pinkney & Patricia McKissack *The Last Book in the Universe* by Rodman Philbrick *The Giver* by Lois Lowry *Fahrenheit 451* by Ray Bradbury *Z for Zachariah* by Robert C. O'Brien *The City of Ember* (Books of Ember Series) by Jeanne DuPrau
I Is for Idea by Marcia Schonberg & Kandy Radzinski	*The Invention of Hugo Cabret* by Brian Selznick. *What a Great Idea! Inventions That Changed the World* by Stephen M. Tomecek & Dan Stuckenschneider *Mistakes That Worked* by Charlotte Jones & John Obrien *Girls Think of Everything: Stories of Ingenious Inventions by Women* by Catherine Thimmesh & Melissa Sweet
A Woman for President: The Story of Victoria Woodhull by Kathleen Krull & Jane Dyer or *The Buck Stops Here* by Alice Provensen	*The Kid Who Ran for President* by Dan Gutman *Madam President: The Extraordinary, True (and Evolving) Story of Women in Politics* by Catherine Thimmesh & Douglas Jones *First Dogs: American Presidents and Their Best Friends* by Roy Rowan & Brooke Janis *Teen Power Politics: Make Yourself Heard* by Sara Jane Boyers *The Kid's Guide to Social Action* by Barbara A. Lewis
The Bat Boy and His Violin by E. B. Lewis & Gavin Curtis or *Ellington Was Not a Street* by Ntozake Shange & Kadir Nelson	*Bronx Masquerade* by Nikki Grimes *Bud, Not Buddy* by Christopher Paul Curtis *The Music Thief* by Peni R. Griffin *Jazmin's Notebook* by Nikki Grimes *Duke Ellington: I Live with Music* by Carin T. Ford *Marsalis on Music* by Wynton Marsalis

You might also consider inviting a special guest reader to present a book hook in your classroom. Students love listening to their principal, another teacher, the librarian, a parent, or an older student from a nearby middle school or high school. You might ask parents to consider planning a ten-minute book hook on a favorite childhood book or ask a librarian to do a book hook that might tempt some of your resistant readers by appealing to interests you have found in their Reading Interest-a-Lyzers. These kinds of book hooks can be very enjoyable for students and can motivate and inspire *you* as you watch students react to different adults as they present book hooks, helping you to vary the reading experiences and recommended books for more of your students.

Some of the many teachers who have implemented the SEM-R have asked about having students conduct book hooks, and it is important to note that our experiences in this regard are quite mixed. Few young students have the storytelling talent and oral reading fluency needed to pull off an effective book hook! Occasionally, however, we have found that rare youngster, a budding actress or actor who can excel in front of her or his peers and have given that child an occasional opportunity to hook the other students in the classroom on a favorite book as an appropriate way to motivate readers. Keep in mind that you can provide different kinds of opportunities for students to share books with one another in Phase Three while maintaining the integrity of the book hooks in Phase One.

In our many years of experience with helping hundreds of teachers implement the SEM-R, we have only observed one teacher who has been a failure at doing book hooks. In this one case, the teacher read in a monotone, had little affect, and seemed to expend minimal effort on trying to motivate his students to read. Guest readers and the regular use of audio books saved Phase One of the SEM-R program at this site, but it should also be noted that in this classroom, students began reading for longer periods of Phase Two supported independent reading very soon! The hundreds of other teachers we have observed during Phase One book hooks have been motivating and exciting readers and have used their own creativity to inspire their young charges. Some have brought in their own treasured, favorite children's books, and others have worn funny hats or costumes to make their students take notice. Some very quiet teachers have transformed in front of their students' astonished eyes, emerging as dynamic actors and actresses who have exposed beautiful literature with drama and unique voices.

Other tips may make implementing this phase of the SEM-R easier for you. For example, when you have found an author who seems to be popular with your students, try to read selections from books written by the same author as part of your book hooks. This practice, of course, models what we do as mature readers and exposes students who like a particular author to a series of books that they might enjoy while also helping them gain an understanding of the author's voice. Students can learn comparison skills and gain insights into critical analysis, enabling them to compare one text with another. Some authors also write books at varying levels of complexity, and exposure to books of differing levels of depth will enable students of varying abilities to gain access to the same author.

Integrating Reading Strategies and Skills into Book Hooks

Phase One provides an opportunity for instruction and guidance in reading skills and strategies along with exposure to books and how to select them. Within the context of book hooks, you can provide your students with challenging questions to consider and discuss, with examples of strategies that they can use while reading, and with modeling that shows how to draw connections across books and from books to their own lives.

Using Bookmarks During Phase One of a SEM-R Program

As we briefly discussed earlier, we have developed a series of reproducible bookmarks that can be used in Phases One and Two of a SEM-R program (see Appendix A). Each bookmark contains several questions that guide students to think more deeply about what they hear or read, to analyze their response to a book, to generate creative ideas based on the book's ideas, or to draw connections with other books. These bookmarks encourage students to explore a variety of literary genres and promote high-level critical thinking and creative thinking skills. During Phase One of a SEM-R program, the bookmarks can assist teachers in the following ways:

- Help to develop a repertoire of higher-order thinking questions that can be employed during read-aloud sessions with the class

- Help to model questioning that will enable students to gain skills in focusing attention and higher-order thinking

- Help students to develop self-questioning techniques to assist them in future literary analysis

When a teacher uses questions from a bookmark during a book hook, she helps to stimulate student thinking and provides practice in applying complex comprehension strategies. Using the bookmarks to model high-level questions also demonstrates to students that they can use self-questioning strategies when reading on their own to enrich their thinking about what they read. To make the purpose of particular bookmarks clear, each has been categorized with a heading indicating the literary element or genre on which that particular bookmark focuses. Our research on SEM-R programs has demonstrated that the bookmarks are good tools for both teachers and students to use, resulting in the use of high-level questioning skills by students of all levels of achievement. The following suggestions have helped teachers to assist students who need additional support in thinking about their reading.

- During the read-aloud, teachers can model their own process of applying comprehension strategies or high-level thinking by thinking aloud as they answer some of their own questions. This practice enables teachers to model critical thinking and creative thinking processes as they answer questions themselves or as they coach students in these strategies as part of an open-ended discussion in a classroom, as the following example illustrates.

  Bookmark example: How would the problem change if the story took place elsewhere?

  The teacher might respond to a student who is struggling to answer by saying, "Let me give you one example of how I might answer that question. First, I would think of a different place or setting—maybe a place in our town. Then I would think about what is different between that place and the setting in the book. [She could talk about some of these differences.] Now, I would think about how these differences might change the problem."

- When students answer questions during the read-aloud session, teachers can ask them to explain what evidence from the text they considered and what thinking processes they used that led them to their response. Teachers can help students reflect on how they answered the question, thereby encouraging the strategy of metacognition.

- Teachers can provide students with practice in using more advanced strategies by asking and answering similar types of questions on consecutive days or for multiple books.

- When working with students on responding to bookmark questions (whether orally or in writing), one important concept that teachers should emphasize is moving beyond providing a plot summary. Students who have difficulty with critical analysis or synthesis should be encouraged to provide opinions and hypotheses, supported by evidence that they have collected from the book.

- A blank bookmark template can be used to encourage students to create their own questions about literature and to help them build a deeper understanding of both literary analysis and higher-order thinking. This exercise may also serve as a way to generate new enthusiasm if students reach a stage at which answering bookmark questions becomes routine. A sample of a blank and some of the filled-in bookmarks is provided in Appendix A.

Creating Themed Book Hooks

A themed book hook is another excellent way to increase the complexity of Phase One as well as to explore major themes or subjects in depth. Weekly book hooks can be based on author studies or themes (such as the idea of struggle for power or the notion of prejudice and its interaction with race). Teachers can use themed book hooks to introduce "big questions" about hatred and man's inhumanity to man or about the redemptive power of love. Book hooks can also focus on historical events, such as the Gold Rush, the Civil War, or events during World War II. Book hooks can be used to introduce pertinent social and emotional issues such as bullying or making courageous choices; literature can provide a helpful context for examining life and for helping students address areas of personal concern. Table 4.2 provides an example of a theme with related books, along with the strategies and standards that can be supported through themed book hooks on the given concept.

Themed book hooks are intended to expose your students to a big idea or a broad concept such as prejudice and to present several books from different genres and ability levels that illustrate this big idea. In the example in Table 4.2, each themed book hook focuses on varying details or plots that relate to prejudice, and exploration of this big idea continues for a week, targeted by different books each day.

A book hook theme can also be used to explore an idea from another discipline more thoroughly, thereby giving the content more attention and fostering interdisciplinary connections. For example, while studying weather in science, you might augment the science unit with literature during your book hooks. One day, you might do your

TABLE 4.2. EXAMPLE OF A THEME FOR BOOK HOOKS

Theme: People's Harsh Treatment of and Inhumanity to Others: Prejudice

Book Titles	Comprehension Strategy	State Standards
• *Martin's Big Words* • *I Have a Dream*	• Making connections — Text to text — Text to self — Text to world	• The student develops vocabulary by listening to, reading, and discussing both familiar and conceptually challenging selections.
• *My Brother, Martin* • *The Voice That Challenged the Nation: Marian Anderson and the Struggle for Equal Rights*	• Making connections — Text to text • Making inferences	• The student identifies specific personal preferences relative to fiction and nonfiction reading.
• *Maniac Magee* • *The Watsons Go to Birmingham* • *Roll of Thunder Hear My Cry* (author study of Mildred Taylor) • *Let the Circle Be Unbroken* • *Song of the Trees* • *The Well* • *The Land* • *Witness* • *The Diary of Anne Frank* • *Butterfly* • *Six Million Paper Clips*	• Making connections — Text to text — Text to world — Text to self • Questioning • Making inferences • Visualization • Synthesizing	• The student identifies and discusses the author's purpose in text. • The student recognizes similarities and differences of events presented within and across high-level selections. • The student knows that the attitudes and values that exist in a time period affect stories.

TABLE 4.3. THEMES FOR BOOK HOOKS

Theme: Overcoming difficulty in life (using the Great Depression as a case in point)

Books:	*Out of the Dust*	by Karen Hesse
	A Year Down Yonder	by Richard Peck
	Bud, Not Buddy	by Christopher Paul Curtis
	The Dust Bowl	by David Booth & Karen Reczuch

Theme: Human connections to nature (focusing on Native Americans)

Books:	*The Birchbark House*	by Louise Erdich
	The Desert Is Theirs	by Byrd Baylor & Peter Parnall
	Kokopelli's Flute	by Will Hobbs

Theme: Overcoming difficulty in life (using weather as an example)

Books:	*The Log Cabin*	by Ellen Howard
	Snow	by Uri Shulevitz
	Snow Treasure	by Marie McSwigan
	The Winter Room	by Gary Paulsen
	Snowflake Bentley	by Jacqueline B. Martin & Mary Azarian

book hook on tornadoes and hurricanes; the next day, on snow; another day, on clouds; and you might conclude the week with a book about the effects of drought. The books that you use might be nonfiction, but they might also include poetry about the sky, fiction books about snow, nonfiction and fictional books about snowboarding, or historical fiction selections about the Dust Bowl. The themes and big ideas that can be used are unlimited, and some of our most creative and insightful teachers have presented book hooks that have engaged and excited every child about reading. The examples in Table 4.3 can help you get started.

The ideas are endless, and we have found many additional resources for ideas about themed book hooks on the Web; in lists of books; in books that win contests, awards, and competitions; and in our own school libraries. One of our favorite Web sites for lists of books is Carol Hurst's Children's Literature Site at http://www.carolhurst.com/subjects/subjects.html. On that site, among other things, there are multiple book lists organized by theme and content.

Bookmarks with Embedded Reading Strategies

As part of both Phase One and Phase Two of the SEM-R, we have created a series of bookmarks that elicit reading skills and strategies that can be applied across many

FIGURE 4.1. BOOKMARKS WITH READING STRATEGIES INTEGRATED IN THE QUESTIONS.

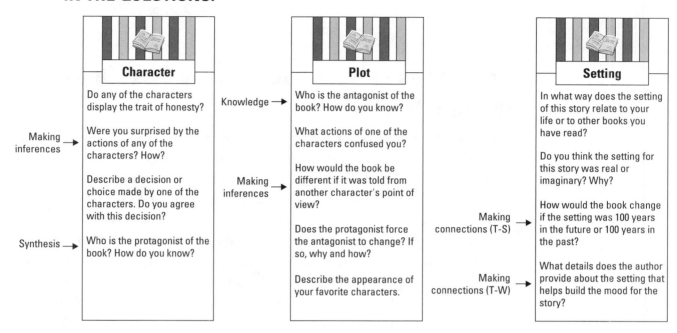

different books. The bookmarks include specific questions that require students to use and apply skills and strategies. The questions are arranged by literary element or genre—for instance, there are bookmarks on setting, character, the theme of power, nonfiction, philosophy, and biography. Each bookmark lists several generic questions that can be used to begin a conversation or assess a child's knowledge of the particular element or genre. The bookmark questions also were developed to integrate the reading strategies discussed in Chapter Three. Figure 4.1 includes notations that illustrate how reading strategies have been integrated in all of the SEM-R bookmarks.

Some teachers ask why we do not just create a set of bookmark questions arranged by reading strategy. Although it appears that this might make things easier, it would actually be impossible because the strategies vary depending on the book and the use of strategies at the highest level requires the use of multiple strategies simultaneously. A bookmark question might require an inference for one book but not for another. For example, a question from one of the bookmarks asks, "Do you think the setting for this story was real or imaginary? Why?" In some books, this might require an inference in which the reader pieces together information from the story to provide an answer. In another book, however, the author might have used a real location, so the question would not require the reader to make an inference. For these reasons, the bookmark in question has been organized around the literary element of setting rather than the reading strategy of inference.

Teachers must understand what they are asking students and what strategies students will need in order to answer their questions. Students should learn to make inferences and connections because one or the other might be important at any given time. In order to use the SEM-R, teachers must become familiar with their students' use of reading skills and strategies and be able to incorporate any missing knowledge into either their Phase One book hooks or their Phase Two conferences.

Resources to Help You Find the Best Books for Your Book Hooks

Which are the best books for hooking your students? Of course, the answer is that there is no one best book but rather many books that will help your children learn to listen, begin to find books they will want to read themselves, and experience a wide range of books that will inform, entertain, and make them think and reflect for more than three seconds! Thousands of children's and young adult books are published annually in all genres and at a wide range of reading levels. Given the wealth of print material for young people available today, how can teachers and parents help young people find an appropriate book that will both challenge and interest them? The first step is to consider your students' interests. As we noted earlier, a simple Reading Interest-a-Lyzer has been included in Appendix B for you to use with your students. In order to learn more about their interests, have each student take fifteen or twenty minutes to begin filling in the survey. If some of your students have difficulty reading the words, read it aloud to them and discuss what some of the items mean. Tell them to take enough time to respond thoughtfully, and if they need to think about some of their responses, collect their Reading Interest-a-Lyzers and tell them that you will give them time in a day or two to reflect and then complete the questions they could not finish. Once some or all of your students have finished this process, you can consider both their collective and their individual interests. Which genres do they seem to like? What are their favorite books and authors and characters? Do you notice patterns across different readers in your classroom (or classrooms)? Which types of books would interest all, most, some, or just a few of your students? You might begin your book hook list with the books you believe might interest or intrigue the largest number of your students. You also might decide to start your book hooks with a book that you think will engage the student you consider to be your biggest challenge: the nonreader who cannot stay still, who may have few friends in the classroom and little patience with or interest in being a student, or who prefers to clown around during class rather than connect with a learning experience. Selecting a book for this student might enable him to understand, implicitly, that you have made an effort on his part, or you may want to tell him that this selection is for him and explain why, making him feel special by allowing him to understand that you were thinking about him outside of school as you were planning your book hook.

Each teacher who has used the SEM-R has a suggestion about how and where to find the best book hook selections. Some begin with their students' Reading

Interest-a-Lyzers. Some ask other teachers, colleagues, or friends. Some ask their students to select sections of the books they are reading that can be used as book hooks during Phase One. Still others explore the available materials in their school library or public library. Teachers often ask librarians about new audio books or newly published books that are popular with children. Many teachers try to find books from different sections of the library each week for themes or specific events. Recently, when Sir Edmund Hillary died, a teacher who heard about his life made a special effort to find a book that could be used to expose her students to the gentle explorer who, with his Sherpa guide, was the first man to successfully climb Mt. Everest. Many teachers have explained to us how they have browsed through shelves of books with a list of their students' interests in hand in an effort to find something that might light a spark. Teachers often spend some time during their searches trying to find books that are of appropriate levels of challenge for their talented readers, who are often particularly grateful for exposure to the complex ideas or information found in adult nonfiction or other more challenging sources.

Still other teachers use the Internet, which can be an excellent source of information on numerous children's writers and illustrators. Entering an author's name into a search engine can bring up a broad array of personal Web sites as well as Web sites maintained by publishers, fans, scholars, and readers. Fortunately, many of these sites are designed to promote enjoyable reading experiences and encourage growth in reading. Some popular children's authors have attractive Web sites that encourage students to continue to learn about them and the books that they have written; a few of our favorites are listed in Table 4.4. Some include personal glimpses into the life of the author, biographical information, illustrations, and even explanations of books they have written. Such Web sites can provide teachers with ideas for book hook selections as well as information for book chats, and the Web sites can also help students become more personally involved with their favorite author during activities in Phase Three. Many of these authors, especially those who are less well known, respond to e-mails sent to them by their fans, especially when these readers are young children.

Some publishers of children's literature (such as DK Publishing and Random House) have excellent Web sites that are designed to engage kids in reading and, of course, promote their own books and publications in the process. We encourage students and teachers to check out their favorite publishers when searching for new electronic reading sources. A few of our favorites are shown in Table 4.5.

Book award winners are also popular for book hooks, and although many teachers know the popular book awards, such as the Caldecott and the Newbery, lesser-known book awards offer exciting books that can be used in Phase One of a SEM-R program. Hundreds of awards are given to outstanding books annually. Some of the most prestigious awards for authors and illustrators of children's and young adult fiction are less known, such as the Pura Belpréacutee Award or the Coretta Scott King Award. Some of our favorite awards are listed in Table 4.6.

TABLE 4.4. AUTHOR WEB SITES

Author	Web Address
Judy Blume	http://www.JudyBlume.com
Gary Paulsen	http://www.randomhouse.com/features/garypaulsen/
Beverly Cleary	http://www.beverlycleary.com/index.html
J. K. Rowling	http://www.jkrowling.com

TABLE 4.5. PUBLISHER WEB SITES

Random House

The resources for teachers on the Random House Web site are organized by grade level from preschool to twelfth grade and include reading programs, classroom clubs that teachers can join, links to author sites, and even book talks that are searchable by title or author.
http://www.randomhouse.com/teachers/

Dorling Kindersley (DK)

Originally a Dutch publishing company, DK has become a leader in publishing nonfiction children's literature. Their Web site provides an overview of the many nonfiction titles available from DK.
http://us.dk.com/

Scholastic

Scholastic's Web site is full of great resources for SEM-R teachers. The book match tool in the Online Activities section allows teachers or kids to search for books.
http://bookwizard.scholastic.com/tbw/homePage.do

We have included a list of Web sites to assist you and your students in choosing high-quality, high-interest books at appropriately challenging levels. The sites in Table 4.7 include lists of recommended books that will provide you with many ideas for book hooks. Additional book lists can be found at our SEM-R Web site at www.gifted.uconn.edu/semr.

Phase One: Indicators of High-Quality Book Hooks

Our research on the SEM-R has demonstrated that teachers who devote time to planning and implementing the SEM-R achieve better outcomes in the classroom. We have been inspired by these teachers and have watched with wonder and joy as

TABLE 4.6. PRESTIGIOUS AWARDS IN CHILDREN'S LITERATURE

Caldecott Medal

This medal was named in honor of Randolph Caldecott, a nineteenth-century English illustrator, and is awarded annually by the Association for Library Service to Children, a division of the American Library Association, to the artist of the most distinguished American picture book for children. For more information about the Caldecott Medal, see http://www.ala.org/ala/mgrps/divs/alsc/awardsgrants/bookmedia/caldecottmedal/caldecottmedal.cfm

Newbery Medal

Named for John Newbery, a British bookseller who lived in the eighteenth century, this award is given annually by the Association for Library Service to Children, a division of the American Library Association, to the author of the most distinguished contribution to American literature for children. For more information about The Newberry Medal, see http://www.ala.org/ala/mgrps/divs/alsc/awardsgrants/bookmedia/newberymedal/newberymedal.cfm

Coretta Scott King Award

Commemorating and honoring the lives of Dr. Martin Luther King Jr. and Coretta Scott King, who fought for peace and brotherhood, this award recognizes outstanding African American authors and illustrators for noteworthy contributions to children's and young adult literature. The Coretta Scott King Award is presented annually by the Coretta Scott King Task Force of the American Library Association's Social Responsibilities Round Table. Recipients are authors and illustrators whose books promote an understanding and appreciation of the American Dream. For more information about the Coretta Scott King Award, see http://www.ala.org/ala/mgrps/rts/emiert/corettascottkingbookaward/corettascott.cfm

Pura Belpré Award

This medal was named for Pura Belpré, the first Latina librarian at the New York Public Library, and is awarded biennially to a Latino or Latina writer or illustrator whose work best portrays, affirms, and celebrates the Latino cultural experience in an outstanding work of literature for children and youth. For more information about the Pura Belpré Award, see http://www.ala.org/ala/mgrps/divs/alsc/awardsgrants/bookmedia/belpremedal/belpreabout/index.cfm

Scott O'Dell Award

This prize is awarded nationally to writers of historical fiction. Scott O'Dell established the award himself in order to promote more writing in this genre.
http://www.scottodell.com/odellaward.html

their classrooms became magical places where children listen to wonderful literature and become excited about reading. Phase One of a SEM-R program hooks children on books, and over our years of research, we have watched many wonderful teachers make SEM-R time a magical part of the day. These teachers helped us to identify the indicators of a high-quality book hook. For some teachers, excelling at some of these indicators will be easily achieved because they are similar to current teaching methods. For others, some or many of the indicators will be more challenging because using a more individualized reading program is a radically different approach to teaching for them. We include these guidelines for Phase One book hooks in order to give you goals and standards for a high-quality implementation of the SEM-R.

TABLE 4.7. BOOK LISTS ON THE INTERNET

American Library Association (ALA)

This list is maintained by the Association for Library Service to Children (ALSC), a division of the ALA. Click on "Building a Home Library" for several lists.
http://www.ala.org/ala/mgrps/divs/alsc/compubs/booklists/homelib/alacbcbuildinghomelbry.cfm

This list is maintained by the Young Adult Library Services Association (YALSA), a division of the ALA. Remember when looking through these book lists that they are slightly more advanced in content and may contain subject matter not appropriate for some readers.
http://www.ala.org/ala/mgrps/divs/yalsa/booklistsawards/booklistsbook.cfm

This list, also maintained by the Young Adult Library Services Association (YALSA), lists Outstanding Books for the College Bound. The book lists are separated into content areas, including history, humanities, literature and language arts, science and technology, and social science.
http://www.ala.org/ala/mgrps/divs/yalsa/booklistsawards/outstandingbooks/outstandingbooks.cfm

The Bulletin of the Center for Children's Books

This list is maintained by *The Bulletin of the Center for Children's Books,* a journal dedicated to reviews of children's literature.
http://www.lis.uiuc.edu/puboff/bccb/

Carol Otis Hurst

This comprehensive site features reviews of hundreds of children's books, as well as ideas for integrating them into a curriculum.
http://www.carolhurst.com

Children's Book Council

This Web site provides links to a variety of book lists, including "Graphic Novels for Young Readers," "Not Just for Children Anymore!" and "Hot Off the Press."
http://www.cbcbooks.org

Children's Literature Web Guide

Another great guide with many resources, this Web site has a conference bulletin board on which users can post messages, plus specialized book lists, including a list in which famous children's authors name their own favorite children's books.
http://www.ucalgary.ca/~dkbrown/

International Reading Association

This site is maintained by the International Reading Association and includes many wonderful book lists and teacher resources.
http://www.reading.org/resources/tools/choices.html

National Council of Teachers of English (NCTE)

The NCTE maintains this comprehensive site where teachers can search for book lists generated by teachers at the elementary level or the middle school and high school level.
http://www.ncte.org

Also powered by NCTE, the Read Write Think site has a calendar that shows literary events throughout the year, including birthdays of famous authors.
http://readwritethink.org

Notable Trade Books for Young People

The lists of social studies books at this site are maintained by the National Council for the Social Studies and include biographies of famous people as well as books on a wide range of societal issues, including homelessness, civil rights, and women's rights.
http://www.socialstudies.org/resources/notable

Outstanding Science Trade Books for Children

The book lists at this site are maintained by the National Science Teachers Association and include biographies of scientists, as well as books in the various science content standards, including life science, earth and space science, and science and technology.
http://www.nsta.org/ostbc

Indicators of Success in Phase One

During book chats, the teacher models book selection behaviors and shows that her book choices are effective in demonstrating an identified purpose.

- The teacher engages students in a discussion of genre characteristics, including comparisons and contrasts with other texts.

- The teacher conducts read-alouds in such a way that his expression enhances listeners' connection with the text.

- The teacher observes that most of her students regularly demonstrate visible excitement or emotional involvement with the book.

- The teacher models higher-order thinking skills and encourages students to apply those thinking skills as well as literary concepts to frame discussion of the read-aloud.

- The teacher uses open-ended questions or strategies that allow entry and challenge at multiple levels.

- The teacher enables his students to make multiple connections (text to text, text to self, and text to world) through modeling, direct questions, and ongoing discussion.

Over time, the teacher presents book hooks that provide access to a wide variety of titles, authors, genres, and themes.

Summary

In this chapter, we have introduced you to the many creative opportunities that will arise as you plan Phase One book hooks, designing them to excite your students about reading and introduce differentiated reading strategies that are linked to state and national standards. In the next chapter, we discuss the heart of the SEM-R: differentiated reading strategies, delivered in individual reading conferences.

Supporting Independent Reading: Phase Two

Why has independent reading become such a controversial issue in classroom instruction over the last year or two? In this chapter, we introduce you to supported independent reading (SIR), Phase Two of the SEM-R, with a focus on differentiated reading conferences. The chapter also includes three mini-lessons about the purpose of independent reading, the right match, and ways to develop self-regulation that can be used to implement Phase Two.

When we discuss Phase Two with the many teachers who have participated in our research, they often tell us that they use independent reading regularly and mention programs such as DEAR (Drop Everything and Read) and SSR (Sustained Silent Reading). When we question them more closely, we find that these programs are used intermittently and that no guidelines are provided about which books can and cannot be read during this time. We also consistently learn that no instruction is provided during DEAR or SSR. When we ask teachers what they do while students are reading during DEAR or SSR, they often look at us as if we should know the answer. Sometimes, they tell us, they also read, but usually they explain that they use this time to catch up on their own work, correct papers, do organizational work in the classroom, or clean their desks!

Currently, little scientific evidence supports the long-held belief that increases in independent reading will lead to improved reading fluency and comprehension. Tim Shanahan, former president of the International Reading Association, caused quite a stir when he wrote about the lack of evidence in favor of the idea that silent reading, either with or without programs like DEAR or SSR, actually increases reading achievement. He was and still is correct. After a large-scale analysis of the limited research on this topic, the National Reading Panel (2000) concluded that "there is a clear need for rigorous experimental research on the impact of programs that encourage reading on different populations of students at varying ages and reading levels . . . and where the amount of independent reading is carefully monitored" (pp. 3–4). To date, limited findings suggest that neither resources nor additional time allocated to independent reading *alone* is sufficient to promote reading growth in students (Anderson, Wilson, & Fielding, 1988; Taylor, Frye, & Maruyama, 1990). Phase Two activities in the SEM-R are quite different from the other independent reading programs mentioned earlier because teachers actively scaffold students in their supported independent reading and also conduct differentiated individual reading conferences in which a variety of goals are introduced and met.

In a SEM-R program, during Phase Two, teachers conduct individual conferences with students and provide individualized instruction that focus on reading strategies and higher-order questions that challenge, instruct, and engage readers. The idea behind these conferences is that students receive differentiated instruction based on their needs, which are assessed through a variety of ongoing assessment methods. Individual student conferences also provide time for teachers to assess the match between students and the books they have selected. The conferences emphasize student self-selection of appropriately challenging material that is personally interesting; teachers invite students to share their reasoning for choosing a particular book and whether the book has turned out to be a good choice. Such discussions, along with other components of the conferences and Phase Two, help to promote self-regulation and metacognition in students on their choices for reading. In addition, teachers may use conference time to discuss student interests and the possibility of pursuing independent work during Phase Three.

Phase Two in a SEM-R program focuses on the development of students' ability to engage in structured, independent reading of self-selected, high-interest books and to sustain the reading for increasing periods over time. Throughout Phase Two, teachers work with students to select books that are slightly above their current reading level, to ensure optimal learning opportunities and continued development of vocabulary knowledge and the use of reading strategies for readers at all levels, including talented readers. As you begin to use this phase of SEM-R in your classroom, you may want to use the following mini-lesson that engages students with a discussion in class about the reasons that people read.

Mini-Lesson #1: Discussing the Purpose of Reading

Goal: To set the stage for extending supported independent reading in class

Objective: To develop students' understanding of the purpose of SIR through a teacher-facilitated class discussion

Supplies needed: Reading materials representing a variety of genres from the school library and classroom collection

Activity: Begin by sharing with your students a variety of reading materials that represent a variety of reading purposes—for example, fiction and nonfiction books, manuals, handbooks, magazines, or newspapers. As you display each type of reading material to the class, empha-size the variety of reasons for reading. Some possible discussion questions:

- Why would you read this?
- What might someone learn from reading this?
- Where might you find this reading material?

Next, focus the discussion on students' personal reasons for reading and have students brain-storm responses to the following questions:

- Why do you read?
- Why do you think that being able to read is important?

Student responses will vary but may include the following:

- To learn
- For enjoyment
- To find out things
- To build vocabulary or language skills
- To share thoughts or ideas with others

Book Match: Finding Appropriately Challenging Reading Material

An essential feature of Phase Two is student selection of books that are sufficiently challenging. SIR is based on the premise that students will benefit more from the experience of reading independently if they are challenged by complex content, ideas, and language in the text. This premise is especially true if the book is of personal interest to the student and he is motivated to read it. However, if books are too challenging, students may become frustrated and their fluency and comprehension will fail to improve. Evaluating the appropriateness of student book selections is challenging, yet it is a critical aspect of ensuring the success and effectiveness of SIR.

The process of deciding whether a book is an appropriate choice for SIR will be different for each student. For example, a talented reader may choose a book that is at or above grade level in difficulty but may not be sufficiently challenged by the book's content. Because of her strong word-reading fluency, she should be encouraged to choose a book with more complex content.

On the other hand, a struggling reader might select books with more challenging content and ideas. Because his reading skills are not fully developed, he may have to expend a great deal of energy simply to decode words that he then is unable to understand. He should be supported in choosing books with equally challenging content but with vocabulary at a level that he can read fluently.

Because students in your class will have very different reading skills and comprehension, there are no specific rules for deciding whether a book is an appropriate choice for Phase Two SIR. Nonetheless, we consider four factors in trying to provide challenging material for every student: readability, complexity, appropriateness of a text's subject matter, and each student's interests.

Readability

Word-reading level refers to the readability of the words in the text. The readability level is designated on many texts in today's classrooms to help teachers match readers with books. When trying to determine the appropriateness of texts, teachers usually expect their students to be able to read most of the words on a page with little difficulty in decoding. They also expect that students should be able to read with a moderate degree of fluency (that is, smoothly and quickly).

Teachers have long used the "five finger rule" to help learners determine whether a text will be too difficult for them. Typically, readers are asked to hold up five fingers as they read a page of text. Each time a reader sees a word that he or she cannot read, the child puts one of her fingers down. At the end of the page, the student should determine, based on the number of fingers left in the air, whether the book is too difficult. Most teachers tell students that if they have put all five of their fingers down when reading a page that the text is too difficult for them to read. In many cases, this is true. What teachers often do not mention to students, however, is that if only one or two of their fingers are down at the end of a page of text, the book may be too easy. Moreover, students may simply assume they do not know a new word without attempting to use contextual clues to determine its meaning, which will change their assessment of text difficulty. Our experience in classrooms indicates that teachers usually tell a student not to read a text that is too difficult but rarely encourage them to read a book that is challenging.

In an appropriately challenging book, students should encounter some words that are unfamiliar and new to them. Students will learn to read new words when they are fluent with the other words in the sentences and paragraphs. Growth in reading will also occur when students are encouraged to read appropriately challenging texts in the context of a supportive environment that engages students as they learn the new words they are reading. The rule of thumb for students in a SEM-R program is that if they can already read most of the words on a page, the book they have selected is likely to be too easy.

A common mistake is assuming that a text that has more difficult words is an appropriate match for a talented reader. Often, as the word-reading level increases, the complexity and difficulty of the subject matter also increase. Just because a talented reader can decode difficult a text does not mean that it is appropriate reading material for him. For instance, we have seen very young children (aged four or five) who can accurately decode text to "read" the *Wall Street Journal*. We can all agree, however, that the *Wall Street Journal* is not appropriate reading material for a four-year-old. Though a young child may be able to accurately read the words, perhaps even with a great deal of fluency, he usually cannot understand the complex ideas in the text, so the subject matter is neither appropriate nor interesting for a young child.

Complexity of Content

Complexity of content refers to students' understanding, appreciation, and critical thinking about the content of their reading selection. After reading any passage, students should be able to answer basic questions about the character, setting, and plot of the passage. In addition, students should be able to interact with a text at a more complex level by making inferences, analyzing and synthesizing information, and relating the content to their own experiences. The content, ideas, and language in a book should challenge the boundaries of what students can understand easily or with little effort. Books should encourage students to use and develop critical thinking skills, expand their knowledge and understanding, and think about ideas differently.

A teacher will be able to gauge whether a text is sufficiently complex for a student during each conference. If a student reads fluently and responds to questions with answers that come easily and require little thought, the text is most likely too easy. Teachers should ask their students whether they have questions about what they have read. A text that is read without any effort and that does not leave some questions in a student's mind does not present an opportunity for the reader to grow.

Appropriateness of Content or Subject Matter

A major concern when working with readers, especially talented readers, is finding material with both complexity and age-appropriate subject matter. Searching for a text that is sufficiently complex may lead to story lines and topics that are not appropriate for young readers. For a late primary reader or an early intermediate talented reader, for example, the options may include literature that is written for adolescents and young adults. However, themes like dating and choosing whether to use drugs are not necessarily topics that teachers and parents would select for younger students.

Finding books with appropriate subject matter may be the most challenging piece of the puzzle that teachers face when matching books to individual readers. Educators may feel cautious about making recommendations, especially in communities where parents have raised questions about reading materials used in schools. Age-appropriateness of reading material is influenced by many factors, including the beliefs and culture of a student's family. It is also important to consider a student's social and intellectual levels of development, not just her chronological development. For that reason, the appropriateness of a text becomes a decision that teachers should make with each child and in some cases, in consultation with parents. The challenge for educators is twofold—knowing and understanding both individual students and the literature that children enjoy. You may find that your school media specialist or local children's librarian is a helpful resource. Teachers facing the dilemma of young, talented readers often revisit beloved classic literature from authors such as

L. M. Montgomery, Jules Verne, and Charles Dickens with success, and some also try to turn students' attention to nonfiction reading material.

Engaging Reader's Interests

The final consideration in helping children choose books is personal interests. Most students have or are developing interests to which teachers can match any number of books. The Reading Interest-a-Lyzer (Appendix B), a helpful tool that was developed as part of the research on the SEM-R, can be used to pinpoint students' reading interests. Some students will indicate their preferences for certain genres of text. Other students might indicate that they only enjoy reading about one topic. It may be more difficult to find books for these students than for other students with more diverse reading interests; however, the effort will be worth it once these students begin to enjoy the process of reading. Remember that the more types of books you introduce in Phase One, the more likely students are to diversify their reading tastes. Interest identification and development are crucial to knowing students as readers and necessary to honor the foundational goal of the SEM-R: encouraging students to enjoy reading.

We conclude this section with a mini-lesson that you could use to help students better understand the types of book choices they might make to have a good match with their interests, reading level, and ability to focus and read for extended lengths of time.

Mini-Lesson #2: Making Appropriate Book Choices

Goal: To improve the quality and quantity of student engagement with books

Objective: To provide students with strategies for choosing a challenging, enjoyable book to read

Supplies needed: A collection of books representing a variety of genres and styles from the library, classroom collection, or other sources

Activity: Begin by asking students to work with a partner to brainstorm a list of strategies that students can use to decide whether a book is right for them (for example, examining cover art or reading a summary). As a class, discuss student responses and compile a list of strategies on the board.

Next, provide each pair of students with a book and ask them to employ some (or all) of the strategies listed on the board to make suggestions about who might be interested in this book. (You may find it helpful to model this process for your students before they begin.)

Have each group share their recommendations as well as the strategy and information gained that led to the decision. You may discover that some students are able to make very specific suggestions (for example, "We think Marc will like this book because we have heard him say how much he likes books written by Andrew Clements, and this is his newest novel.")

Finally, discuss with students how they determine if a book is a good match for reading during SIR time, emphasizing the idea that there is an appropriate level of challenge. You may find the following questions helpful.

- Have you ever read a book that was too hard for you to read by yourself? How did you know that it was too difficult? What advice would you give me if I had a book that I *really* wanted to read but it was just too tough for me to read right now?
- Have you ever read a book that was too easy for you to read? How do you feel when you are reading an easy book? Why do you think I might ask you to pick a more challenging book during independent reading time?
- Are there any strategies on our list that you could use to help you decide whether a book is too easy or too difficult for you to read during independent reading time? [Circle those strategies on the board.] Are there any other strategies we should add to help us decide whether a book provides the right challenge level?

Reading Conferences: Differentiating Instruction to Meet the Needs of All Readers

Most teachers in our studies faced the challenge of teaching a heterogeneous class with eight to ten grade levels of reading achievement and instruction in the classroom; in many of the heterogeneous third-grade classrooms, students were reading from a kindergarten or preschool level all the way to an eighth-grade or ninth-grade level. The prevalence of such a wide range of student proficiency levels in today's classrooms makes it necessary for teachers to use varying methods and processes to reach learners. Teachers must target instruction toward differing levels of skills in order to ensure that those who enter school ahead of their peers will be sufficiently challenged and that those who are behind their peers will also be challenged at an appropriate level. Using conferences in Phase Two of a SEM-R program will help to differentiate the reading instruction and materials that students receive.

We have found that when they begin using the SEM-R, many teachers share a common concern that they will not be able to conduct conferences on books that they have not read. They worry about having to read every book that their students are reading in order to be able to determine students' comprehension of plot, characterization, and author's message. Of course, such expectations are unreasonable. In fact, all of the teachers we worked with could conduct challenging, high-level conferences on books they had not read. Teachers have learned that while teaching reading without an answer key can be challenging, it also encourages thoughtful, reflective practices.

Though a conference assumes the feel of a conversation about the book, it also provides instruction for the student and specific feedback for the teacher on the student's progress. Though conferences may appear to be somewhat informal, remember that they are a crucial component of Phase Two supported independent reading. During this time, students should be asked to use higher-order thought processes, read challenging selections, and integrate new reading strategies into their repertoire. A SEM-R student log is also given to each child who participates in the

SEM-R program. A sample page from this log is included in Appendix G. When teachers sit next to students to begin a SEM-R conference, the students often hand their teachers both the book they are reading as well as their student log. Students are often eager to share a specific part of the book that they want to discuss. Their responses usually often draw on the book they were reading as well as their background experiences and interests. An examination of students' reading logs will let their teacher know that they are reading every day and their weekly written reflections will help teachers to assess students' use of reading strategies and their enjoyment of and interest in reading.

Format for Reading Conferences

In our experience with the hundreds of teachers who have used the SEM-R in their classrooms, the most successful teachers have developed a standard format or expected routine for the conferences. Although the order of the components described here may vary, each is likely to occur during a conference. Teachers may vary the parts of the conference based on a student's need. For example, if a child is struggling with fluency, her teacher may spend more time providing strategies, modeling, and practice to help her develop greater fluency. In other conferences, teachers may spend very little time working on the fluency of a student's reading, choosing instead to spend the majority of time building comprehension strategies by asking the student to synthesize information or make connections. The format of the conference should be easily differentiated to meet the needs of the student.

Suggested Format for Conferences

- When you begin a conference, sit down with the student and ask him to tell you a little bit about his book. Keep in mind that you are asking the student to synthesize information from the book rather than recount every detail.
- Ask the student to describe whether he likes the book so far, and why.
- Ask the student to read a little bit of the book aloud to you, starting wherever he stopped when you dropped in. Have the student read about a page or two for about a minute.
- If the student comes to a word he does not know, wait a few seconds and then tell the student the word. Allow the narrative flow to continue instead of interrupting it by spending too much time on trying to figure out the word.
- If the student is missing so many words that it is impossible for a narrative flow to occur, stop the student and suggest that maybe this book should be saved to read later on, after there has been time for more reading practice. Have the student write the name and author of the book on the sheet "Books I Want to Read Later" in the student's log and then help the student choose a new book.
- Pay careful attention to how the student reads the passage. Listen for the number of words that are difficult for him, for expression, and for other indications of comprehension.

- When the student finishes reading, offer some comments that reflect praise. Try to be specific (for example, "I really liked how you used different voices for the characters!" or "I liked how you went back and corrected yourself on a word that you missed!"). Then ask the student a few follow-up questions about the reading. You may want to use one of the SEM-R bookmarks (see Appendix A) as a guide, or you may want to ask some questions that are more specific to the passage itself.

- The questioning portion of the conference should take about three minutes. The overall conference should take only about five or six minutes at the most.

- Try to ask questions that go beyond simple recall of what happened in the narrative. Ask "why" questions, and remind the student to support answers with evidence from the book.

- Try to ask questions that are individually challenging for the student. Varying your questions will help to differentiate conference discussions.

- A good source of questioning is the connections that can be made with the text (that is, text-to-text, text-to-self, and text-to-world connections).

- The follow-up questioning time is also a good time to review words that the student might have missed. Go back and point out some words that were challenging, and ask the student how he might have tried to figure out the words. Talk about strategies for figuring out words, such as using context clues, using pictures, or looking for parts of the words that are familiar.

- In some cases, the reading and discussion portions of the conference, together or separately, might indicate that the book is too hard or too easy for the student. If this is the case, encourage the student to try a different book. In the case of books that are too easy, talk to the student about the importance of reading challenging books while at school, where someone can help him with his reading, and encourage the student to read the easier book at home.

- Initial the student's conference record on the appropriate date to show that the conference was conducted. You may want to list any major strategies that you worked on or difficulties the student had and write them in the student's log. You should also thank the student for sharing some reading time with you.

During conferences, it is important that strategies such as making inferences, predicting, making connections, higher-order thinking, and self-questioning be used. It is also important that the student understand how to apply strategies appropriately. To achieve these objectives, it is helpful for the teacher to explicitly instruct the student on these strategies as well as to model good reading habits by using the strategies. During the conferences, you will want to ask questions that incorporate and identify strategies. For example, the questions, "What do you think will happen next?" and "What is your prediction about what will happen next?" essentially have the same meaning; however, the second question explicitly names the strategy being used and therefore provides the student with a clearer understanding of how these strategies are used on a regular basis.

During each conference, you should use informal assessment measures to determine the student's reading progress and her ability to use reading strategies. You will be able to assess a student's reading fluency, her comprehension of the selected text, and her other reading experiences, including enjoyment of and engagement with the book. You will read more about documenting student progress and ways to manage student conferences in Chapter Seven.

Assessing and Improving Reading Fluency

The concepts of reading fluency and comprehension are closely intertwined. Readers who struggle with fluency concentrate on deciphering and identifying words rather than constructing meaning. Fluent readers, on the other hand, have achieved automaticity—that is, they automatically decode and recognize words, enabling more cognitive resources to focus on high-level thinking and interpreting the text. Therefore, helping students increase their ability to read fluently should be an important goal for teachers of young readers. Readers should be able to read at a pace that enables them to connect phrases together, contributing to meaningful comprehension of the text.

At the beginning of each conference, have each student read a short section from her current book. This allows you to make a quick determination about the appropriateness of the book based on what you have heard in just that minute of reading. If a student can read every word with a high rate of fluency and with expression that matches the text, it is obvious that the book's readability is high or that the text might be too easy. This judgment about readability, however, should also be combined with a comprehension check.

On the other hand, when students struggle to decode the text they are reading or cannot read with any degree of expression, the readability level of the text may be too difficult for them. Again, the appropriateness of the book should be determined only after you have had a chance to gauge the student's comprehension of the text and consider the students' interests. If, for instance, you have a student who struggles with decoding the text but accurately answers questions about the plot and seems interested enough to keep reading, you should provide the student with some strategies for increasing fluency and encourage him to keep reading. Even though he may be missing words occasionally as he reads, it has not hampered his ability to comprehend.

When conducting a conference with a student who is misreading words, it is usually better to write down the words as you hear them rather than interrupt and correct the student each time he miscues. Once the student has read a paragraph or two, stop him and begin to talk about some of the words he missed. Ask him to go back to the text with you, to examine the context of the sentence that might have helped him determine the word's meaning. Or ask the student to chunk the word into smaller and more manageable pieces. For example, if a student has missed the word *unforgivable,* ask him if he can see part of a smaller word within. Once he has identified *forgive,* discuss the meaning of both the prefix and the suffix. Modeling the process of self-correction shows the reader that this is what good readers do when they read. Once you have modeled self-correction, ask the student to read a bit more and try to use the new strategy if he runs into a word he does not know how to read.

If, however, the student reads a word and seems to hesitate or goes back to self-correct, this is the perfect opportunity to stop the student and model the behavior of self-correcting. You might ask the student how he knew that he had read the word incorrectly or whether he noticed that it did not make sense in the context of the rest of the text. You might also give him additional strategies to use when fluency breaks down. Remember, the best way for students to increase reading fluency is to practice!

Using Questioning and Conversation to Assess Comprehension

Another purpose of SIR is to help students develop their ability to comprehend text. Students who understand what they read actively construct meaning as they interact with text. They have an in-depth understanding of story elements such as character, setting, and plot as well as the structure of nonfiction work. They are also able to think critically about what they are reading, know when they have problems with understanding, and know how to resolve those problems as they occur. Strengthening the reading comprehension of students enables them to become better readers of both creative and expository texts and provides students with greater access to information from both the literary world and the realms of content areas such as science and history.

Part of the conversation between the teacher and the student in Phase Two is like any conversation that two readers would have about a book. In adult conversations about books, readers might try to get a sense of the story, the author's purpose, and possible connections with their own life. It is probable that the bulk of the conversation would focus on big ideas like these, rather than small details such as the color of shoes the character wore or the name of the cousin who attended the party. The readers would almost certainly discuss whether they were enjoying the book. Conferences during SIR should have a similarly important tone and should not simply become oral recitations of multiple-choice tests.

Ideally, the conference should involve an authentic conversation as well as strategy instruction; initially, however, these conferences may be difficult to conduct. In the beginning, you may be trying to integrate several reading strategies into the conference, thereby losing the authentic feel of the conversation. Conversely, some teachers become so involved in listening to a child talk about his book, that they forget to integrate strategy instruction and appropriately challenging questions into the conference. Although this occasionally happens at the beginning of SEM-R implementation, teachers quickly adapt and integrate all aspects of the conferences. The SEM-R bookmarks discussed in the preceding chapter on Phase One have been instrumental in helping teachers integrate higher-order questions throughout their conferences with students.

We have found that the most effective conferences begin with the teacher warmly greeting the student and trying to establish some type of connection. Next, the student is asked to read a brief selection from the book she is currently reading. Then, the teacher often comments on the student's reading and offers suggestions on the use of reading strategies or on vocabulary that she has missed. At this point, the teacher might ask a question that requires the student to use high-level reading skills or that challenges the student to use analysis, synthesis, or evaluation. At the end of the conference, the teacher may use the bookmarks to ask the student to consider a new skill or a new literacy approach. Again, it is important that strategies used in the conference be made clear by explicitly stating which strategy is being used and why that particular strategy is appropriate.

The bookmarks (Appendix A) can be used to identify higher-order thinking questions that are appropriate for use in the conferences. The questions on the bookmarks can also be used to assess students' use of reading strategies. To accomplish this objective, you must be clear about which strategy you intend to assess. For instance, to determine whether a student was able to make connections between personal experiences and the story characters, you might ask, "Did you relate to the main character of this book? If yes, in what way? If no, why not?" This question asks the reader to make a direct comparison of his own feelings with those of the main character, and the following question might ask him to identify the strategy he used to answer the question. However, if you intended to find out whether the same reader could make an inference, you might ask a slightly different question. In order to answer the question "When does the main character feel the saddest in the story, and why?" the reader would need to infer the answer. A follow-up question might be "Which strategy did you use to answer this question?" Such fine distinctions in questioning illustrate the importance of teachers' understanding of the reading strategies and the assessments they hope to conduct during each conference.

Modeling Strategies by Thinking Aloud During Conferences

When a student is unable to answer comprehension questions, a teacher can provide a model by "thinking aloud"—that is, narrating the thinking process of the strategy step by step so that the student can follow the process. The following case provides a detailed example.

> Emily's teacher, Mrs. Dahl, sat down next to Emily to begin her reading conference. Emily was nearly finished with *The Higher Power of Lucky* by Susan Patron and Matt Phelan, and she told Mrs. Dahl that she was really enjoying the book. Mrs. Dahl asked Emily to briefly summarize what had been happening in the story. As Emily summarized, it was clear to her teacher that though Emily could provide a cohesive summary of the plot, there were overall themes that Emily might not be recognizing. When Mrs. Dahl asked Emily to read a page of text, Emily read fluently and with expression. Emily's teacher decided to ask Emily some questions about theme and the authors' message to see if she could provide enough scaffolding to get Emily to think at a deeper level about why some of the events in the story had occurred. She began by asking Emily why she believed that the main character, Lucky, felt worried so much of the time.
>
> Emily thought for a while. Finally she said, "I think that Lucky was sad that her mother had died."

"What makes you say that?" asked Mrs. Dahl.

"I'm not sure. I just know that if my mother died, I would be so sad all of the time just like Lucky," Emily responded.

Mrs. Dahl, who had not yet read the book, decided to probe further, realizing that Emily was using only her own experiences to judge the actions of the character. Mrs. Dahl decided to make her own thinking transparent in order to help Emily reason an answer to the question. "I think you're partially right, Emily. She probably was thinking a lot about her mother, just as you would if your mother weren't with you. But I'm thinking about the word *worry* and wondering why Lucky might feel worried if her mother were gone. Certainly she would feel sad, but worrying is a bit different from sadness, isn't it? Let's see if we can look back in the text to see if we can figure out what might have made Lucky feel worried."

Together, the pair leafed through the pages that Emily had already read. As they did so, Mrs. Dahl asked Emily to discuss elements from that part of the story to see whether they could discover the answer. At one point, Emily mentioned that Lucky often thinks that her guardian will leave her to go back to live in France. Emily's teacher knew then that Emily had not connected the potential leaving of the guardian to Lucky's feeling of worry. Emily had not had experiences similar to Lucky's and had difficulty making a text-to-self connection to better understand the story. In addition, the author probably had not explicitly written "Lucky was worried" in the text, instead planting clues for the readers to find and make inferences from. Therefore, Mrs. Dahl concluded that Emily needed additional coaching in making inferences.

As the conference continued, Mrs. Dahl made another attempt to show Emily her thinking. "Emily, when people worry, they are thinking about something that might happen that would be unpleasant. You told me that the author has given some clues that Lucky's guardian might be moving back to France. As I think about what I know about Lucky, I can tell that she is feeling sad and alone in the world after her mother's death. She also has a guardian. However, she thinks that this guardian might be moving away, thus leaving her alone. Now, can you think about all of those clues and infer what might be worrying Lucky?"

With such strong scaffolding, Emily was easily able to determine that Lucky's worry was due to the fact that she was unsure about whether her guardian would be leaving her. They went on to discuss how Lucky's worry affected the rest of the story and how to use that information to make predictions about the ending of the story. Mrs. Dahl's ability to detect only a surface level of understanding in Emily's responses led to the scaffolding. This practice later enabled Emily to make an inference about the author's intent and understand the story more deeply.

Teachers must learn to make their thinking transparent to their students. Often, this type of "thinking aloud" will be done in Phase One through modeling answers to bookmark questions, but it should also be done with readers of all achievement levels in Phase Two. Please note that this is not a strategy reserved for use with struggling readers. *All* students will need some scaffolding and coaching if they are reading sufficiently challenging books.

Gauging Enjoyment of Reading

You will recall that the first goal of the SEM-R is to promote enjoyment of reading in students. Therefore, teachers should also use the conferences to gauge students' enjoyment of their reading. In most cases, teachers will begin each conference by asking the student, "How do you like the book so far?"

A sixth-grade teacher's experience with her student, Tony, provides a good illustration of the importance of reading enjoyment:

> Tony was a struggling reader. He had achieved low scores in reading throughout school, and his reading interest scores, taken on his entry to sixth grade, showed that he did not enjoy reading. Early in the school year, Tony was having a conference with his teacher, Mrs. Karnes. During that conference, the pair was discussing the text *Mick Harte Was Here* by Barbara Park. Mick's sister narrates the story and describes the fatal accident of her brother. Mrs. Karnes began the conference by asking how the character Mick had died. Although he was more than halfway through the book, Tony indicated to Mrs. Karnes that the character hadn't died. Though she had never read the book herself, Mrs. Karnes was able to deduce from the title of the story that Tony's comprehension had broken down somewhere along the way. The teacher worked with him to review the text and discover the sister's memories of Mick's death in the first few pages of the text. When Mrs. Karnes asked Tony if he was enjoying the book, he admitted that he'd never really gotten into it. She suggested that he find a book that he enjoyed.
>
> Later in the semester, Mrs. Karnes sat with Tony as he excitedly described to her the plot from the book *Monster* by Walter Dean Myers. This time, Tony knew every detail and plot twist of the novel, a novel that was more complicated than the other had been. When his teacher asked him whether he was enjoying *Monster,* Tony emphatically nodded and indicated that he planned to read every book written by Walter Dean Myers.

Tony's situation could confuse any reading teacher. Why was it that he could read a more difficult text more successfully than one that was slightly below grade level? We would have expected that the more appropriate book for a struggling reader like Tony would have been the easier one. Because the word-reading level, complexity, and subject matter were all more difficult in the second text than the first, only the interest level of the student seems to have changed the result. Interest seems to have complicated the matter of book match. In Tony's case, a simple formula involving word-reading level and complexity and subject matter was not enough; finding an appropriate text for Tony also involved considering his interest in the text.

The lesson that we can learn from Tony's case is the guiding principle behind the SEM-R: interest often mediates ability. In other words, an otherwise struggling reader will be able to read a high-interest text that she could not normally access without the strong interest. Likewise, a perfectly capable reader may have lower comprehension of a text in which he is not engaged.

During conferences, we have found that teachers are more likely to make a connection with students when the teachers reveal their own reading likes and dislikes. You might talk about which genres or types of characters that you enjoy. As you share your preferences, be sure to discuss the reasoning behind your preferences, to demonstrate to your students some of the ways that you interact with texts.

Self-Regulation and Supported Independent Reading

Supported independent reading is most effective when all students are engrossed in their reading. Experienced teachers know that there are always a few students who need additional support to stay on task. Advance planning and practice in using techniques that can help students focus and regulate their learning and behavior can help teachers to lay the foundation for success in reading for students.

Defining Self-Regulated Learning

As we discussed in Chapter Two, successful students use self-regulated learning strategies (Zimmerman, 1989). Self-regulated learning can help students develop a set of constructive behaviors that positively affect their learning. Several processes have been identified that enable students to pursue and achieve personal learning goals and adapt their environment to support such outcomes. Self-regulation skills can be taught, learned, and controlled by students, and research on self-regulation (Zimmerman, 1990) has found that successful students use self-regulation strategies in three categories: personal, behavioral, and environmental. *Personal strategies* involve how students organize information and include strategies related to classifying and coordinating information, setting goals, and planning work. *Behavioral strategies* occur when students check their own progress or the quality of their work by examining what they do when they learn, identify consequences for work not done, and use self-reinforcement and delay gratification until they have achieved their specific goals. *Environmental strategies* for self-regulated learning involve the use of external resources and the methods that students use to change or adapt their environment to achieve more positive results.

Developing Self-Regulation Using the SEM-R

When you are introducing the SEM-R to a new group of students, Phase Two should be implemented gradually. Eventually, most of the time you allocate to your SEM-R program will be spent in Phase Two, but initially, your students may not have the self-regulation necessary to read for long periods of time. In fact, our experience has shown that some students may not be able to read for more than four or five minutes at a time. This lack of staying power may be due to the challenging books you are asking them to read. Students may be able to read unchallenging books for long periods of time but may not have developed the skills necessary to do so with more challenging texts. Students may simply lack experience with independent reading for long periods of time. In Phase Two, students will begin to develop the self-regulation necessary to read self-selected, challenging texts for sustained periods of time. For some students, however, this will be no small undertaking!

When the SEM-R was first implemented in most schools, many students were only able to read for three or four minutes at a time during the first few weeks. After only a few minutes, they would begin to squirm and demonstrate off-task behavior. When the teachers noticed that the students were getting off task, they ended Phase Two and moved on to another SEM-R task or another activity altogether. The teachers realized that once students were no longer focusing on the task of reading, they were not developing the self-regulation necessary to participate successfully in SIR. When the majority of students are off task, it is best to end Phase Two and move to more Phase One read-alouds or to Phase Three activities. The following suggestions can help you to manage students' independent reading and increase their self-regulation:

- Proximity to students is the most proactive measure you can take to help them maintain their focus on reading. Rather than calling students to your desk for individual conferences, we suggest that you move quietly throughout the room and sit beside a student to conduct each conference in a quiet tone of voice. Your presence can help to keep your students on track and provide other students with the opportunity to learn when they overhear your comments and suggestions to their classmates.

- Work collaboratively with students to set goals for SIR target time, and celebrate on the days in which everyone exceeds expectation. Younger students in particular have a difficult time gauging the amount of time that they are actually reading quietly and on task. Providing students with a visual reminder of their goals (like a stop time written on the board, a timer, or a sticky note placed on the clock to mark the end of SIR time) may help them to sustain a focus on reading throughout the designated SIR time.

- Some children may need to have their SIR time broken into smaller chunks of reading time. The goal is to build reading stamina in all students, but it will be necessary to make accommodations for some readers. For students who have great difficulty sustaining their reading for an extended period, you may want to give them the option of listening to an audio book for part of the SIR time, working with a buddy to read for a portion of the time, or working on a written response followed by more SIR time.

- Encourage students to focus on one particular bookmark or bookmark question, to provide a purpose as they begin their reading for the week. As students find evidence in the book to help them answer a question, they can either mark the spot with the bookmark or make note of the page in their reading log. They will then be prepared to discuss their ideas with you during their reading conference.

- Provide students with sticky notes or scratch paper on which they can jot questions, concerns, or unfamiliar vocabulary so that they can continue to read until an adult is available for assistance or a discussion.

- Many teachers have explained that during self-directed activities, they know that students cannot both raise their hand and continue to be productive at the same time. Sun/cloud cards can be used as an unobtrusive cue to indicate whether a student wants assistance. The sun side indicates that the student is doing fine with reading independently. The cloud side indicates that the student wants assistance. A template for the sun/cloud card is provided in Appendix D.

- Proximity to other students may be distracting to some children. Work with students to consider the spaces within the room where they will be reading. Have them consider how their choice of reading location might support continued focus or lead to distractions. To support the goal of having spaces that support a focus on reading, you might try to create some spaces that limit distractions yet are inviting.

When introducing the SEM-R program and SIR to students, it is important to engage them in several discussions that will set the stage for self-regulation in your classroom. These discussions will help students understand what is expected of them in terms of behavior during SEM-R time. Moreover, they will help you achieve the goals and objectives that you have set forth for the program.

Establishing a Routine with Clear Expectations

One of the most important things to do when you begin to use the SEM-R is to create a structure with clear expectations. Establishing a routine will help students understand what is expected of them during the class period. Clear expectations will help students envision and imagine what it means to get into the groove of self-regulated reading and also provide a structure within which both you and your students can solve problems when difficulties arise.

Teachers should strive to give students all of the tools that will enable them to stay on task during their independent reading time. See the box for an example of an expectations chart that could be posted in a SEM-R classroom.

Behaviors Expected During Supported Independent Reading

- You must have a book to read at all times.
- If you aren't enjoying a book and have given it a fair chance (read at least ten pages), ask the teacher to help you choose a new one.
- Select and remain in one reading area during SIR.
- Only reading is happening. (You may talk quietly with your teacher during conferences.)
- Do your best reading the whole time.

Managing Interruptions

There are times when students are more likely to be off task, such as when they require teacher assistance, need permission to go to the bathroom, or want to select a new book. There are several management strategies you can use to keep students on track, even when they require your attention. First, you can adopt a policy of no interruptions during your conferencing time. Without such a policy, it is very likely that you will receive frequent requests from students for help with tasks that they can manage on their own. If students must ask permission to use the bathroom or get a drink of water, for instance, you are likely to be interrupted several times throughout the period.

Effective SEM-R teachers have developed systems in which students are able to excuse themselves without disturbing the teacher. In most classrooms, it is important that the teacher be able to see at a glance which student is in the bathroom or at the drinking fountain. Therefore, some teachers have developed systems in which students must hang a card with their picture on a hook when they are in the bathroom. This method is especially effective for large classrooms because the teacher can immediately see who is not in the classroom. A sign-out log can be effective because teachers can see whether there are certain students who seem to make frequent bathroom and fountain trips; these are possible signs of inattentiveness to reading, which may have many different causes.

Teachers should also establish procedures for using the classroom and school library during SIR. Without guidelines, some students may abuse the privilege and use the library as an excuse to be out of their seat rather than a resource for finding books. In addition, some students may develop the habit of "book shopping," in which they choose a new book every period instead of completing books. Teachers have developed several ways of dealing with this behavior. If you find that you have a chronic book shopper in your room, it will be necessary to diagnose the reason for the behavior and then apply an appropriate remedy.

For students who are easily pulled off task, it is important to try to figure out why they are not finishing or engaging with books. The books may be too challenging, too boring, too easy, or just not what they were hoping to read. Knowing the problem will help you find a solution. For instance, the teacher might use the student's conference time to aid the child in finding appropriate books. You and the student might discuss ways to find books that are neither too difficult nor too easy. You might also encourage the student to use different strategies, perhaps bringing several books back to his or her seat for reading time.

In some cases, however, chronic book shoppers do not easily shake the behavior! In such cases, it becomes obvious that these students are less able to self-regulate reading than their peers and that teachers need to provide additional support. In some cases, teachers require students to finish their current book before they begin a new one. In other cases, students are asked to write a letter to the teacher requesting permission to abandon a book. Both strategies have been helpful in lessening book-shopping behaviors. Some teachers also discourage this behavior, as well as interruptions throughout the period, by having a rule that students can only visit the class library during the first five minutes of the reading period.

Interruptions can also occur when students become confused by the text they are reading. At times, they may get hung up on a word that they cannot decode or an idea that doesn't seem to make sense. Teaching students how to deal with these types of content difficulties is an important step in teaching them to self-regulate their reading. If we continue to allow students immediate access to answers when they have these questions, it may discourage them from figuring out the answers for themselves. Thus, independent processing is an important step in helping them become self-sufficient readers who will continue to enjoy the process long after they leave our classroom.

Several teachers have developed strategies for dealing with students when they have questions during SIR. One fourth-grade teacher allows her students to "phone a friend," a takeoff on the popular game show *Who Wants to Be a Millionaire?* In her classroom, a student can ask a friend one question during the period. Some students might ask a friend to clarify the pronunciation or meaning of a word. Others might seek out a peer who has read the same book to get clarification on something that wasn't understood or to ask for a book recommendation.

Many teachers have employed the use of sticky notes. In these classrooms, each student has his own supply of sticky notes so that if he runs into something that doesn't make sense, he can mark the spot to ask the teacher in a free moment or during his own conference. In addition, teachers have also asked students to use sticky notes to mark sections of the text that illustrate their use of a reading strategy or that provide evidence to answer a bookmark question. For example, sticky notes can also be used to mark the sections that raised questions for the student or where they made an inference or drew a connection.

Teachers can also use the time between conferences to answer questions for students. Teachers using the SEM-R have developed different management strategies for recognizing which students are in need of some attention. As an alternative to the sun/cloud card, students in some classrooms alert teachers that they are in need of help by turning the "Stop" side up on a card, while the "Go" side is used when all systems are go and reading is going smoothly. Teachers duplicate the symbols on card stock and laminate them for durability. With either symbol system, teachers can see with a glance across the classroom whether a student needs help.

Managing Off-Task Behavior

Students may develop off-task behaviors for many reasons. They may be unable to concentrate on their reading for long periods of time because they don't know how to manage their own behavior. There are many behavioral strategies that you can use to help students manage these issues in order to help them develop self-regulatory behavior for reading. Some students realize when they are off task, and others do not. In any case, it is necessary to increase the student's metacognition about her off-task behavior. If she does not know that it is occurring, there is less chance that it will decrease. However, if the teacher is able to cue the child about the interruption, she will be more likely to realize when it is happening and will learn to curb the same behavior in the future.

Teachers can increase students' metacognition about off-task behavior. A simple tally system may be developed for students who occasionally lose their focus. Every time students find themselves off task, they make a check mark or write the time on their paper. This system helps students become aware of how often they are distracted, and they may be able to determine whether some pattern exists. For instance, they may find themselves off task at the same time during each period. Or they may be off task more frequently on certain days of the week. Such record keeping will raise the students' metacognition about their own self-regulation. If students are unable to redirect their behaviors by themselves, proximity can be used to remind them that you are aware of their actions and expect them to get back on task. It may be as easy as walking to that side of the room or placing a hand on a shoulder.

Several options can be employed for students who require a more stringent system. A teacher may need to use a behavior modification technique, such as the behavior tally system described earlier, to document the amount of time a student spends on task. In a technique that is similar to when a student monitors his own behavior, a teacher may check whether a student is on task at five-minute or ten-minute intervals. There may be consequences or rewards based on the information that the teacher gathers. Another excellent strategy is to set time goals for individual students. Teachers can provide timers for these students so that they can see exactly how long they must read in order to meet their goal. After each goal is successfully reached, students can be provided with a rest break or other appropriate reward.

Conferences, by their very nature, are collaborative. Having students participate in assessing and understanding their own actions and providing students with explicit feedback are fundamental to increasing their self-regulation of behavior. Take, for example, attempting to set a goal for the student as opposed to collaboratively setting a goal with the student. The collaboration empowers the student and often requires her to take more responsibility for the outcome. Therefore, the more collaborative goal setting and assessment are, the more able students are to achieve the desired outcome of focus and engagement for extended periods of time.

Increasing Reading Time

Remember that the goal of SIR is to increase the amount of time that students are able to self-regulate their reading of challenging material. If you can increase students' reading time gradually in small increments, it will make the additional effort of tackling appropriately challenging texts more manageable for them. Extending the reading time by a minute each day is one way to accomplish this objective. If, at the beginning of your implementation of SIR, students are able to read for five minutes, by the end of one week of reading, their reading time will have doubled.

To illustrate their progress, students can create graphs that show the amount of time spent reading daily or weekly. A template of a chart for recording students' reading minutes is included in Appendix E.

The following mini-lesson to help students develop and increase their self-regulation in reading has been useful in our work with teachers who have students who need to increase their supported reading time. It can be used with all students or with a group of students who struggle with focus and concentration in reading.

Mini-Lesson #3: Using Specific Self-Regulation Tools

Goal: To increase students' self-regulation of their reading behavior

Objective: To develop students' ability to use the sun/cloud signs and sticky notes to identify reading difficulties during SIR time

Supplies needed:

- Classroom set of sun/cloud cards
- Several sticky notes for each student
- Book for SIR time

Activity: Begin by discussing instances in which students may get off track in their reading. Ask students to share examples of times when they have become confused while reading. Ask them questions like these:

- What do you do when you can't read a word?
- What do you do when you don't understand what is happening in the text?

Next, remind students of the need to self-monitor their reading. This is important because they may often be reading when no one is around to help (for example, at home or while the teacher is conferencing with a classmate).

Role-play two scenarios in which a lack of comprehension or fluency impede your progress in reading a text selection. Be sure to include the following points:

- Model the use of sticky notes to mark the locations of unknown words in order to refer back to them in a conference.
- Demonstrate the use of the sun/cloud card for getting a teacher's attention between conferences.

Discuss with your students the possible benefits and drawbacks of each system. Ask them to name instances when the use of one or the other might be better.

Most teachers using the SEM-R have been successful at helping students increase their self-regulation of reading by including their students in goal setting. Each day, you should work with students to set a reasonable goal for the day's reading period. After your students reach the goal, be sure to recognize their effort. By working with students to set and reach a goal, you show them that at times SIR will be hard work and that SIR (and goals that they set, too) should be something that will challenge them. You also reinforce for students that their success is the result of their behavior.

Self-Regulation Can Be Learned: A Case in Point

Jamie is an eighth-grade student who was identified as academically talented in first grade. She read at the seventh-grade level by the time she finished second grade and consistently scored at the highest level on all areas of standardized achievement tests. Jamie did not like to read challenging material but had coasted through her school district's reading curriculum from first through seventh grade, doing minimal homework and getting top grades. Because of her high scores on achievement tests in previous grades, she was recommended for an advanced reading class in eighth grade, and in a SEM-R class, she encountered, for her first time in school, some challenging reading. She struggled with reading material that had some words and ideas that she did not rapidly understand and began to tell her parents that they had erred in their assessment that she was smart. Jamie gave up almost immediately whenever she encountered challenging reading. After a few minutes of reading, she would become distracted and try to switch to an easier book. How could Jamie gain the self-regulation skills she needed to succeed in a more challenging class?

Jamie's teacher worked with her to help her develop self-regulation. With patience, she encouraged Jamie to start by reading a high-interest book that was slightly above her current reading level. Initially, Jamie gave up after reading just a few minutes each day from the more challenging book, but her teacher, using humor and attention, encouraged her to increase the time she spent in trying to read the more challenging book. When Jamie became frustrated, her teacher suggested she think about how she could control her temper if she could not easily solve a hard problem. Her teacher discussed her own challenges with hard work and the role of effort in her own work, and she encouraged Jamie to do as she had done—that is, think about what strategies worked for her and consider how she could modify her study strategies by considering when she was successful in reading the more challenging book. Over the course of a few months, Jamie learned to spend more time reading challenging literature, to carefully consider how and when she could become more successful, to discuss the problems she had in concentrating with her friends, and to try different approaches to extending the time she spent on reading the challenging literature. By the end of eighth grade, she had become a very successful reader and had mastered a number of the self-regulation strategies discussed in this chapter. She was also much better prepared for the challenging honors and Advanced Placement classes that she would encounter the next year.

As we noted earlier in this chapter, self-regulation enables children to develop and learn constructive behaviors that affect their learning. These behaviors are planned and adapted to support the pursuit of personal goals in changing learning environments. Learners with high levels of self-regulation have good control over how they attain their goals. Conscious self-regulation requires a student to focus on the process of how to acquire these skills. Many researchers agree on the importance of self-regulated learning for students at all academic levels. Remember, self-regulation can be taught, learned, and controlled. In fact, in Zimmerman's studies (1989, 1990), successful students reported that the use of self-regulated learning strategies was directly tied to their success in school.

Phases of Self-Regulation

Acquiring self-regulation skills seems to proceed through three phases (Zimmerman, 2008):

Phase One: Forethought   In this phase, the student thinks about learning and the tasks at hand. This phase precedes the actual performance, sets the stage for action, maps

out the tasks that will minimize the unknown, and helps to develop a positive mind-set. Realistic expectations can make the task more appealing. Goals must be considered as specific outcomes, arranged in order from short-term (tomorrow and this week) to long-term (next month and next year). As students begin to receive harder work, they can be taught to consider how they will accomplish their work and finish their assignments.

Students have to consider which conditions will help or hinder their learning activities. Jamie had to think about her reading and reflect on what she could do to be more successful. She learned to consider whether there was a better place for her to read in the classroom and whether it would help her to sit near friends who were successful in Phase Two reading. She learned to spend five minutes and then seven minutes and then at least ten minutes on her work before feeling frustrated enough to quit. The teacher suggested that she talk with a friend, either in person or on the phone, who could be available to talk about some of the steps she might use to continue to do this more challenging reading.

Phase Two: Performance Control   This phase involves the student's processes during learning and the active attempt to use specific strategies to become more successful.

Teachers should ask their students to consider the following questions:

- Are you accomplishing what you hoped to do in reading?
- Are you being distracted?
- Under what conditions are you able to accomplish the most?
- What questions can you ask yourself while you are working?
- How can you encourage yourself to keep working (including self-talk: "Come on, get your reading done so you can watch that television show and read that magazine!")

Jamie, for example, had to consider her performance in reading as opposed to other content areas. When frustration increased, she had to consider whether she should stop and take a break. She had to think about how she could continue learning to read challenging material without encountering frustration. Should she have background music or work in silence? In Phase Two, Jamie also needed to consider and use the successful strategies she had developed in Phase One of her process of learning self-regulation.

Phase Three: Self-Reflection   This phase involves reflection after the performance—a self-evaluation of outcomes compared with goals. Teachers can ask their students to consider the following:

- Did you accomplish what you planned to do in your independent reading?
- Did you become distracted? If so, how did you get back to reading?
- Under what conditions do you accomplish your best reading?

If she was successful in reading the more complicated material for a longer period of time, Jamie might ask herself questions such as these:

- How did I read differently to make my reading more effective this time?
- Did I change my work habits to make my reading more focused?
- Did sitting next to a friend who was very focused on her reading make a difference?
- Did setting a minimum time frame ("I am going to extend yesterday's reading by three minutes") help?
- Did using self-talk to praise myself ("All right, I did it! I read the harder material for fifteen minutes!") have a positive impact?

The development of good self-regulation usually involves *self-observation* monitoring one's performance by keeping records. It also involves gaining *self-judgment*—comparing performance with a standard or goal that may involve re-examining what one has done and the process one has used. Learning self-regulation also involves *self-reaction*—self-administered praise or criticism, rehearsing or memorizing, structuring the environment (for example, changing the difficulty of the academic task, changing the academic setting or the environment, creating a study area), or asking for help. When teachers help students to learn self-regulation, students are more likely to take responsibility for reading challenging material for longer periods of time in Phase Two of the SEM-R program.

Assessing Phase Two of a SEM-R Program

The teachers who have implemented Phase Two of a SEM-R program have used many different opportunities to assess students within the parameters of the SEM-R. While high-stakes assessment may seem to run contrary to creating a love of reading, it is helpful for students to receive feedback and participate in the assessment process. Several teachers have adopted rubrics for assessing their conferences with children, and in the companion to this book, *The Joyful Reading Resource Kit*, we provide an SIR rubric that can be used as a student assessment tool in its current form or modified to suit your needs. Each conference can be graded, enabling you to compile a group of grades that can be used for report card purposes, if necessary. The rubric that we have developed has items related to self-regulation, such as the student's ability to work independently without prompts from the teacher; reading fluency, with attention paid to vocabulary development; reading comprehension, including use of reading strategies; and challenge and enjoyment of books selected.

Phase Two: Indicators of High Quality in Supported Independent Reading

Phase Two of the SEM-R has produced some of the most impressive gains in reading comprehension and fluency in our experience of working with the SEM-R. Phase Two results in students with better self-regulation and reading automaticity and gives students the time to read challenging content every day. The highest level of implementation of Phase Two occurs when the following indicators occur.

Indicators of Success in Phase Two

- Most students start to read at the beginning of the SIR period without any reminders beyond initial directions.

- Teachers conduct conferences without interruption throughout Phase Two.

- Teachers communicate a purpose for each student's oral reading before listening to the student read.

- Teachers extend discussion beyond each student's next book choice to address book selection habits in general.

- Teachers ask questions at multiple levels across conferences and use one or more higher-order questions in every conference.

- Teachers identify individual needs based on students' oral reading and integrate varied strategies that are clearly connected to demonstrated reading behaviors.

- Teachers provide verbal guidance or environmental reminders about self-regulation strategies for reading (for example, verbal reminders at the start of Phase Two, use of sun/cloud cards, self-regulation strategies posted in the classroom).

- All or most students can self-regulate their behavior throughout Phase Two.

Summary

In this chapter, we have reviewed Phase Two of the SEM-R, in which students have the opportunity to gain reading fluency and increase comprehension, as well as learn how to self-regulate their feelings and behaviors pertaining to reading, their time spent reading challenging material, and their use of reading strategies to help them improve their performance. In the next chapter, you will learn about the exciting opportunities for independent choice and challenge in using reading to pursue individual interests using Phase Three of the SEM-R.

Facilitating Interest and Choice: Phase Three

6

When you use the SEM-R for part of each day, your reading classroom can become a place where both individual and small groups of students explore new ideas while building new literacy skills. Imagine the enthusiasm and learning that will occur when you and your students have the time and freedom to work independently on projects based on students' interests and preferred styles of learning. In this chapter, you will learn how to implement Phase Three of the SEM-R, in which you will create these opportunities for students to explore their strengths and help them pursue and discover their interests. As you will see, Phase Three enables your students to discover joyful learning and literacy experiences, as well as gives you the time to work with students who are engrossed in challenging learning opportunities and who actually groan when the class period ends.

The Rationale for Phase Three

The ultimate goal of Phase Three is for students to progress from teacher-directed learning opportunities to independent, self-chosen activities. As students' self-regulation skills and enjoyment of reading develop during the first two phases of a SEM-R program, they learn to select books in their areas of interest and many begin to have a desire to investigate new topics and ideas in these areas. Phase Three uses this growth, encouraging students to explore their personal interests through self-selected literacy pursuits. However, like other developmental capacities, student independence does not happen overnight—or even at the same predictable rate for all students—making your role as a facilitator and coach vital during Phase Three of a SEM-R program.

With your help, students can use Phase Three explorations to further understand, analyze, synthesize, and evaluate some of the information they have encountered in the books they have read during Phase Two. The options for Phase Three are diverse and unlimited; the information provided in this chapter will help you select a structure and successfully launch this phase of the SEM-R in your classroom. Phase Three can include a myriad of options for student explorations: creativity training activities, reading on the Internet, book discussion groups, audio books, investigation centers, independent or small-group enrichment projects, Renzulli Learning activities, or other creative explorations that require students to further extend their thinking. You may wish to review the rightmost column of Figure 1.1 "Components of the Schoolwide Enrichment Model for Reading" in Chapter One, which lists these options in an easy-to-read format.

It is important to remember that the SEM-R evolved from the Schoolwide Enrichment Model (SEM) (Renzulli, 1977; Renzulli & Reis, 1985, 1997), an enrichment-based approach that is widely used to provide self-selected activities for all students based on their interests. This talent development approach provides enriched learning experiences and high learning standards for all children with a focus on a broad range of enrichment experiences in order to expose students to new ideas and skills and to provide advanced learning for academically talented children who are interested in further investigation. The SEM-R focuses on enrichment for all students through engagement in enjoyable, challenging learning experiences based on students' interests. As you continue reading and begin to plan activities for your own classroom, keep the helpful acronym ICE in mind to remind you of the importance of interests, choices, and explorations in Phase Three.

Interest

Activities in Phase Three should be based on student interests because interest provides motivation for students to tackle increasing levels of challenging work. Some students may explore areas of interest that existed for them prior to their participation in the SEM-R program. Alternatively, students may develop new interests based on books they encounter during Phases One and Two. Quite often, students recognize the types of books or information they like and dislike, but they cannot always focus on an activity or exploration that requires them to do something with their interests and growing knowledge. The SEM-R approach to teaching reading focuses on helping students become aware of how the books they are enjoying might relate to other literacy skills and explorations.

Various questionnaires can be used to help students identify their interests as well as their learning and expression styles (Renzulli & Reis, 1997). One of these inventories, the Reading Interest-a-Lyzer, is included in Appendix B. That inventory and others that summarize student interests, learning styles, and product styles are also available in electronic format with a subscription to Renzulli Learning (www.renzullilearning.com). Information from these instruments will allow you to better understand your students' unique strengths and create opportunities for their individual growth while simultaneously helping students better understand themselves.

Choices

A SEM-R program provides students with choices for exploring their interests in independent or small-group work. This concept begins in Phase Two as students read books of their own selection and is more fully explored in Phase Three. As students are provided with additional choices, the goal is for them to begin to develop independence in their exploration of interests. Phase Three of the SEM-R creates a safe environment in which students can investigate their own topics and activities of interest. Generally, in the first few weeks of Phase Three implementation, teachers have found that students are more productive and engaged when they are provided with structured activities that are designed to give them practice in independent work skills such as task management, self-regulation, and creative problem solving. As students (and teachers) become more comfortable with students' independence and decision making, Phase Three activities can progress to involve less teacher scaffolding and more student choice. The goal in Phase Three is to promote creative productivity in the hope that many students will choose to conduct their own self-directed activities.

Explorations

Often, a student's love for a book stays with her long after she finishes reading the last page; however, time to act on this passion during the school day is a rare gift. During Phase Three, teachers who use the SEM-R make a conscious decision to create opportunities for students to investigate and explore what they love about literature. Rather than providing strict project guidelines or a format for a book report, students are encouraged to use their own interests and skills as a map to guide their explorations; it is the developmental journey, not the destination, that we value in Phase Three. SEM-R classrooms provide time for deep and meaningful investigations that build on students' newfound enjoyment of reading and extend beyond the regular curriculum. Teachers can support and encourage students in delving deeper by providing the tools, scaffolding, and coaching necessary for students to explore and develop their interests.

Implementing Phase Three: Stories from Two Classrooms

Perhaps one of the best ways to envision how interests, choice, and explorations can be coordinated during Phase Three is to review examples from two SEM-R classrooms in which all three are working in concert.

A fourth-grade class that uses Phase Three for one hour each Friday. In Mrs. Patrick's fourth-grade classroom, students participate in Phase Three activities for one hour each week, on Friday. At the beginning of Phase Three time, students know exactly what they are supposed to do, and they begin working with little hesitation. According to Mrs. Patrick, having an extended time period enables students more time to get the creative juices flowing and work on projects with less time spent on management of materials. After administering the Reading Interest-a-Lyzer online through Renzulli Learning, Mrs. Patrick discovered that half of her students had interests in performing arts. She suggested that the students might be interested in the production of a class play, a suggestion that was greeted with both high levels of enthusiasm and outstanding results. One pair of students began writing a series of scripts based on books they had read during Phase Two, while a group of three students decided to use their talents and interests in creating set designs and learning about how professionals build props. Another group was interested in acting out the parts created in the student-written scripts. From this group, one student with strong leadership skills emerged as director of the plays. Meanwhile, another group of students began designing playbills and advertisements for the productions.

Although the play eventually involved most of the class, some students demonstrated very different interests, and their Phase Three activities reflected this divergence. One group of three students decided to create a project that highlighted the use of simple machines in everyday objects, while another group of four students scoured the Renzulli Learning Web site for information and projects on topics ranging from starting a business to Mars exploration. Mrs. Patrick structured the classroom environment of Phase Three to support the individual choices of each of her students. This structure was accomplished by the use of learning management plans, which were completed by the teacher and each student or group of students, ensuring that the students were aware of their tasks and timelines. The classroom was arranged to allow multiple groups of students to work together simultaneously. To facilitate the management of group materials, each group also had its own stackable container for supplies.

A fifth-grade Phase Three implementation of twenty minutes each day. After easing students into the SEM-R routine during the first two months of school, Mr. McMillian began each hour of the SEM-R program with a ten-minute book hook that exposed his students to two carefully selected books. Then, his boisterous fifth-grade class read quietly for thirty to thirty-five minutes each day in Phase Two, and he usually reserved twenty minutes each day for Phase Three activities. At the conclusion of Phase Two, Mr. McMillian announced that it was time for students to wrap up their independent reading time. Every day, Mr. McMillian quickly reviewed the menu of choices, and each Phase Three time began with a proclamation that each student should "Go and do what makes you special!" With these words, students moved with purpose and enthusiasm to their activity of choice.

When students were unable or unwilling to put down their SIR books in Mr. McMillian's classroom, they were encouraged to simply continue reading during Phase Three. Three of the four computers in the classroom were quickly occupied by students who wanted to continue their online independent projects using Renzulli Learning. In another corner, a group of four students invested their time in playing a stock market game, and they used the remaining computer station to track how their stocks were performing.

In another part of the classroom, a group of students gathered in the art investigation center to continue designing board games based on their favorite books. Close by, a trio of students played a game that the group had previously created based on their favorite novel, *Eragon*. Finally, a group of five students rehearsed a commercial they had written that encouraged students to read more nonfiction. This commercial was to be filmed by the students for the school library.

As students worked on their chosen activities, Mr. McMillian circulated throughout the classroom to provide guidance and encouragement. Not only did Mr. McMillian answer questions, but he also asked students probing questions that extended their thinking skills, further developing their metacognitive strategies.

Getting Started with Phase Three

As we mentioned earlier, at the beginning of the SEM-R implementation, you may want to offer fewer choices at the start of Phase Three and then expand the choices over time. Starting with a smaller number of choices will help students learn skills (such as creativity training) that will be embedded in subsequent activities. This transition time should still enable students to make choices about activities, taking into consideration learning styles and interests. Some students may be able and willing to work independently for long periods of time, while others may not be ready to handle an unlimited number of choices, particularly if they have little experience with choosing work to do in school. For a successful implementation of Phase Three, give specific choices of both group and individual activities in the beginning and work up to a full-scale implementation with a broad menu of options. Many teachers have successfully introduced the process over a period of four to six weeks. The timeline in Table 6.1 illustrates how this method of implementing Phase Three might be organized.

A Continuum of Services

Students vary in abilities and interests, as well as levels of self-regulated behavior, necessitating a continuum of services (from very independent to very structured) for students. This continuum can range from simply allowing students to continue with their Phase Two independent reading and listening to audio books all the way to providing students with time to conduct independent investigations. In much the same way that a restaurant offers a menu of choices, the ideal SEM-R classroom

TABLE 6.1. TIMELINE OF PHASE THREE ACTIVITIES

Week	Duration of Phase Three	Activities	Instruction
Week 1	15–20 minutes per day	• Interest assessment (Appendix B) • Self-regulation skill lesson (Chapter Five mini-lesson #3)	Whole-class participation and instruction
Week 2	10–15 minutes per day	• Creativity training activities	Whole-class training, with follow-up choice of three independent creativity exercises
Weeks 2–3	15–20 minutes per day	• Introduction to investigation centers (students rotate through each of three centers)	Teacher assigns and organizes small groups of students to ensure that each student explores all investigation centers
Weeks 3–4	15–20 minutes per day	• Investigation centers • Creativity activities • Computer training (3–5 choices each day)	Teacher directs students to sign up for one of the following choices: • Independent reading • Art investigation center • Poetry investigation center • Animals in literature investigation center • Creativity activities • Renzulli Learning
Weeks 5–6	15–20 minutes per day or 1 day per week	• Training on how to develop independent activities • Free choice from a menu of options	Students are guided to work independently or in small groups. Choices include • Independent reading • Audio books • Buddy reading • Poetry investigation center • Animals in literature investigation center • Renzulli Learning • Independent or small-group projects

offers a menu of activities from which students can make selections. No one activity will satisfy all of your students' tastes. Moreover, while students may want to try particular menu items, it is unlikely that they will be satisfied if they have to choose the same menu item day after day. At some point, they will want and will also enjoy some variety in their intellectual diet. You, as the academic chef, will want to prepare a collection of rich and inviting options for your students and establish a balance between standard menu choices and special Phase Three opportunities.

The following sections describe some of the most popular and successful Phase Three options (see Figure 6.1). As we have seen, these options are often pursued for fifteen to twenty minutes daily or for an entire period once a week, but they can be implemented on any other schedule that works well, too. This is not, by any means,

FIGURE 6.1. PHASE THREE MENU CHOICES.

	Phase Three Menu *Use for 15 minutes daily, or 1 period a week*	
Student–Selected Activities	Continued Independent Reading Listening to Audio Books Buddy Reading with someone of similar levels of reading achievement Literature Circles or Novel Discussion Groups	Increasing Student Independence
Teacher Directed	Creativity Activities	
Activities to Move Students Toward Independence	Investigation Centers Independent Investigations SEM-Xplorations (See Appendix G) Renzulli Learning	▼

an exhaustive list, and you should use your own creativity to develop and expand your own classroom menu.

Student-Selected Activities

In Phase Three, students move from teacher-directed opportunities to self-choice activities over the course of the intervention. Activities include (but are not limited to) opportunities to explore new technology, discussion groups, advanced questioning and thinking skills, creativity training in language arts, learning centers, interest-based projects, free reading, and book chats. The intent of these experiences is for teachers to give students time to pursue areas of personal interest through the use of interest development centers and the Internet to learn to read critically and to locate other reading materials, especially high-quality challenging literature. Options for independent study are also made available for students during Phase Three. During the SEM-R intervention, Phase Three activities are fluid, as teachers modify the lengths of the phases to accommodate students' interests and increasing ability to engage in independent work.

Continuing to Read

An easy choice to implement in your classroom is allowing students to continue their Phase Two reading. Frequently, students become engrossed in their SIR books and the thought of stopping troubles them; therefore, this choice in Phase Three is often welcomed. Although many talented readers will be satisfied if they are able to continue reading a book that is both challenging and interesting to them, not all students will be able to maintain focused reading, making other options necessary as well. You should encourage all readers, at some point, to investigate topics of interest and extend their reading in varied ways. This type of investigation allows students to see connections between reading and creative productivity.

Audio Books

In addition to serving as an effective scaffolding tool for struggling readers in Phase Two, audio books can provide an opportunity for students to experience literature coming alive as they listen. Many of the popular book choices for children are available in both unabridged and abridged audio versions. Teachers can encourage students to read along in the book as they listen, or they can allow students to listen to a segment or chapter of the book as a pre-reading activity. In either case, listening to fluent reading and new vocabulary serve as scaffolding and motivation, both of which will further students' enjoyment of reading.

Portable CD players have become quite inexpensive, and students may choose to listen independently or as part of a small group with the use of an auxiliary headphone jack. These small adapters are available from any consumer electronics store, and multiple headphones can be plugged into a single headphone jack to enable several students to listen simultaneously to the same book. To investigate affordable sources of audio and print materials, check with your school media specialist or local public librarian; you may be surprised at what you discover. Numerous audio books are also available online.

Buddy Reading

Many students want to share their reading experiences with their friends. A simple and effective option for Phase Three is buddy reading. Rather than being assigned to do this, students often choose to read a book aloud together. In fact, during one implementation of the SEM-R, two students spent the day reading a book to each other over the telephone on a day when school was closed due to weather. While this may not be common, this strategy may serve as an excellent outlet for more social students and as a way to maintain a sense of purpose and order about reading in the classroom. However, we do suggest that you try to help students select partners who have similar reading levels. For example, it has created conflict for some struggling readers to be paired with very talented readers; struggling readers have explained that they feel both embarrassment and angst in these situations. Therefore, some teacher guidance is needed in order to match students who will work well together for buddy reading.

Literature Circles

Literature circles provide an opportunity for students to discuss either a book that they have read in the past or one that they are currently reading. Initially, you may want to provide a structure by providing a series of open-ended questions for students to discuss during their literature circles. There are many good books and articles that explain how literature circles should work in classrooms, but all seem to agree that they include the following characteristics:

- Students choose their own books.

- Groups are temporary and based on the choice of book.

- Different books are read by each group.

- Students use written notes to guide their discussion on a regular basis.

- Students choose their own discussion topics.

- Conversation is open and natural and includes open-ended questions.

- Students assume different roles on different days.

A literature circle is created to develop an open conversation among students about a commonly read book. During literature circles, one student usually assumes the leadership position in the group. Other group members are assigned different roles, such as acting as the group leader and developing the prompts and questions with accompanying prompts that are used to enable each student in the group to respond to questions about the book. Everyone in the group then responds to questions raised by the other students, leading to meaningful conversations. After this discussion, group members decide how much reading will be accomplished before the next meeting. Students in the group may write a response to the book discussion in their journal at the conclusion of the meeting.

The SEM-R bookmarks (see Appendix A) can also provide questions for discussion among a small group of students. As your students become more accustomed to conferences during Phase Two, literature circles will increase in complexity.

Teachers can access more information about literature circles on the SEM-R Web site at www.gifted.uconn.edu/semr.

Teacher-Directed Creativity Activities

Creativity training activities can be used during the first few weeks of implementing Phase Three to provide teacher-directed activities that encourage students to expand their thinking and develop innovative ideas. In creativity training, teachers encourage students to be more fluent thinkers and to practice flexibility, elaboration, and originality. Fluency activities would guide students in coming up with many responses to a question that is posed. Flexibility would encourage students to try to think about different categories of responses to questions. When students elaborate, they learn to add on and extend their own or other students' responses, and when they learn about originality, they are encouraged to try to come up with ideas or responses that are completely new and different from others in their class. The benefit of creativity training is twofold. Students will develop skills that will help them explore new literary ideas. At the same time, teachers gradually create less structured opportunities in which students practice the problem-solving and self-regulation skills needed for a successful implementation of Phase Three. As students become more comfortable with independent work, the creativity activities will become one of the options available to students.

Additional creativity lessons can be found in the *New Directions in Creativity Package* (Renzulli, Callahan, Smith, Renzulli, & Ford, 2000) and in *The Joyful Reading Resource Kit* that is available as a supplement to this book. Above all, you should use your own creativity to modify these kinds of activities and lessons to meet the needs and encourage the interests of your students. During these training exercises, establish guidelines for your students that will create an open, supportive, and nonjudgmental environment.

Independent Student Activities

Independent student activities include enrichment choices to give students the opportunity to pursue interest-based reading activities. There are many options for these activities, including using teacher created investigation centers, going online to use Renzulli Learning for independent projects, reading and discussing a book in a book club format, reading with a buddy, creating a completely new independent project, and listening to audio books.

Investigation Centers

As students become more comfortable with working independently, Phase Three activities can be expanded to involve more self-directed explorations. One way to ease the transition is to use investigation centers in your classroom. Investigation centers are an instructional component of the SEM-R that are designed to create and develop interest in and enthusiasm about a particular topic or theme. The goal is to engage students actively in reading, thinking, and researching. Books, magazines, newspapers, computer technology, and specific exploratory activities can be included as part of a thematic collection of reading investigations designed for your students. Investigation centers can be as simple as a collection of high-interest nonfiction materials based on student responses on the Reading Interest-a-Lyzer or a space in the classroom devoted to audio equipment and a selection of audio books. Students' interests should be a driving force when you are creating investigation centers. An example of how to create an investigation center is provided in the box.

Investigation Center Example: Investigating Art

Begin by assembling a variety of resources to spark the curiosity of your students. Organize the materials so that students can easily peruse the resources and ponder. An art investigation center might include the following:

Books

- Biographies of famous artists such as Pablo Picasso, Vincent Van Gogh, Edgar Degas, and Frida Kahlo are featured in the Getting to Know the World's Greatest Artists series by Mike Venezia
- *Art Fraud Detective: Spot the Difference, Solve the Crime* by Anna Nilsen
- *The Great Art Scandal: Solve the Crime, Save the Show!* by Anna Nilsen
- *Who Can Open Michelangelo's Seven Seals?* by Thomas Brezina & Laurence Sartin
- *Who Can Save Vincent's Hidden Treasure?* by Thomas Brezina & Laurence Sartin
- *From the Mixed-Up Files of Mrs. Basil E. Frankweiler* by E. L. Konigsburg
- A collection of art history reference books borrowed from the art teacher

How-to Books

- *Discovering Great Artists: Hands-on Projects for Children in the Style of the Great Masters* by MaryAnn Kohl, Kim Solga, & Rebecca Van Slyke
- *Introduction to Art Techniques* by Ray Smith, Ray Wright, James Horton, Michael Wright, & the Royal Academy of Arts (Great Britain)
- *Career Ideas for Kids Who Like Art* by Diane Lindsey Reeves
- *Looking at Art* by Laurie Schneider Adams

Web Sites

- National Gallery of Art for Kids

  Take this virtual tour and learn all about different paintings located in the National Gallery of Art in Washington, D.C.! Just click on any painting to begin. See close-ups of many famous works of art housed in the museum, along with a description and history of each. You can also try the Art Zone, which lets you make interactive art online!

  http://www.nga.gov/kids/kids.htm

- MoMA: The Museum of Modern Art—Destination Modern Art

  Join a friendly alien from outer space in a journey to Earth to learn about modern art! On this Web site, you will guide the little alien as you both walk through the museum. As you look at each piece of art, you can use your senses to see the art, hear what the art may sound like, and use your hands to create your own art.

  http://www.moma.org/destination/

- From Cave Art to Your Art

  This site is for those of you who like to create interactive art projects. Check out instructional videos about different art techniques. You can choose the ones you find most interesting or influential in your artistic life, add music and a title page, and create your own informational video timeline of how art has evolved and how this has affected you as an artist.

  http://www.sanford-artedventures.com/play/caveart/index.html

- The Louvre

  Take a virtual tour of one of the greatest art museums in the world, the Louvre. Online exhibitions include Egyptian antiquities; Greek, Etruscan, and Roman antiquities; Islamic art; sculptures; paintings; and much more! Choose a tour from the list on the left of the screen to start.

  http://www.louvre.fr/llv/musee/visite_virtuelle.jsp?bmLocale=en

Independent Investigations

One goal of Phase Three is to promote independence in students as they develop their interests. Ultimately, you want your students to progress to conducting their own independent investigations. Rather than assigning a topic or project, you should encourage students to develop their own questions and goals. The following detailed process can help you teach students how to produce quality enrichment projects. This process, which has been applied in classroom and resource room settings, has evolved over several decades and countless activities. Two comments should be made on the steps of the process. First, the steps do not have to be followed in the order given; and second, some steps can be eliminated if students can accomplish the learning objectives in other ways.

Guiding Students Through Independent or Small-Group Study

1. **Help students identify interests and connections to possible explorations that culminate in a product or a service.** Interest often drives effort; therefore, students should be encouraged to select topics in which they have an intense interest and investment. Book hooks during Phase One and individual conferences during Phase Two are ideal times for teachers to help students uncover the connections between the content (problem they want to investigate, story or poem that want to write, interest area they want to pursue) and form (auditory, written, oral, presentation) of the projects they are enjoying to create possibilities for explorations during Phase Three.

2. **Find questions or problems to research.** Consider what happens when you type the term *science* into an Internet search engine; you are faced with thousands of pages of pertinent information through which you must sift if you wish to locate useful details. However, if you were to use the same search engine to research *genetic engineering and biodiversity,* the resulting Internet resources would be more relevant because you focused your search on a more manageable collection of knowledge. This skill of winnowing down resources and ideas is essential to independent explorations. Nevertheless, most students have difficulty moving from a broad interest area to a specific one. One way to help young learners focus general historical, mathematical, musical, or athletic interests is to translate their interests into a question or questions to research.

   Brainstorming a list of potential research questions will also encourage students to identify specific investigation topics. You can help students find how-to books to examine the methodology employed in specific fields of study. For instance, students who want to ask the right questions about problems in anthropology would start by looking at how anthropologists work and what kinds of questions they investigate.

3. **Make a plan.** Once students have brainstormed a question, they will need a plan to assist them in locating needed resources, identifying important tasks, and managing time. This plan should not be set in stone. Like assessing the book match in Phase Two, it needs to be revisited regularly so that scaffolding can be provided and modifications can be made to ensure student success. Many students and teachers have found success through use of a learning contract, journal, or log.

4. **Work with students to locate resources and organize information.** Your students may not believe it, but there is a wealth of information and ideas beyond encyclopedias and Internet search engines. As you help students identify the many other available sources of information, you may need to explain possible investigation techniques and the importance of keeping track of resources to avoid plagiarism. Remember that librarians and media specialists can help steer students toward sources beyond encyclopedic references and of varying degrees of difficulty. You can help with this task by making your students aware of resources such as atlases, letters, surveys, films, periodicals, and personal interviews.

5. **Identify final products and audiences.** A sense of audience is integral to students' concern for quality and commitment to their tasks. For example, students' attitude and attention to detail change when they know that their writing may be published in a children's magazine instead of simply remaining within the confines of the classroom. With this in mind, teachers should guide students in their identification of possible audiences and outlets for their independent explorations. Students should be aware that a job well done can bring more than individual expression and personal satisfaction; it may benefit others by changing how they think or feel or enhancing quality of life in other more tangible ways.

6. **Offer encouragement, praise, and constructive criticism.** Almost every student project can be improved through revision, rewriting, or closer attention to detail. When you convey feedback to students, be sensitive; they should feel that their teacher's greatest concern is helping them achieve excellence and should understand that constructive feedback is vital to that process.

7. **Escalate the process.** Some students resort to simple or unimaginative research methods because they have not explored or experienced more advanced ones. You should assist students in phrasing their questions, designing research, gathering and analyzing data in an unbiased way, drawing conclusions, and communicating their results. This is also an excellent time to encourage students to go beyond first drafts and to incorporate more advanced uses of resources in their work.

8. **Help students evaluate and assess their work.** We discourage formal grading of independent projects because no letter grade, number, or percentage can accurately reflect the knowledge, creativity, and commitment that students develop during an independent investigation. Nonetheless, evaluation and feedback do promote growth and should be used. The ideal process actively involves students and familiarizes them with evaluative procedures. To help students appraise their own work, we suggest a short questionnaire such as this one:

   • How did you feel about working on your project?

   • What did you learn through your study?

   • Were you satisfied with the final product? In what ways?

   • How were you helped with your project?

   • Do you think you might like to undertake another project in the future? Do you have any ideas about what that project would be like?

SEM-Xplorations

Designed as guides for students' exploration of a topic of interest, SEM-Xplorations provide students with a template for independent and small-group investigations. Several of these independent or small-group project activities are included in *The Joyful Reading Resource Kit,* the companion book to this one. These activities cover a wide range of topics, and each self-contained unit encourages students to investigate a variety of resources. Each unit begins with a brief overview that is designed to pique student curiosity. In the "Charting Your Course" section, background knowledge is reinforced and resources for further information are presented. After developing their background knowledge, students are ready for the "Exploration" stage. In this section, SEM-Xplorations present a variety of short-term and long-term projects for students to consider and create. Each unit focuses on helping students create something meaningful and put their knowledge to work. While the students are creating a product, they consider how and why they will share it with a real-world audience. Each SEM-Xplorations project concludes with a "Treasure Chest of Tools" that features a list of books and Web sites to help students locate resources that may prove helpful in their explorations.

Renzulli Learning

Renzulli Learning (www.renzullilearning.com) is an electronic search engine and profiler that matches students' interests, abilities, learning styles, and expression styles to thousands of enrichment activities. Renzulli Learning (RL) is based on the Enrichment Triad Model (Renzulli, 1977) and the Schoolwide Enrichment Model (SEM) developed by Renzulli and Reis (1985, 1997), which represents more than thirty years of research conducted by the University of Connecticut's Neag School of Education. In their original paper-based format, the SEM instruments that are now a part of Renzulli Learning have been field-tested for more than twenty years in thousands of schools. RL is currently being used in more than 1,200 schools across forty-three states.

Many teachers who have used the SEM-R have used RL as a part of their implementation. Renzulli Learning is an interactive online program that matches student interests, learning styles, and expression preferences with a vast array of educational activities and resources that are designed to enrich students' learning process. As part of their SEM-R program, students have been provided with RL, giving them opportunities to explore, discover, learn, and create, using the most current technology resources in a safe environment. Many students spend hours reading independently on the Internet while using Renzulli Learning on a weekly basis, and new research indicates that use of RL can increase reading fluency and reading comprehension (Field, 2007).

Renzulli Learning uses a three-step procedure to identify talents and interests and promote advanced thinking skills, motivation, creativity, and engagement in learning. Step One consists of a computer-based diagnostic assessment that creates a profile of each student's academic strengths, interests, learning styles, and preferred modes of expression. The online assessment, which takes about thirty minutes for most students to complete, results in a personalized profile that highlights individual student strengths and sets the stage for Step Two. Student profiles can also be used to form groups of students who share common interests.

The student profile acts as a compass for Step Two, in which a search engine presents thousands of resources that relate specifically to each student's interests, learning styles, and product choices. These resources are grouped into fourteen enrichment categories: virtual field trips, real field trips, creativity training activities, training in critical thinking, independent study, contests and competitions, interactive Web sites, fiction books, nonfiction books, how-to books for conducting research, summer programs, research, videos and DVDs, and online activities. All Web sites are carefully selected, screened, and matched to students' areas of highest interest, learning styles, and product styles, providing personalized and differentiated learning opportunities.

These resources are not merely intended to notify students of new information or to occupy them in surfing the Web. Rather, they are vehicles for helping students find and focus on a problem or creative exploration of personal interest that they might like to pursue in greater depth. Many of the resources provide methods of inquiry, sharpen advanced thinking and creative problem-solving skills, and offer investigative approaches. The resources also suggest outlets and audiences for students' creative products. The resources made available in Step Two also inform students about places where they can pursue advanced training in their areas of strength and areas of personal interest.

Step Three in Renzulli Learning is an automatic compilation and storage of all student activity into an ongoing student record called the Total Talent Portfolio. Teachers and parents can access the portfolio at any time, allowing them to view students' work and provide guidance to individual students. This feature also provides parents with information about students' work and opportunities for parental involvement. In this step, students can pursue a variety of projects by using the Wizard Project Maker. Renzulli Learning includes dozens of previously written high-interest projects as well as opportunities for students to select and develop their own project ideas.

The Renzulli Learning Wizard Project Maker is designed to help students explore their interests and passions with varying levels of support. Students who are ready for independent study can create their own Wizard Projects, while those who need more support can start with the more structured Super Starter Projects. Using one of these two options, students can complete an interest-based project, using the steps outlined both in this chapter and in Renzulli Learning.

Phase Three: Indicators of High-Quality Facilitation of Independent Student Work

Throughout our development of the SEM-R, Phase Three has evolved based on our observations of the needs and differences among teachers, classrooms, and students. While Phase Three is focused on student choice and interests, there are common characteristics of highly effective interventions that have been observed in multiple classrooms. The following list of characteristics is intended to serve as a benchmark for successful implementation of Phase Three. Developing a quality Phase Three implementation is a process that takes time. When teachers introduce the process of independent exploration gradually, students are able to make a natural transition. Creating structure and organization by clearly communicating expectations to students is critical to success in Phase Three.

Indicators of Success in Phase Three

- Most students start to read without any reminders beyond the initial directions.
- Teachers offer activity choices that include open-ended options and complexity in order to extend the challenge of previous phases.
- Teachers provide activity choices that demonstrate responsiveness to specific student interests and varied expression styles in product development.
- Teachers provide verbal guidance or environmental reminders of self-regulation strategies for activities (for example, verbal reminders at the start of Phase Three or self-regulation strategies posted in classroom).
- All students self-regulate their behavior throughout Phase Three.
- Teachers create an environment that enables students to demonstrate visible enthusiasm and task commitment for their chosen activity.
- Teachers enhance Phase Three activities through physical organization of resources to facilitate student access.

Summary

In this chapter, we have presented many ways that teachers can enable students to find engaging opportunities to use literacy for practical and joyful purposes—that is, reading to pursue interests and gain needed information. By scheduling a time for individual exploration each day or each week, teachers give students the time to pursue their interests through independent work. In implementing Phase Three, teachers can start slowly, offering a few choices at first and increasing the number of choices as students are better able to self-regulate and work independently.

In the next chapter, we present a number of strategies that will help you organize your time, resources, and classroom to make all phases of the SEM-R easier to implement.

Succeeding with the SEM-R

Library and Classroom Management Strategies

7

In our many years of researching the SEM-R in classrooms across the country, we have observed that teachers who discover and develop their own systems for organizing materials, structuring activities, and providing individualized support and guidance for students create a successful classroom environment for a SEM-R program. In this chapter, we discuss the best organizational strategies that classroom teachers have used. It includes many exciting ideas for using the SEM-R as a practical solution to their own organizational dilemmas. Among the suggestions introduced are the creation of a classroom library and various ways in which the classroom can be organized in order to encourage enjoyment in reading. We want to remind you, however, that the SEM-R is designed to be flexible. In this chapter, we share several examples from elementary and middle schools to help you understand how some teachers have enhanced and modified this enrichment approach by organizing their classroom differently and adjusting reading instruction according to the needs of their particular group of readers.

Creating and Organizing Your Classroom Library

The creation of a classroom library is a very important facet of the implementation of a SEM-R program. When teachers begin using the SEM-R, they often find that their students quickly outgrow a classroom library that was once sufficient when used as a supplement to a basal reading or guided reading program. However, a classroom library need not consist only of expensive book collections purchased out of pocket. A fabulous classroom library can be obtained through yard sale finds, trading books with another teacher, or borrowing books from your school or public libraries. Especially when using the SEM-R, teachers may need to rethink their idea of the classroom library, changing their notion of a long-standing collection to a concept of something more fluid and able to change as the needs of readers change.

The classroom library that is most successfully used to support a SEM-R program and other related reading activities includes a variety of selections (based on genre, topic, text length, and reading level) and is designed to meet the needs and interests of the students (Fountas & Pinnell, 2001). Such a library should include a balance between fiction and nonfiction and should represent multiple genres. When you create your classroom library, we suggest the inclusion of genres that will interest a vast array of readers. These genres include realistic fiction, historical fiction, biography, poetry, periodicals, graphic novels, fantasy, informational texts, and mixed-text formats.

Within each of these genres, we suggest that you also include some of the following types of publications in order to engage the majority of your students as well as to expose them to diverse and well-respected literature.

- **Award winners** (for example, winners of Newbery, Caldecott, Coretta Scott King, Pura Belpré, Robert Sibert, or Michael L. Printz awards)
- **Classics** (for example, *Stone Soup, The Polar Express, Black Beauty, The Call of the Wild*)
- **Picture books** (for example, *Amazing Grace, The True Story of the Three Little Pigs, Built to Last, Strega Nona, Art Fraud Detective*)
- **Chapter books** (for example, *Anne of Green Gables, The BFG, Holes, Walk Two Moons*)
- **Books in a series** (for example, the Little House books, the Redwall series, the Eragon series, *The Chronicles of Narnia*)
- **Books with predictable and repetitive text** for students who read close to a first-grade or second-grade level (for example, *Tikki Tikki Tembo, Why Mosquitoes Buzz in People's Ears, If You Give a Mouse a Cookie*)

As you select books for your classroom library, consider including books on social or cultural issues that will help to engage and involve all of your students. Children's engagement with literature grows when they discover books that contain characters and individuals with whom they can identify. Having access to books about people from a broad range of racial and ethnic backgrounds and with main characters of various ages and genders will enable you, at times, to match them with your students. Because of the independent nature of students' SEM-R reading selections and behaviors, pay special attention to stereotypes in literature. Although we want to include classic books in our collections, we also want to avoid unguided student encounters with books that perpetuate hurtful or negative stereotypes or attitudes.

Often, teachers encourage students to select books with characters that they can identify with or feel connected to; however, skilled educators also recognize that engaging experiences with literature can help readers better understand people and cultures that are very different from their own. Ensuring a diversity of content, cultural representation, points of view, and author voices and languages in your library will help you and your students move beyond the boundaries of your classroom to learn about and celebrate the diversity in literature—and human nature. For some of our favorite literature related to diversity, see the themed book hook recommendations in Chapter Four.

Another source for classroom library selections might be your own reading history. If you want to include some of your favorite books from childhood in your library, consider the context of the story, plot, characters, and language. You may want to ask yourself whether they are still relevant and understandable to students today; if they are, you may want to use one of your favorites in a book hook. Do not be disappointed if some of your students do not follow up and read the book; our experience suggests that students in today's classrooms find many popular children's books from the 1950s, 1960s, and 1970s too difficult to relate to or to fully understand. However, some talented readers in your class may be eager for the additional challenge or historical understanding that is readily available in older literature without the more mature themes or language found in some of today's adolescent literature, as we discuss in the next chapter.

Organizing Your Library for Optimal Matches in Reading

Work in the SEM-R is undertaken with a clear goal: student choice in reading that is supported by adult evaluation of independent performance. Therefore, two central challenges for teachers are identifying the correct level of academic difficulty for each student and determining whether texts are appropriately challenging. As we explained in Chapter Five, because students in your class will have very different reading skills and comprehension, there are no specific rules for deciding whether a book is a good match for SIR. Nevertheless, there are four general categories to consider as you think about helping a student find the right book in your classroom library: readability, content complexity, appropriateness of subject matter, and each student's interests.

Reading educators usually determine the appropriateness of a text based on factors such as sentence length, vocabulary, word-level readability, student skill development, and content. Readability generally refers to how easily a student can read the words and understand the text, based on the writing style, the content of the text, and the student's interaction with the text (Fry, 2002).

Graves, Juel, and Graves (2001) recommend fluency tests to determine the text level that is comfortable for a student to read. This method primarily addresses how easily the student can read the words, but it does not specifically address content difficulty or a student's interest in the text. In our research on the SEM-R, we have learned the importance of emphasizing students' interest in the process of finding the optimal match between each student and the challenge afforded by the books selected by that student. Our recent research on the SEM-R has found that students who make their own reading choices based on their interests not only enjoy reading more but persist longer when faced with challenging text (Reis and others, 2005).

Choosing challenging books requires sensitivity to a variety of factors that are individual to each student and environment. Assessments that measure students' fluency and comprehension through formal and informal means provides information on the difficulty a student has reading the words, but the challenge of a text and its appropriateness for an individual student must be judged holistically. The content or topic should be considered, as should the emotional or thematic elements, the language used, and the writing style. These elements considered individually or in combination may influence how challenging a book may be for a student to read. For example, if the content of a book is particularly difficult to understand, wading through complex syntax may further obscure comprehension. When a teacher selects texts on the basis of ongoing assessment of reading behavior, she can help to identify the text, provide scaffolding, teach background knowledge, engage student interest, and encourage the student to make connections to personal and prior knowledge. Graves, Juel, and Graves (2001) agree that a key force in comprehension and finding the optimal match is helping students to access prior knowledge and experiences in order to bring meaning to a text, suggesting that if we support a child enough, he will be successful. In other words, there must be a supported struggle.

Given the variety and quantity of books in any classroom library, it may seem challenging to create an optimal match. There are methods to help both teachers and students in this process, and in our work on the SEM-R, we found that teachers needed to consider three factors when assessing a book match: the qualities of the book, the student's interests, and predetermined leveling systems. Keeping these three factors in balance enables teachers to help students choose appropriately challenging reading material.

Publishers and reading experts use many different systems for leveling of books, as summarized in Table 7.1. Each system is designed to assist teachers and students in locating books that are appropriately challenging. We have included a second column in Table 7.1 that could be used to indicate the SEM-R level of the book by designating a color to match a level. Several teachers used this strategy in our research on this approach. The letter corresponds to the Fountas and Pinnell reading levels but can be easily cross-referenced to either Developmental Reading Assessment (DRA) or Lexile leveling systems by moving horizontally across the chart. The color designation, on

TABLE 7.1. SYSTEMS FOR CODING LEVELS OF BOOK DIFFICULTY AND READABILITY

Grade	SEM-R Color-Coded Level	Fountas & Pinnell Guided Reading Level	Developmental Reading Assessment (DRA) Level	Lexile Level
Kindergarten		A	A	200–400
		B	1–2	
		C	3	
			4	
First Grade			A	200–400
		B	1–2	
		C	3	
		D	4	
		E	6–8	
		F	10	
		G	12	
		H	14	
		I	16	
Second Grade			6–8	300–500
			10	
			12	
		H	14	
		I	16	
		J–K	18–20	
		L–M	24–30	
Third Grade	J–K (Green)	J–K	18–20	500–700
	L–N (Yellow)	L–M	24–28	
		N	30	
	O–P (Orange)	O–P	34–38	
			40	
Fourth Grade			24–28	650–850
			30	
	O–R (Orange)	O–P	34–38	
		Q–R	40	
	S–V (Red)	S–T	44	

(*Continued*)

TABLE 7.1. Contd.

Grade	SEM-R Color-Coded Level	Fountas & Pinnell Guided Reading Level	Developmental Reading Assessment (DRA) Level	Lexile Level
Fifth Grade	Q–R (Orange)			750–950
	S–V (Red)	S–V		
	W–Z (Purple)	W	40	
	Z+ (Blue)		44	
Sixth Grade	T–V (Red)	V		850–1050
	W–Z (Purple)	W–Y		
	Z+ (Blue)		44	
Seventh and Eighth Grades	Z+ (Blue)	Z	44	1050+

Sources: Fountas & Pinnell, 2001, p. 228; MetaMetrics, Inc., 2004; Scholastic, 2007.

the other hand, indicates the relative difficulty of the books in one range compared with another. For instance, the easiest books found in a third-grade SEM-R study classroom would be coded green, whereas in the fourth-grade classrooms in the study, the easiest books would be coded yellow. The yellow coding represents books that are slightly more difficult than those found in the green range, as indicated by the ascending letter order. It is also important to note, however, that the levels of books are not always the best predictor of the level of personal challenge that we hope children will encounter in a SEM-R program. Interests, prior knowledge, and the desire to read something all contribute to the right match. Therefore, most of the teachers who use the SEM-R have used the opportunity to listen to children read in order to help them choose books at the right level of challenge.

Another way to estimate the challenge level of a book and, thus, whether it is the right match for a student is to use the Scholastic Book Wizard tool (http://bookwizard. scholastic.com/tbw/homePage.do), which enables a teacher to enter the title of a book and obtain its level. You can find the DRA level, the Guided Reading level, the Scholastic Lexile level, and the grade equivalent level, and the Book Wizard also suggests other books that are at the same level, as well as enables you to find books that are just slightly below or above that book's level. This could be an extremely helpful tool for SEM-R teachers! We sometimes imagine the day when all teachers will have PDAs and will be able to find challenging books and identify good matches right during a conference—oh, the possibilities!

Some might wonder why a teacher should bother having a color-coded system at all, when it seems to be so random. The advantage of such a system can be illustrated by taking a closer look at Ms. Johnson's classroom. Ms. Johnson is a third-grade teacher whose students' reading abilities vary widely. Some of her third graders are quite proficient in both fluency and comprehension and have been reading novels for a few years. She also has students in her class who struggle with comprehension because they must devote so much effort to reading fluently. Using the SEM-R color-coding system, Ms. Johnson is able to recommend books with green stickers to the students who would struggle to read fluently in a typical third-grade book. Likewise, she is able to recommend that a talented reader in her classroom browse through the books with red stickers to find an appropriate match. The color-coding system enables teachers to provide students with a range of books that may be appropriate.

One informal method that you can use to understand the level of books in your existing classroom library is to gauge the reading difficulty level of the text based on the experiences of previous students or in comparison to grade-level textbooks or other books in the classroom library. You also might want to work with other teachers or the school media specialist to divide the books into three or four general categories based on readability, complexity, and your own experiences with the text (for example, at grade level, challenging). Though slightly less defined than the color-coded or Guided Reading levels, these general categories will still represent a range of options and ease the process of book selection, giving you and your students a head start in finding the right match. Once you are having regular conferences, you will be listening to students read and talking to them about the books they are reading, thereby becoming even more familiar with the range of books in the library. Over time, in using book hooks and in holding conferences with students, you will develop an even better knowledge of the books in—and the changing needs of— your classroom library. For teachers who prefer a more detailed or specific approach to book leveling, many online resources are available for checking the reading levels of books or learning more about the process of leveling (see Table 7.2).

Selection of the right level of book does not have to be scientific; we have found that finding the right match often can be accomplished through a hunch on the part of the student or the teacher. Common criteria for selecting a book include the overall length, the number of words on a page, font size, pictures that tell parts of the story or support the story, and the results from skimming a page for difficult words or new vocabulary. Our experience with the SEM-R has validated our belief and knowledge that children are astute observers who typically want to read more sophisticated or important books. Books with large print and few words, while appropriate in terms of their readability for some students, will appear to be appropriate for younger children and may turn off some struggling older readers. Teachers should be sensitive to this and seek out high-interest books with a low reading level that are formatted to appeal to older readers.

Looking up the readability level of each book can be time-consuming, and taking time to read each book, or at least a portion of it, also takes more time than

TABLE 7.2. RESOURCES ON LEVELING BOOKS

Content	*Description and Web Address*
Discussion of book leveling	This site provides a summary of book leveling and a discussion of developmental reading levels and ways of matching readers to text. A variety of leveling systems are described. http://www.literacy.uconn.edu/month2.htm
Description of how books are leveled	The Center for the Improvement of Early Reading Achievement (CIERA) details leveling of books for first-grade students. Nevertheless, useful information about the leveling process, which is applicable to many grade levels, is provided. http://www.ciera.org/library/reports/inquiry-1/1-010/1-010.pdf
Book leveling database	This database allows users to search for a book and its corresponding guided reading level (in English or Spanish) by title, author, subject, key word, and publisher. http://registration.beavton.k12.or.us/lbdb/
Lexile levels	The Lexile Framework for Reading site allows users to search for the Lexile reading level for books based on title, author, Lexile level, or ISBN. http://www.lexile.com/DesktopDefault.aspx?view=ed&tabindex=5&tabid=67

most teachers have available. However, some time invested in becoming more familiar with the reading levels of the books in your classroom library before SEM-R implementation will actually save time once you are conferencing regularly with students in Phase Two. The goal when helping students choose books is to match each student's interests with a text at an appropriate reading level so that he becomes fully engaged in the process of reading. The use of a leveling system is intended to facilitate this process and to be used simply as a guide. Teachers and students should take care to understand that a book must hold the reader's attention and that even if a book is at the appropriate level of reading difficulty for a student, the book is not a good match unless its subject interests the student.

The SEM-R framework is designed to provide teachers and students with dedicated time during the Phase Two conferences to have conversations about the books that students are reading. This time also provides teachers with the opportunity to listen to a student read in order to evaluate whether the reading level of the book is commensurate with the student's skills and reading ability. Through these conversations and evaluations, the teacher and the student, working together, determine the best match of texts for the student as an individual reader.

Physical Setup of the Classroom

Part of planning for success during Phase Two is developing a room arrangement that complements and supports the self-regulation behaviors that students are developing during SIR. Ideally, the teacher should be able to see students from any area in the room so that help or guidance can be given quickly and easily. Therefore, consider how you can arrange furniture and reading areas so that students have the space they need and are visible to the teacher. You may also wish to designate or create special reading areas in your classroom, but be sure to also develop a system for managing fair access to these areas. For example, if you have a couch, a rug area, and comfortable pillows, you may want to make a chart that enables an orderly rotation of students in each area. Students may also read at their desk. The choice of reading spaces should be determined by your classroom's physical and logistical setup, your style and preferences, and your students' ability to self-regulate their behaviors.

As you consider how to organize your room for the best implementation of a SEM-R program, remember that students should have easy access to the book that they are reading, ideas about the next book they want to read, their reading log, and any other materials that they use on a regular basis, such as sticky notes or a reading response journal. Some teachers provide a book bin for each child, in which all these reading materials are kept. Other teachers who have used the SEM-R have students keep all their materials in their desk. However, you may find that a central storage area for all reading logs, organized in alphabetical order, is a good way to help students keep materials organized. Consider the space in your classroom, the organizational skills of your students, and ease of access when choosing a system for organizing reading materials.

Most important, books should be easily accessible to students. Elementary school students are still very visual, and they rely on the covers of books to help them choose what to read. Bins or small boxes of books enable students to see the books available and to easily sort through titles. This system is usually preferable to keeping books shelved in the traditional manner in which the reader has to rely solely on the text on the book spine. Consider the height at which books are placed, and make sure they are spread out so that students are not jockeying for access in tight quarters. Books can be arranged alphabetically by author name, grouped together by genre or series, by type (picture book, chapter book), by level, or grouped by some criterion determined by the teacher and the students—for example, class favorites. The teacher or students can label the bins of books according to the chosen criteria. Students will need to become familiar with the range of titles and subjects in the classroom library. By enlisting students to help organize the collection, you provide them with an opportunity to identify books of particular interest to them, to feel some ownership of the library, and to recognize that the library is an important part of their classroom community. In recognition that students' reading interests and abilities change over time, we recommend that you keep some books stored away for the first half of the year. By adding these books to your classroom library midway through the school year, you can create excitement about the new titles and offer an opportunity for students to resort to the books available to read. At this time you might ask the students to select some books to retire for the remainder of the year and then put those books into storage. These suggestions are designed to keep students interested in the books in the library and invested in the process of choosing and caring for books.

Managing Conferences

The individual reading conferences during Phase Two are where the majority of reading instruction occurs. The conference is an opportunity for the teacher to provide one-on-one instruction, targeting the needs of each student in an atmosphere of support and collaboration. Having a conference with each student on a regular basis (two times each week) is quite possible, provided that the teacher puts certain supports in place.

Teachers should feel confident that the rest of the students are reading independently while reading conferences are under way. This will require teacher modeling and support at the beginning of the SEM-R implementation because the students will need to work up to reading for extended periods of time. The initial amount of time spent during supported independent reading will depend on the age and reading stamina of your students. If they have not spent a good bit of time on independent reading, you should begin by allowing them to read for as long as they remain focused. Once students begin to lose focus, encourage them to stay focused for a brief amount of time (two to three minutes). Following the brief time extension, you should endeavor to collaboratively set goals for systematically increasing SIR time in the future. Working with students to set goals for incrementally increasing the SIR time is an important step toward increasing student self-regulation and allows students to influence their environment, thus increasing their locus of control.

Students who are accustomed to reading for longer periods can start out with a longer block of reading time, with similar incremental increases in reading time and a similar goal-setting process. Because students are already reading for longer periods of time, the incremental increases should be longer as well (three to five minutes). Once again, when students lose focus, encourage them to refocus for a brief additional period of time and then engage students in a goal-setting process for incrementally increasing the duration of SIR time in the future. One effective strategy for encouraging students to focus longer is to provide a twenty- to thirty-second stretch break about halfway through the reading period, during which students can stretch, look around, and then return to their reading material. By breaking up the reading time into smaller chunks, the teacher can provide scaffolding for building more stamina for reading. Other strategies that support students as they work to self-regulate their behavior include writing the names of students who will participate in conferences on the board, setting a timer or indicating the stopping time on the clock, and writing the starting time with a clearly established stop time that is based on the goals set in conjunction with students.

During the initial SIR sessions, teachers should circulate through the room to make sure that students are actually reading and to determine whether students are struggling with their reading. At the end of the SIR session each day, students can record the name of the book they are reading, the total time spent reading, and the number of pages read in their reading log. By circulating around the classroom, the teacher is able to monitor students' time on the task of reading and ensure that students are properly recording their reading progress in their reading log. This monitoring at the beginning of the SEM-R implementation helps to set the expectations for reading in the classroom.

On the second day of implementation, try to increase the first block of time by two to five minutes. By the third day, you should be holding one or two conferences during SIR time. During each subsequent day, lengthen the block of SIR time until students are reading continually for thirty to forty-five minutes each day. Initially, it is important to circulate among the students to monitor their work and provide positive feedback as they become more proficient at regulating their time on task and increasing their stamina as readers. Although this will limit the time you have available for formal conferences during the first weeks of SEM-R implementation, you must establish the "rails" of self-regulation and routine during Phase Two before you can successfully set the "train" of conferences in motion. The following suggestions can help you to achieve the goal of meeting with each student several times per week.

Establishing a weekly record-keeping system will help you to keep track of the students with whom you have met, to remember the focus of the conference, and to keep other notes about the content of the conference and the student as a reader. This organization system is the first step to managing Phase Two conferences. The style or preference of each teacher will determine the method chosen, but based on our experiences and what we have observed in successful SEM-R classes, we can offer a few suggestions:

- Use the Phase Two spaces provided in the Teacher Log (see Appendix F) to list the students with whom you want to hold a conference each day of the week. Post the corresponding list of student names on the board each day.

- Create a list of all the students in your class, with some space next to each name for your notes. Keep this list readily available (for example, on a clipboard or in a notebook). Use this list to determine the next student with whom to confer. After you have met with each student, start a new list!

- Put the name of each child in your class on a full sheet of labels. Write your conference notes on the label, making sure to include the date. Once all the labels are full, transfer the label for each student to a page with that student's name. This will provide you with a record of all the conferences for that student. Once all of the labels from a sheet have been completed, repeat the process.

- Create a chart titled "Conferences" for your room, and use magnets or clothespins with the names of the students. Students can move their name to the bottom of the list once you have held a conference with them. This provides a visual reminder for you and the students.

- Write the name of each student on a tongue depressor. Label two cups "Waiting to Conference" and "Conference Complete." Place all the names in the first cup. Draw names one at a time for a conference. Place the names of students whose conference is complete in the "Conference Complete" cup. Once all of the names have been drawn from the "Waiting to Conference" cup, transfer the names back to that cup and repeat the process.

- Use sun/cloud cards (Appendix D) to enable you to quickly see how many students need help so that time can be made to meet with a student or answer urgent questions.

Regardless of which management technique you use to select students for conferences, it is essential that you keep a written record of the conference you have completed with each student. Some other suggestions for how to maintain a record of each conference include keeping an index card for each student or including a note in the student's reading log (see Appendix G for an example of a student log). The amount of time that teachers spend with each student during a conference will determine how many students are seen on a daily or weekly basis; our suggestion is to limit each conference to approximately five minutes. Because the conference is the time during which meaningful instruction takes place, it is tempting to make conferences longer, but we have found that fifteen- to twenty-minute conferences are less effective than conferences that are shorter and more frequent. As a general rule, one conference should not exceed ten minutes and our target range is five to six minutes per conference.

Ideally, teachers will have a conference with each student at least twice each week. The key to success in conferences is to provide strategy instruction that is specifically targeted to each individual student's learning needs at the time of the conference. Maintaining a five-minute limit on conferences and focusing on individual needs will enable you to have two to three opportunities weekly to provide explicit instruction for each child. Often, the tendency is to provide students with learning difficulties or behavioral issues with more frequent or longer conferences. One goal of the SEM-R, however, is to provide every student with equal opportunity for instruction and continued growth. Whether a student is a low achiever, a high achiever, or at grade level, continual progress in learning requires instructional support that challenges and extends her knowledge. The needs of students who require specific learning support can be easily addressed by adding a regularly scheduled conference with a learning specialist or other support person for those students.

When you first begin to conduct conferences, you may want to use a timer or stopwatch to keep track of the time spent with each student, in order to maintain equality in teacher-student contact time. Another strategy that you can use is to predetermine the amount of time allotted for Phase Two, divide it into five-minute or seven-minute increments, and schedule one student in each slot. This method provides a few extra minutes of time to complete conference notes between conferences and check on the reading progress of students as they read independently. You should anticipate slightly longer conferences at the beginning of your implementation of the SEM-R program. As you become more accustomed to the process and more knowledgeable about the specific reading needs of each student, conferences can become shorter and more explicit.

Helping with Transitions Between Phases in a SEM-R Program

Smooth transitions enable teachers to optimize learning time within an increasingly hectic and busy school day, and transitions are made easier when students have ready access to the materials they need and knowledge of the procedures to follow. Our experience in managing the transition into Phase One book hooks leads us to make the following suggestions:

- Designate one area in the class for book hook time, and have students practice gathering in this area in a controlled, timely manner. Consider assigning some or all students to seats or places in the classroom.

- If students have individual bins for their reading materials (such as their reading log and books), consider placing these bins in close proximity to their desks. You might also consider placing the bins in two or three locations throughout the room to avoid having too many students trying to retrieve items from their bins in the same area at the same time. Students can access their bins when they enter the classroom at the beginning of the school day or prior to joining the class at the book hook area.

- If all materials are kept in a central location, you also can assign two students to distribute the reading folders that include students' reading logs and independent reading books. The folders can be delivered to students' desks while the rest of the class assembles in the book hook area.

- If students are going to remain at their desks during book hook time, establish guidelines to minimize distractions (for example, have desk cleared, keep hands on top of desk).

- To facilitate the process when multiple students want to read a book from your book hook, create a way to manage sharing. Procedures that we have seen work well include these:

    - Place all books from book hooks along the chalk tray or in a designated book bin. A student can take the book once he is finished with the book he is currently reading, or you may choose to give the book to one student and ask that student to pass the book along to another classmate when she has finished the book.

    - Create a chart of books that have been read during the book hook phase. Post this near the book bins where students would look for the books. You can also leave space for students to clip a clothespin with their name on it next to books they want to read.

    - Put a sticky note with a list of the students who want to read the book inside the front cover. When one student finishes reading the book, it can be passed along to the next student on the list.

- Desk placement, classroom library location, and additional reading spaces should be arranged to facilitate traffic flow as students move from Phase One to Phase Two. Try to avoid bottlenecks!

As you finish the Phase One book hooks, students will need to get their books and move to their designated reading spots to begin independent reading. During the initial days and weeks of the SEM-R implementation, you will want to provide guidance, praise, and redirection to students during this transition. Make your expectations clear and easy to follow. You may also want to work with your class to create a list of guidelines to be followed during the transition to SIR. The list might look like this:

1. Have your book with you.

2. Keep your reading log and pencil with you.

3. Be settled and ready to read within two minutes!

Students will also need time to select the book they want to read during SIR—particularly in the first few weeks. You might consider allowing students to choose books at other times of the day to minimize the amount of SIR time they spend in looking for a book. There are several times when students might be able to browse for a book, including when they arrive in the classroom in the morning, when they finish with other work, or during designated free time. After the first week or so, Phase Two becomes a time for students to be reading quietly, not a time for selecting books. We recommend that students have their current reading selection along with the next book they plan to read close at hand. If students are reading longer chapter books, you may want to set a guideline for an appropriate time to select the next book (for example, when only three or four chapters remain in the book, it is time to select a new one). If one or more students seem to always take a long time to select a book, you can take time during your individual conference with those children to discuss book selection strategies. Finding the optimal match in terms of reading level and an interesting genre or subject should help alleviate a prolonged selection process in the future. Teachers who have used the SEM-R have found it useful to create the expectation that book choices must be made within five minutes.

You may want to assign jobs to students to facilitate the transition from one phase to another. Here are some possibilities:

- Classroom librarian (makes sure books are returned neatly and to the proper place)

- Book hook manager (straightens up books returned to book hook bins, announces availability of titles to interested students)

- Reading folder technician (distributes and collects reading folders or reading log)

- Reading area supervisor (straightens up pillows or mats in special reading areas)

- Bookmark clerk (collects and organizes the bookmarks that students have used during their reading time)

Each day at the end of Phase Two, students should be given time to write the name of the book they have been reading, the number of pages read, and the amount of time read in their reading log (see Appendix G). This process will take less time as students become more familiar with how to record this information. You also might include extra time once each week for students to prepare a written response in their log, perhaps using a bookmark question.

The ways that you manage the transition from Phase Two supported independent reading to Phase Three free choice activities will depend largely on the choices that you offer during Phase Three. If you plan to provide direct instruction in creative thinking or some other training in a process or skill, the transition will look different than if students are moving to predesignated work stations or centers in the room. Moreover, how you manage student transitions and activities will also depend on whether Phase Three activities are pursued each day or once each week.

You may want to help yourself plan for Phase Three activities by using a posted schedule of options. Your students can then sign up for free choice options in advance or work together during Phase Three to make decisions about their choices. An example of how this might look is presented in Table 7.3.

In highly effective SEM-R classrooms, work areas are clearly defined. Materials are prepared in advance, are organized, and are readily accessible to students. Teachers provide clear instructions and expectations for transitions from one phase to the next. In addition, teachers engage students in the planning process, creating a schedule for all phases in advance.

TABLE 7.3. EXAMPLE OF A PHASE THREE SIGN-UP SHEET

Phase Three Sign-up for Thursday, March 24	
Choice #1: Participate in Reader's Theater	Mark, Janelle, Tammy, Daniel
Choice #2: Use Renzulli Learning	James Sarah
Choice #3: Buddy reading	Joy with Carolyn Louis with Dawn
Choice #4: Listening station	Kristen, Maria, Tomas, Jack

Incorporating the SEM-R in an Elementary Reading Classroom

The SEM-R program was initially designed to fit within the typical elementary school reading or language arts time block and was intended to be used as *part* of a daily ninety-minute or two-hour literacy block. The SEM-R was deliberately designed to be flexible in order to meet the educational needs of students and the scheduling demands of elementary school. The suggested implementation at this level involves five to ten minutes devoted to Phase One book hooks, thirty to forty-five minutes for Phase Two supported independent reading, and ten to twenty minutes for Phase Three independent choice time. Some teachers use their ninety-minute literacy block in two parts—sixty minutes for the SEM-R program and thirty minutes for writing, spelling, or vocabulary work. Some teachers facilitate Phases One and Two four days a week for one hour each day and provide Phase Three independent choice time on the remaining day of each week for one hour at a time. Others use Phases One and Two for thirty minutes and Phase Three for thirty minutes for two days of each week and then use Phases One and Two for the entire sixty minutes the remaining three days of every week. Still others devote one hour every day to Phases One and Two and then do Phase Three for twenty to thirty minutes at another time during the day. The implementation should be organized according to your needs and those of your students; feel free to use your ingenuity to make the SEM-R program a success in your class.

Adapting the SEM-R for Use in a Middle School

Using the SEM-R in a middle school may require some adjustment of current approaches to reading and English language arts instruction. The amount of time allotted to the SEM-R implementation in a middle school will be influenced by the length of class time. For example, in a forty-five-minute block, five to ten minutes can be devoted to Phase One book hooks, twenty to twenty-five minutes to Phase Two supported independent reading, and ten minutes to Phase Three independent choice activities. Another alternative is to organize each week so that SEM-R programming consists of four days of Phase One and Phase Two instruction and a fifth day entirely devoted to Phase Three explorations. In a middle school setting, the latter option is preferred because it allows students to increase their focus and self-regulation by increasing SIR time to thirty-five to forty minutes, a minimum target for middle school students.

In many middle schools, reading and English language arts instruction center on whole-class study of novels and writing instruction. The SEM-R framework represents a shift from whole-class to individualized instruction with a focus on developing enjoyment of reading. Typically in middle schools, teachers use the study of a novel as a vehicle to teach various literary devices. Choosing one novel for a class to read can be problematic because even in classes that are grouped by ability, there is a range of reading proficiency among the students. A book that will be a struggle to read for one group of students will be too easy for others, but it might be just right for the students who read at grade level. Teachers can still teach specific literary devices when students choose books to read independently, but it requires teachers to think carefully about the skills they want students to learn and how readers can demonstrate that they have learned those skills. Options for managing this process include identifying a genre or thematic book list from which students can select a text that interests them. Teachers can also enable students to use the SEM-R bookmarks for conferences during two or three periods a week in which Phase One and Phase Two reading strategies are implemented. During these periods, teachers can use Phase One book hooks to demonstrate how to recognize or apply a literary device and then have differentiated Phase Two conferences with students during SIR. Teachers also can implement this phase as originally designed by selecting several books for book hooks and using the bookmarks as tools for engaging with text. Ultimately, students should be encouraged to choose books that are interesting and appropriately challenging (that is, books with varying complexity and reading levels). This enables students to use the principles of the SEM-R while the class as a whole addresses the goals of the middle school curriculum.

Phase Two supported independent reading in a middle school provides an important opportunity for the teacher to meet with students individually to support their reading growth. Teachers may want to set a focus for conference discussions in advance so that students will have time to prepare and reflect. As noted in previous sections, the teacher needs to record notes about the conference with each student in order to track reading progress over time.

Phase Three independent choice time provides numerous opportunities for students to explore new topics or ideas and to demonstrate their creativity. Early in the academic year, teachers may want to have students write a response to their reading that relates to a theme or an identified literary device. This practice allows students to apply higher-order thinking skills and to use examples from the text as evidence. Teachers may also consider using this time for free writing in different genres or for discussions in which students can talk about their independent reading with classmates. As students become more self-regulated and more comfortable with having choices, more choices can be added. For example, students might choose to do an individual research project, express their understanding visually, explore beat poetry, or compose a song. Teachers are often surprised by the quality and creativity of students' products when they have been given freedom and choice in procedural processes, content, and expression style.

This section has described just some of the ways that middle school teachers have successfully implemented the SEM-R program in diverse classrooms, and of course, there are unlimited creative ways that teachers can use the SEM-R to enhance their classroom practice and reading instruction. The only limitation is the time constraints that some middle school teachers face because they teach reading during a single period.

Summary

As with all worthwhile endeavors, there is a good deal of thought and planning that goes in to creating a successful SEM-R classroom. The flexible nature of the SEM-R allows you to establish routines and organize the learning environment to best match your personality and preferences as well as those of your students. When planning to use the SEM-R, keep in mind that students' voices, interests, and learning needs should be considered in order to increase their participation and investment in reading. The variety of books in your classroom library and their accessibility to students are the first things to consider for a well-run reading program. Next, consider how the environment can be modified in order to facilitate students' retrieval of materials and quiet, focused reading time. Just as students need to learn to manage their reading time, you should carefully plan how you will manage your time to meet with students to provide that one-on-one instruction on a consistent basis. The SEM-R can be used in a variety of school settings because it can be customized to fit into different time frames or English language arts instructional blocks. In the next chapter you will learn how the use of the SEM-R can help you with one of the biggest challenges facing teachers today: differentiating instruction to meet the wide range of reading levels that exist within each classroom.

Differentiated Practices to Challenge All Readers

Continuous progress and growth in reading is important for all students, and in this chapter, we discuss how you can use the SEM-R to ensure that all of your students, including those who are talented, can make continual progress in reading. We discuss ways to match readers with texts that challenge and engage them, as well as specific strategies to help both talented and struggling readers work at appropriate levels of challenge.

Educators and researchers agree that reading and literacy are the gateway to academic success (Snow, Burns, & Griffin, 1998; National Reading Panel, 2000). Being able to read fluently and comprehend written information is the foundation for many other skills taught in school. Furthermore, reading comprehension is key to solid performance on the standardized achievement tests that have quickly become the hallmark of U.S. educational accountability policies. Current legislation and reading policies, which focus on reducing the achievement gap between those who perform at the highest levels and those who perform at the lowest levels on standardized measures of academic proficiency, have widespread support from lawmakers and the public, sometimes resulting in high-stakes pressure on students and educators to perform well.

Unfortunately, there are no easy answers to closing this achievement gap, but the information in this chapter can help you to reflect on the diversity of student needs in your classroom and the support and strategies you will need to capitalize on individualized instructional opportunities during a SEM-R program. Seizing these opportunities becomes even more important when we consider the lack of challenge that often exists for students who are talented in reading. We have been invited to many meetings in which teachers have asked for advice about what to do with talented readers. Sometimes this happens in response to parents' complaints about the lack of challenge in reading instruction for their talented, inquisitive children.

Although some teachers try to differentiate curriculum in reading, many believe that their efforts are not really enough. What can teachers do to challenge children who are reading at a level that is four or five grades above their current grade? What do they do when the differences between a child who reads several years above grade level and her peers make it difficult to provide sufficient challenge? This scenario is playing out in classrooms across the country as talented readers deal with instruction in reading that is well below their challenge level.

A Rich Mix of Students

Today's classrooms include students with many different talents, abilities, and cultural backgrounds. In this chapter, we introduce many creative and exciting strategies that are designed to address the varied reading levels and instructional needs that you will find in any classroom of students. These strategies can enrich students' experiences with the SEM-R program and enable you to reflect on and refine your own instructional methods and strategies to address this diversity.

Given the wide range of skills with which students enter a reading classroom, teaching all students by using the same techniques and the same materials cannot foster increased reading achievement for everyone. These practices result in work that is too easy to provide talented readers with opportunities for continual growth—and too difficult to provide struggling readers with growth. The report *National Excellence: A Case for Developing America's Talent* (Ross, 1993) suggested that enrichment programs like the SEM-R program can make positive changes, having "served as laboratories for innovative and experimental approaches to teaching and learning in the development of complex thinking strategies and problem solving" (p. 23) as well as sophisticated alternative teaching strategies and innovative curriculum approaches.

Although the development of the SEM-R was initially driven by concerns about the neglect of talented readers in classroom literacy instruction, it became apparent to us during our earliest pilot implementations of the SEM-R program that the use of enrichment pedagogy and differentiated instruction benefited almost every student in the classroom, regardless of their level of skill, including students with special needs. In our SEM-R research, we have routinely encountered classrooms with students whose reading differences span eight to ten grade levels, and we have also found that differentiated instruction (that is, instruction designed to meet learners' individual needs within the classroom) has helped teachers better understand and further student growth in and enjoyment of reading.

The SEM-R program enables all students, including those who read several levels above their current grade placement, to select books they want to read, to read content that is above their current reading level, to engage and think about complex texts, and to extend conventional basal reading instruction, which too often

students may not be interested in reading because they experience reading difficulties, and others may avoid reading because of unpleasant reading experiences they have had in the past. Some students, however, may have adequate or above-average reading ability and still choose not to read, a phenomenon that is called *aliteracy.* You might try to motivate reluctant readers by helping them to identify and select high-interest books to read. Audio books can sometimes motivate reluctant readers. We have also found that self-selected Phase Three projects can help to engage some reluctant readers, especially those who develop a passion for discovery on a specific topic or in a particular area.

In the SEM-R, we focus on the necessity of including instruction in high-level strategies for *all* readers. Struggling and talented readers both need the opportunity to discuss the strategies they are using and what they are thinking about a text. Moreover, all readers benefit from the development and practice of self-regulated behaviors that allow them to pursue and enjoy exciting and interesting literature.

Matching Readers to Texts

As we discussed in Chapter Five, finding the perfect book match for a particular reader can be a challenging task. The two keys to matching individual readers with the right book are knowing your students' interests and skills as readers and thinking creatively about the types of books and literature that are readily available to readers. When you are trying to match students with the right books, several of the following characteristics need to be considered in combination:

- Reader (interests, background knowledge, preferences, motivation)
- Reading level (challenge range)
- Content (subject, theme)
- Reader's academic needs (reading support; differentiated, individualized reading strategies)
- Social or affective characteristics or needs (identity, emotions, connections to real life)
- Text (genre, structure, language, style, visual elements)

The Reader

One of the first things you can do to successfully implement a SEM-R program is get to know your students' interests both in and outside of school. Information such as whether a student participates in extracurricular activities, the types of reading material available to her outside of school, or a student's passion about a particular subject or topic may help you identify genres or authors that will spark a learner's motivation to read. Book discussions in Phase One and individual conferences in Phase Two will also allow you to better know and understand your students' reading patterns and to track the growth of reading skills and strategies. Informal conversations and conference dialogues may prove helpful for gauging the depth of background knowledge each reader possesses. Using an interest inventory such as the Reading Interest-a-Lyzer (Appendix B) or the profile system in Renzulli Learning can also help you gather and organize information about students as both individuals and readers.

As an enrichment-based program, the SEM-R program offers challenge and choice as well as opportunities to use imagination and creativity. In essence, tapping into students' interests through formal and informal interest assessments and then providing choice in reading materials makes tackling an appropriately challenging book more palatable for students at all performance levels. In describing her success in a twelve-week intervention with a fourth-grade learning-disabled student, one SEM-R teacher explained the role played by interest: "He did not like to read, and we hooked him. He was a success for me. We talked to him. We got him to read stuff he was interested in, and we found that when he was interested, he could really do well. . . . He is so successful now. He has made major gains in reading."

Reading Level

The second component in finding the right match relies on a teacher's ability to make a determination about each student's current reading level. In many classrooms, this level is identified by using quantitative information from various assessments at the school level or from state tests. These results can be a helpful starting point for you in the first few weeks of SEM-R implementation as you continue to learn more about each student as a reader. In our research on the SEM-R, we have found school-based assessments, in particular, to be helpful in an initial examination of reading levels (for example, Lexile levels) that can be used to match students with appropriately challenging texts. However, it is important to bear in mind that interests and motivation also have an impact on what students can and will read independently.

When you use the SEM-R, you will find that one effective way to determine students' reading levels is to encourage students to select books to read before they have their first individual conference with you. At the conference, you can listen to your student read the book she has chosen and then ask skill-based literal and interpretive questions to determine her levels of comprehension. If the student struggles with numerous words (either decoding or vocabulary) or has difficulty understanding the text, simply stated, the book is too difficult for her.

In the SEM-R, we want all students to be challenged when they are reading during Phase Two and we recommend that students select books that are one to one and a half grade levels above their current reading level. To try to determine whether a book is at this level, we suggest that you listen to the student read. If the student is challenged by decoding a few words on each page or struggles a bit to *fully* understand the meaning or content, then the book is most likely a good match for that student. We often praise students for reading quickly and with ease; however, in our experience in working with the SEM-R, we have found that when students are not challenged, their reading will not improve. In the SEM-R, we also want to encourage students to seek depth in ideas, in the new content in which they have an interest, and in the types of reading they want to pursue because of their interests. So while praising students when they have to work and expend effort in their reading may seem counterintuitive, it is by doing so that we can help them to improve and grow as readers. In addition to carrying out your informal assessment of reading levels (which we believe works efficiently and will help you come to understand your students as readers), you may also wish to revisit the discussion "Organizing Your Library for Optimal Matches in Reading" in the preceding chapter.

Content

A third criterion to consider when matching students with interesting and challenging books is the content—an area in which student interest plays an important role. As we mentioned earlier, one important difference between SEM-R instruction and regular instruction is that students are able to choose what they read—with guidance and support from a teacher. Students with a great deal of knowledge about a topic can usually read more difficult books about a subject; however, they may struggle when they are asked to read books of similar difficulty about topics with which they are not familiar. A SEM-R program encourages students to read books in their areas of interest, and teachers are also encouraged to expose students to topics and genres that students typically would not chose on their own. This exposure is one important purpose of the book hooks in Phase One.

Familiarity with books in the classroom library can make the process of matching books easier for both students and teachers. When you are implementing a SEM-R program, consider different organizational systems for displaying the books, concentrating on creating groupings that make book choice both inviting and practical for students. Books can be organized by genre, series, author, subject, or theme, and we have found that teachers who involve students in the organization of their classroom books help those students to more actively identify books of interest for current or future reading.

Reader Academic Needs

Another area to consider concerns the academic needs of individual readers who need differentiated reading strategies to continue to improve their reading. In our research on SEM-R, we have found wide variations of reading level and cognitive needs in the same classroom. For example, in one school implementation of SEM-R, the range of reading levels spanned twelve grade levels, from grade 1 to grade 13 in the fifth-grade classes. Any teacher who tries to meet the academic needs of such a wide span of students will have to use differentiated strategies. For the most talented students, for example, instruction on academic areas that students have already mastered can be eliminated or compacted. For students who have had content introduced previously but who have not mastered the material, different instruction should be used, rather than repetition of the same style of instruction. In either case, differentiated and individualized reading strategies should be used to challenge all students.

Social or Affective Considerations

Another consideration in helping a student select a book is how the book might help the reader. Books can help students explore their feelings or deal with difficult events, and they can also be an important source of emotional support for students. If a student is new to a classroom or a school, a book about being a new student in school might help to make the transition easier. If two students are having problems in their friendship, books about how other friends deal with similar situations might be helpful. Good readers often make connections from their own life to the lives of characters in books. Talented readers may also develop strong attachments to characters in books.

Knowledge gained from reading nonfiction books can help students feel more confident as they begin to study other content areas in school. Books can help students cope with challenges they face and new experiences they encounter. Exposing students to a wide variety of books provides them with opportunities to reflect on their personal life in different ways.

Finally, the conversations about literature that emerge during all three phases enhance students' ability to choose and recommend books and build a sense of community literacy. Through conferences and conversations, teachers will learn the specific strengths and weaknesses of learners, as well as their reading preferences. In addition, as the SEM-R program continues, students in the program will discover and discuss one another's reading preferences and interests and will be more likely to have conversations about the books they are reading. Teachers can also take advantage of students' expanding knowledge about books and encourage them to make suggestions for one another. In one classroom, the students were so in tune with their peers' reading preferences that they were able to make better recommendations than the teacher.

Text

The final characteristic to consider when matching a reader with a text is the text itself. For a good match, consider the genre, the text structure, the language and style, and visual elements such as headings, bold words, captions, illustrations, photographs, graphs, charts, and tables. Books that have a direct match between the text and the pictures are easier to read and are recommended for struggling readers.

The length of a text or the type of book does not automatically determine the text complexity. For example, a picture book by Patricia Polacco has more sophisticated language and a different style than a chapter book in the Horrible Joe series by Suzy Kline. The pictures in a Patricia Polacco book, however, support the more complex text, whereas the Horrible Joe books have fewer illustrations but more predictable text structure and vocabulary. For English language learners, texts with idiomatic phrases and figurative language can be difficult to comprehend without careful guidance or direct instruction. Organizational features such as headings and captions offer additional support for readers and can provide scaffolding for new learning.

Talented Readers

The most common method of challenging talented readers in classrooms has traditionally involved providing talented students with more difficult and complex literature. While precocious readers need to be challenged by more difficult texts, supplying only books without supplementing them with appropriate instructional support can isolate advanced readers and enable them to use reading as an escape rather than an opportunity for continued growth in learning. Talented readers have the ability to make sophisticated connections between texts and to identify and synthesize multiple meanings contained in complex stories, and they also can learn to analyze and evaluate the use of literary elements and techniques. A SEM-R program allows teachers to maximize the potential of talented readers through appropriate levels of challenge and support.

A Case Study

A pervasive finding that has emerged from the limited research and discussions on instructional practices for talented readers is that regular reading instruction is often too easy for talented readers (Reis and others, 2004). Chall and Conard (1991), too, found that the talented readers they studied were not adequately served in school because their reading textbooks provided little or no challenge. Many students were aware of this deficiency, according to Chall and Conard, who said that in interviews, students commented that they preferred harder books because they learned harder words and ideas from them. A SEM-R program can provide the higher level of challenge that many talented students seem to be seeking. Consider the case study of Alex.

> Alex, an eight-year-old third grader, was reading at an accelerated fifth-grade level and had been previously identified as a gifted and talented student. Alex lived with his mother and stepfather, and he explained that he enjoyed the company of both of his parents and that he was encouraged to read at home.
>
> Alex was an energetic student who had difficulty with being still for any extended period of time. Although he could be quite focused when reading, Alex fidgeted and

often had verbal outbursts during group activities. His classroom teachers had noticed this heightened activity and reported that Alex was often distracted and lacked focus. They had provided him with a squishy ball to squeeze when he felt distracted, in the hope that this action would help him to focus better during group work or any time when he could not be independently engaged in his own work.

In contrast to his behavior during group work, Alex was able to focus well when reading and could read quietly through periods of peer noise. To ask Alex a question about his reading and gain his attention, we often had to call his name twice before he would take his eyes from the page. Unfortunately, although he was capable of reading at a fifth-grade level and despite being encouraged to read at a higher level, Alex's initial choices of books were always from the Goosebumps series, which was well below his challenge level. Alex liked some of the challenging books suggested to him, including biographies of baseball stars, but would discontinue reading if he perceived that he could not finish the book within a half hour or forty-five minutes. He typically read one Goosebumps book in the forty-five-minute reading period and seemed to need the extrinsic praise given when he finished a book in that time period.

On his Reading Interest-a-Lyzer, Alex indicated that he liked books about science or fantasy; comic books; writing activities; and reading books of his choice before going to bed at night. Alex also explained that he liked reading about spiders and frogs and that he often read children's science books he found in the library and the classroom. During the course of the SEM-R intervention, Alex began reading many novels that were suggested to him because they were good matches for him in interest and challenge level, but he stopped reading shortly after he began almost every novel. If he chose a book that was well below his challenge level, he could usually read silently and independently for one hour. At the beginning of the SEM-R program, when a book in one of his interest areas of fantasy, sports, or science that would provide an appropriate level of challenge was suggested, he would lose interest and become distracted after fifteen minutes.

Toward the end of his first six weeks in the SEM-R program, Alex needed to be in a space separate from his classmates in order to focus and had to be encouraged to take more frequent breaks. When the weather was pleasant, Alex asked if the group could go outside for a break and when granted permission, he ran the entire time and had to be cajoled to leave the playground to participate in the SEM-R program. On some spring days, Alex simply seemed incapable of reading anything that challenged him in any way and teachers were forced to let him read Goosebumps books or whatever books might spark his interest. In later sessions, when a book was suggested to Alex in his areas of interest, he would glance at the cover or read one page of a book at or above his reading level and dismiss it as boring. Despite having several conversations about giving books a chance and reading enough so that he could enter the world of a particular book, he did not appear to want to change his behavior. It was difficult to monitor his progress as he tried to read more challenging books because he would ask to bring them home and then fail to return them, saying he had forgotten them.

Based on some of his interests, science fiction or fantasy books, the Harry Potter Series was suggested to Alex, but he became frustrated with the unfamiliar names in the books and made fun of the sounds of the titles. He became discouraged about reading more challenging books when the title looked unfamiliar or the content was too difficult. For example, when the book *The Sands of Time* by Michael Hoeye was given to Alex, he immediately said the book was too hard. When Alex was informed that this book was special because it was the most challenging the program had offered any student, his interest was maintained a little longer; he read for ten minutes, but then lost interest. He initially complained about the length of the book, but in further discussion, Alex explained that he had become accustomed to speed-reading at his comfort level and felt discomfort when he had to read higher content more slowly. After several hours of observation, it became apparent that Alex routinely read books that did not challenge him and that he lost interest in or could not regulate his own reading of appropriately challenging material. When reading material was simpler—for example, when a graphic novel version of *Moby Dick* was suggested to Alex—he read straight through the book for fifty minutes and finished the entire book. When asked comprehension questions about the content of the book, Alex remembered fine details and seemed to understand the plot. He also sped through *The Little Prince* but initially seemed to have a limited understanding of this challenging text and the difficult issues raised within the pages. However, when asked additional questions after he had had a chance to reflect more about what he had read, Alex was able to answer more in-depth questions, again suggesting that he may have initially lacked the experience to respond to challenging questions. Over the time he spent in the SEM-R program, he gained some skills in learning how to think through more challenging questions.

Intensive observations during the SEM-R intervention suggested that Alex was an academically talented student who had the ability to read challenging texts at the fifth-grade or sixth-grade level or higher if he had an interest in the content and could regulate his behavior, but that he lacked the reading and self-regulation strategies to focus on new, more challenging material on a systematic basis. With enough support and with books in an area of interest, and if he was in a positive frame of mind, Alex could be encouraged to read at an appropriately challenging level for up to fifty minutes. This continued to occur over the course of the SEM-R with a great deal of feedback and encouragement. If left to select what to read, Alex consistently read books below his chronological grade level, even though he understood he was reading material that was well below his skill level. He explained that he had learned over time that he could receive positive feedback for little effort because his output exceeded that of the majority of his classmates.

Like Alex, some talented readers may not be accustomed to being challenged by more difficult text and high-level questioning and may avoid reading more complex books when possible. Holding conferences with unmotivated talented readers on a frequent basis will help to promote reading as a valued activity and can help to prevent aliteracy. SEM-R teachers should also ensure that students are reading challenging books during Phase Two and should encourage talented readers to take their books of interest home if the books are too easy. If you find yourself in this situation, simply explain to your talented student that as the teacher, it is your job to make sure she is challenged. Suggest that the student take the book home to read and that while she is at school and has your support, she should be engaging with material that is sufficiently challenging (that is, one to one and a half grade levels above her current reading level).

Instructional Needs of Talented Readers

Alex's story illustrates the need for thoughtful and flexible instructional grouping to be implemented with talented readers. If Alex had the opportunity to be in a group with other advanced readers, he may have had the opportunity to better understand how to react to more challenging content and watched as other students also learned to read more complex reading material, resulting in increased achievement in reading literature (Gentry, 1999). In general, grouping academically talented students together for instruction has been found to produce positive achievement outcomes when the curriculum provided to students in different groups is appropriately differentiated (Gentry, 1999; Kulik & Kulik, 1991). To provide talented readers with multiple opportunities to discuss complex texts, SEM-R teachers may want to provide time for them to discuss books with other talented readers during Phase Three or even as a featured option during Phase One or Phase Two. In groups of talented readers, students can take turns leading the discussion or use the SEM-R bookmarks to formulate questions for the readers who are sharing the book. Teachers are also able to ask more challenging questions and introduce more challenging content and instruction in these groups and the differentiated instruction that occurs within these groups is what makes grouping an effective instructional strategy (Kulik & Kulik, 1991; Rogers, 1991).

A differentiated reading program also enables students to interact with advanced content that has both depth and complexity (Kaplan, 1999), focuses on developing high-level comprehension skills, and engages students with advanced reading skills instruction. Regular reading instruction is often too easy for talented readers (Reis and others, 2004). The optimal match between a learner's abilities and the difficulty of the instructional work occurs when instruction is slightly above the learner's current level of functioning. Chall and Conard (1991) state that when the match is optimal, learning is enhanced. If, however, "the match is not optimal, learning is less efficient and development may be halted" (p. 19). Using textbooks that are several years below students' reading level may result in halted development as well as subsequent motivational problems for talented readers who may think that reading should always be an effortless process. In a longitudinal study of academically talented students who either achieved or underachieved in a large urban high school, underachieving students consistently acknowledged that the easy curriculum they encountered in elementary and middle school failed to prepare them for the rigors of challenging classes in high school, and most mentioned a lack of challenge in reading (Reis, Hébert, DéIaz, Maxfield, & Ratley, 1995). For these reasons, it is evident that higher levels of challenge in reading are very important for talented readers.

Differentiating SEM-R Instruction to Challenge Talented Readers

Using the SEM-R enables classroom teachers to differentiate their instruction to meet the needs of talented readers. Classroom teachers who are trained in the SEM-R use different books for all of their students in order to optimize their individual level of challenge in reading. The teachers encourage rich, complex reading of literature that can challenge students at all levels with the possibility of multiple interpretations. Book discussion groups can also provide talented readers with opportunities to interact with intellectual peers and to discuss their ideas in greater depth. Talented readers benefit from having multiple interpretations of text that encourage them to examine how they have developed their own beliefs and to respond to challenges that they seldom encounter in their classroom (Reis and others, 2005). Book discussion groups can also provide talented readers with opportunities to interact with intellectual peers and to discuss their ideas in greater depth. SEM-R teachers also challenge talented readers with high-level questioning that extends the depth of the students' contact with engaging literature (Reis and others, 2005). The SEM-R also enables teachers to use reading strategies such as making connections, determining the importance of elements of the text, advanced self-questioning, visualization, making inferences, summarizing and synthesizing, and metacognition (Paris, 2004) with talented readers, who will need to use these strategies systematically when they read texts with advanced content.

The SEM-R automatically enables curriculum compacting to occur (Reis, Burns, & Renzulli, 1992) because students are able to move beyond reading at their chronological grade level and, instead, are matched to books that are slightly or somewhat above their independent reading level—a practice known as *acceleration.* The SEM-R enables teachers to eliminate the use of basal or regular classroom reading materials that are usually much too easy for talented readers. A SEM-R program also enables students to individually pursue more challenging writing in their weekly responses in their SEM-R logs and in writing they do during Phase Three. SEM-R programs enable talented readers to pursue high-interest reading, independent project opportunities, and literature circles with their peers, as well as opportunities to respond to high-level questions from their teachers.

SEM-R teachers should regularly use a book hook to introduce a complex story line during Phase One; stories featuring sophisticated plots and literary elements will challenge and motivate talented readers. Phase Two presents teachers with the opportunity to engage talented readers in extended discussions about literary devices and techniques (for example, foreshadowing or the use of metaphor), the author's intention, the relevance of the subject matter to the outside world, or students' appraisal of a book's worth. Such discourse allows talented readers to develop high-level reasoning skills through responding to advanced-level questions. Talented readers may become excited about participating in challenging conferences and may want to engage in prolonged conversations; however, it is important for SEM-R teachers to keep conferences brief. As we discussed in the previous chapter, providing short but frequent conferences allows talented readers to discuss the complexity of a challenging book multiple times. If conferences are not scheduled on a regular basis, talented students may miss the chance to develop complex, high-level thinking because they may finish the book before the next individual conference. If a talented reader is reading entire books between conferences, consider evaluating the student's choice of book; the content and reading level are likely too easy to stimulate reading growth in that student.

Another lesson that can be learned from Alex is the necessity of challenging talented readers early in their school career. A SEM-R program can provide this level of challenge in all phases. During both Phase Two and Phase Three, talented read-ers can be given multiple opportunities to discuss complex stories with each other, both with and without the teacher. Phase Three also provides an ideal opportunity for talented readers to extend analytical thinking, creative thinking, and produc-tion skills. The element of choice in Phase Three allows advanced readers to pursue areas of interest related to books they have read by working independently or with a small group to create a product for an audience. Some activities for talented readers that promote high-level thinking include the following:

- Writing a review of a book to be shared with a peer or to appear in the school newspaper

- Holding a book award ceremony in which students design the evaluation crite-ria and judge books accordingly to make the awards (for example, best picture book, best fantasy novel)

- Adapting a favorite book into a class play

- Completing a biography on a favorite author

- Composing alternative endings for a book

- Generating complex questions about books read that can be answered by the next student to read the book

- Using Renzulli Learning to generate and organize independent projects of interest

Differentiating Instruction to Challenge Precocious Talented Readers

As we have stated, the earlier we challenge talented readers, the more likely they will be to tackle more difficult reading materials. A SEM-R program can be imple-mented in kindergarten through second grade within a cluster group of precocious readers who need additional challenge. We have found that it can be used with a small group of talented readers while the classroom teacher is providing more traditional reading instruction to groups of students who are not yet reading inde-pendently. Like their older peers, young talented readers integrate prior knowledge and experience into their reading; are capable of using high-level thinking skills such as analysis, synthesis, and evaluation; and communicate effectively in responses to ques-tions that require them to use these high-level skills. In our research on the SEM-R, we have found that early readers are able to use colorful and descriptive phrasing, demonstrate advanced understanding of language, have an expansive vocabulary, per-ceive relationships between characters, and grasp ideas that are challenging (Reis and others, 2004, 2005). A SEM-R program can offer these students the opportunity to pursue personal interests in reading through independent choice, as well as provide appropriately challenging reading to ensure continual progress. Reading strategies for young children should also integrate high-level thinking skills such as questioning, making inferences, making connections, understanding one's own thinking processes, visualizing, determining importance, and synthesizing in order to make meaning of text.

Helping young, talented readers make appropriate book choices is an important step toward ensuring both their continuing desire to read and an appropriate level of challenge for them. Books for talented, young readers should be selected with age-appropriateness in mind. Book selections should also introduce them to advanced content, themes, and ideas as well as advanced language. We recommend several books that can challenge precocious readers in Appendix C. It is especially important that young children's first experiences with reading be joyful; they should enjoy reading and anticipate happy times when they think of reading books and listening to stories in the company of classmates. The more pleasurable these early experiences are, the more likely it is that a child will want to read independently and develop the self-regulation necessary to become a lifelong reader. In summary, talented readers who participate in a SEM-R program can benefit from many of the strategies that we use across the three phases of this approach, especially the use of self-selected, individually challenging reading materials based on their interests.

Teachers can use Phase One book hooks for students who read above, at, or below grade level to facilitate whole-class discussion of themes across books (Kaplan, 2001). Talented readers can also be given opportunities to complete different kinds of creative products or alternative writing assignments (Reis & Renzulli, 1989). Talented readers can be encouraged to bring prior knowledge and insight into their interpretations of challenging text. They can use technology to access the Web sites of authors, read challenging books online, or interact with talented readers from other schools, using literature circle discussion strategies. Computers can also be used to access advanced content; to create concept maps or other technological products; or to write and revise stories, chapters, or even books (Reis and others, 2004).

Strategies to Support Students with Reading Difficulties

Our research on the SEM-R has demonstrated that students with reading difficulties also benefit from this approach. After learning more about students' reading levels and interests, you may wish to conduct further assessments to identify the specific nature of the difficulties they are experiencing. Additional assessment can provide information that will help you choose instructional strategies to meet the needs of individual students. The source of reading problems experienced by students can be issues associated with print processing (decoding) or meaning processing (comprehension) (Walker, 2000).

Problems with print processing are usually detected by conducting informal reading inventories to determine reading behaviors (for example, the degree of self-correction, frequency of skipping words or lines, mispronunciations) and by using word-recognition and spelling tests to determine decoding skills (for example, phonological knowledge). Meaning processing should be assessed through both oral reading analysis and silent reading analysis. Oral reading analysis involves asking the student to read a passage aloud and stopping the student regularly to ask comprehension questions about the text (both literal and interpretive). A student may struggle to complete this task; however, this does not always mean that she has a problem with comprehension. Reading aloud places additional demands on memory that can compromise deeper understanding of text. Therefore, a teacher will often follow up with a silent reading analysis in which the student is asked to read a passage silently and is stopped periodically in order to answer literal and interpretive questions. If the student successfully answers the questions, the teacher will realize that she can process the meaning of text when she does not have to read aloud. If the student fails to respond appropriately to questions posed in the silent reading analysis, it may indicate that the student does experience problems with processing the meaning of text and might warrant some instruction in reading strategies, a less difficult book selection, or even testing for learning difficulties.

Teachers should be aware of common signs that might indicate more serious problems. Students who persistently make visual errors (for example, reversing letters or words, skipping words or lines of text) may be experiencing problems with visual processing, while students who commonly mispronounce and misspell words may be experiencing problems with auditory processing. Students who exhibit difficulties in comprehending written and verbal instructions may be experiencing problems with language processing. Students with any of these problems should be referred to a reading specialist or special education teacher for further assessment.

Using the information gathered from the assessments described earlier, a teacher may choose instructional strategies to support the specific problems experienced by individual students. Reading specialists and other support personnel can also be invited into the classroom to help support these students during Phase Two conference time. You may want to use some conference time during Phase Two or Phase Three to implement specific instructional strategies to individually support struggling readers. Some suggested strategies to help students with print processing problems and meaning processing problems are listed here.

Instructional Strategies to Help with Print Processing

- **Echo reading** occurs when a novice reader echoes the reading of a proficient reader. This strategy helps a student to learn sight words, improves his reading fluency and phrasing, helps him to read text that is too difficult for him to read alone, and develops his reading confidence.

- **Chunking** involves grouping words in a sentence into short meaningful chunks (usually three to five words). Chunking helps students to read in meaningful units rather than word by word, which assists improvement in both fluency and comprehension (Walker, 1996).

- **Paired reading** starts with the student and teacher reading together in synchrony; then, after some time, the student continues to read on his own. The teacher commences reading again when the student experiences difficulty in decoding the text. On average, children involved in paired reading make three times the normal reading progress in reading accuracy and five times the normal progress in reading comprehension (Topping, 1995).

- **Repeated readings** involve students' reading the same book several times. Familiarity with the text after repeated readings improves fluency and reduces the demands placed on working memory; therefore, students can dedicate more attention to comprehending the text on subsequent readings. Young, Bowers, and MacKinnon (1996) found that the use of repeated readings improves the reading rate, accuracy, and comprehension of students with reading difficulties.

- **Word walls** are displays made up of unknown words that students encounter while reading; students may add to the wall after completion of Phase Two independent reading each day. Teachers may select words from the wall during Phase One to discuss with the class, defining the words (or having the class help define them) in order to develop vocabulary and sight word recognition.

- **Readers theater** occurs when students take on the roles of characters in order to read a familiar story, fable, or play to an audience. The purpose of this activity is to develop students' reading fluency and expression. The general rules of readers' theater include limiting students' movement to provide a focus on using voice and facial expression to enrich the telling of the story. Many students enjoy participating in readers' theater, and it can be a motivational activity for students who experience reading problems.

Instructional Strategies to Help with Meaning Processing

- **Cloze instruction** is an instructional technique in which words are deleted from text (covered by the teacher), and students are asked to insert words that would make sense. Cloze instruction encourages students to make predictions and monitor for meaning while reading, and it is particularly effective for students who read fluently but struggle to comprehend text.

- **Directed reading-thinking activity** is an effective method of improving students' prediction skills. After reading the title and cover of a book, students make initial predictions about the content of the book (plot, characters, settings, and so on). The students then read a section of the book, stop, and review their initial predictions (Were their predictions accurate? What happened that they did not predict?). The students then make new predictions as to what will happen next in the story. They recommence reading and then stop again later to check their predictions. This pattern continues during the reading conference and throughout independent reading as students develop self-regulation skills.

- **SQ3R** is an instructional method that helps students to comprehend and retain information that they read. This strategy is primarily used with nonfiction texts but may be applied to fictional works. The first step in SQ3R requires a student to *survey* the chapter and develop an idea of the main ideas presented by the text. The student then generates *questions* about what she wishes to know (she may record these in writing). Next, the student *reads* the chapter to learn the content of the text. The student then *recites* her understandings of the text by discussing the chapter with others or by making summaries of the information that she has learned. The final step involves a *review* of the chapter and her notes the following day (or on several days) to reinforce learning.

- **Triple read outline** is a strategy to assist students in identifying the main idea of a passage and the details that support the main idea. There are several forms of this technique; however, the goal of the first reading is for students to identify the main idea of the passage. The second reading of the passage requires students to identify the details that support the main idea. The students then read the passage a third time to confirm their outline of the main idea and supporting details. Students may then use their outline to write a summary of the passage or engage in a discussion about a pre-selected bookmark question. This instructional strategy helps students to develop comprehension and study skills.

- **The K-W-L-H technique** is a strategy that helps students to activate prior knowledge before reading and to ask questions that will promote engagement with reading material. Students first list what they *know* about the subject matter of the text; then, they record questions about what they *want* to learn. The students then read the text and look for answers to their questions. After the conclusion of the reading, the students discuss or record what they *learned* about the subject from reading and then list *how* they could learn more about the subject (for example, read other books about the topic, conduct a Web search to find more information).

In Phase Two of a SEM-R program, when teachers have conferences with struggling students, they should continue to use high-interest and personally challenging books, keep the conferences brief, focus on use of reading strategies, and provide specific feedback about reading performance. Short but frequent conferences help to promote reading as a valued activity, and teachers who provide regular feedback to struggling students about their reading also send a message about the value and importance of reading. Words of encouragement and regular feedback about their use of reading strategies can be powerful motivators for struggling readers. Increased levels of motivation to read may help the struggling student read independently for longer periods, which should be positively reinforced by teachers. Finding books for struggling readers can be difficult; however, school librarians and reading specialists can help locate suitable texts.

All three phases of a SEM-R program can be successfully used with struggling readers; however, some of the activities may have to be modified to meet their individual needs. During Phase Two, some students with similar patterns of reading difficulties may occasionally be grouped together in order to receive specific mini-lessons on print processing strategies or meaning processing strategies. However, these groups should not become the norm; conferences with individual students to provide differentiated instruction and encouragement are essential. Teachers can also support students who are not able to maintain independent reading throughout Phase Two by offering alternative activities (for example, audio books or computer programs that reinforce reading skills and strategies). Nonetheless, teachers should set a goal for the amount of time that students spend reading independently, which should be increased on a weekly basis for struggling readers. It is essential that the SEM-R teacher assess students with reading difficulties during each conference and, when appropriate, promote them to a higher reading level. Frequently increasing the difficulty of text encountered by struggling readers to just beyond their comfort zone will improve both their reading skills and their confidence.

Struggling readers may view reading as something to be endured, and in regular reading instruction, they often miss out on participating in more enjoyable activities because they are required to complete remedial work. It is important to offer choices for struggling readers during Phase Three because pursuing areas of interest related to the books they read can improve their motivation to read. Struggling readers can experience success by completing independent and small-group projects, although they may also benefit from participating in more structured activities such as readers theater or paired reading, which help them improve specific reading skills.

Students with reading problems may continue to experience difficulties despite the efforts of the SEM-R teacher. Teachers should consult a reading specialist for advice about additional strategies and resources; further assessment and support may be warranted in some cases.

Summary

This chapter has discussed the ways in which the SEM-R can help you to ensure that all of your students, from those who struggle in school to those who read several grade levels above their chronological grade, make continuous progress and continue to grow in reading. Also discussed were the ways to match readers with texts that challenge and engage them as well as specific strategies to help both talented and struggling readers work at appropriate levels of challenge. In the next chapter, we discuss the role of the SEM-R coach and how a coach can help teachers who may need support for one or more of the phases of the SEM-R.

The Role of the SEM-R Coach

As teachers implement a new instructional framework such as the SEM-R, questions inevitably arise about how best to make the strategies work within their own classroom and with their own students. For example, a teacher might ask herself, "How will I be sure to cover all the elements in the reading standards? How can I ask students challenging questions when they are reading a book I have not read? What kinds of reading strategies should I be teaching when I work with highly advanced readers? What kinds of options can I provide for Phase Three?" This guidebook is intended to answer some of these questions, but having the support of other collaborative professionals can be vital in helping teachers become more comfortable with new ideas and instructional strategies.

Literacy coaching is becoming an accepted model for support and professional development in reading education, and the idea of coaching has many applications within the SEM-R framework. This chapter explains the roles and responsibilities of a SEM-R coach.

A SEM-R coach is a professional in the school environment whose role is to support implementation of a SEM-R program by facilitating teachers' goal setting, classroom practice, and reflection. Coaches work with teachers during and outside instructional time to help them understand the framework, find answers to questions that arise during implementation, and develop activities and resources. Coaches are not supervisors or evaluators; rather, they are colleagues who can offer another perspective on classroom practice and assist in seeking resources and answers.

Recommendations for SEM-R coaching are grounded in more general strategies for literacy coaching as well as experience with the implementation of the SEM-R framework in a number of school settings. Following are some examples of a SEM-R coach's activities:

- Gathering a group of teachers together to discuss how the SEM-R relates to their current reading instruction

- Documenting alignment of the SEM-R program with district and state expectations in the area of reading

- Working with school administrators and librarians to find ways to add to the school's collections of books

- Modeling a book hook or a conference in a particular classroom, then following up with the teacher for a debriefing conversation

- Working collaboratively with teachers to plan Phase Two conferences and Phase Three activities to respond to a student with special needs

- Covering a SEM-R teacher's class to allow him to observe another colleague who is implementing the framework

- Helping teachers search for books to match the special interests or ability levels of some students

Our experience has demonstrated that a SEM-R coach can help to make implementation of a SEM-R program easier and more effective by supporting teachers as they develop their own sense of efficacy and by linking the SEM-R to the overall reading instruction program of the school.

Role of a Coach

Our research on the SEM-R demonstrates that the support of a coach can help you become more comfortable with the new ideas and instructional strategies that are embedded in this approach to reading. Indeed, this is the role of a coach as is explained in this chapter.

Who Is the SEM-R Coach?

A literacy coach is not the same as a reading specialist, although many literacy coaches are or have been reading specialists. The main distinction between the roles is the difference between the audiences they work with to facilitate reading. While reading specialists generally focus on helping students, providing small-group or individual instruction for struggling readers, literacy coaches focus primarily on supporting teachers (Toll, 2005).

A SEM-R coach's primary responsibility is to help teachers implement the program effectively; the coach does this by facilitating teacher goal setting and reflection, by modeling and discussing classroom activities, and by helping teachers to link the framework authentically into their existing repertoire of skills. The following research-based characteristics and skills (International Reading Association, 2004; Toll, 2005) are important ones for a SEM-R coach.

- Strong background and experience in teaching reading

- Comprehensive knowledge of the SEM-R

- Thorough knowledge of reading strategies, from foundational strategies to more advanced strategies for critical reading

- Understanding of the special needs of students with exceptionalities, including struggling readers and advanced readers

- Experience with facilitating discussions among groups of teachers

- Strong habits of reflection

- Ability to model goal setting and reflection

- Well-developed skills in observing classroom activities and problem solving related to classroom events

- Experience with providing feedback to colleagues in a collaborative manner that facilitates reflection and problem solving

Although the SEM-R coach will take on a leadership role in SEM-R implementation, the coach can also be someone who is just beginning to develop expertise in the SEM-R framework through professional development activities related to the program. The person who serves as the SEM-R coach in a school must have dedicated time within the school day assigned to the role, to allow classroom visits as well as meetings with teachers individually and in groups during planning time. In our research on the SEM-R, reading specialists, administrators, and gifted resource teachers have volunteered or been assigned to assume the role of SEM-R coach in their school.

Although most coaches will have other responsibilities beyond supporting the SEM-R program, it is important that the coach not have responsibility for supervising or evaluating the teachers who are implementing the SEM-R framework. While it is important for SEM-R coaches to spend time in classrooms, working with teachers and becoming familiar with their practices, that time should not be viewed by coach, teacher, or administrator as an evaluative experience. Having an evaluative role can limit development of the professional relationship needed for collaboration (Joyce & Showers, 1995; Toll, 2005).

Why Is a Coach Necessary?

Part of the reason for the genesis of the coaching model is the difficulty in converting skills presented in professional development workshops to changes in classroom practice. Professional development research has consistently demonstrated that without follow-up after new strategies are presented to teachers, classroom implementation tends to be limited (Joyce & Showers, 1995). The coaching model responds to this issue by having a professional support person who is knowledgeable about best practices in reading, well-versed in the new strategies that are being implemented, and able to assist teachers in changing their classroom practice. In-class coaching promotes the transfer of newly learned skills or ideas into classroom practice, in part because of the opportunity for coaches to guide teachers in recognizing the linkages between past practice and new strategies. Coaches also work to develop teachers' confidence and comfort with changes in practice. As teachers begin to try out a new program, coaching can provide validation of what the teachers are doing, as well as support and feedback in areas in which teachers might be struggling or unsure. During and following the implementation of new strategies, a teacher and coach can talk together about what worked, what could have gone better, and how to improve (Joyce & Showers, 1995; Toll, 2005).

Defining the Coach's Role

One of the difficulties related to the literacy coaching model is ambiguity in the definition of the coach's role. Dole (2004) discussed the many questions that persist in relation to literacy coaching, such as the issue of whether the coach should be working primarily with groups or individuals and the question of how much time should be spent in classrooms demonstrating lessons as opposed to co-teaching or observing. The literature on coaching has consistently highlighted the importance of establishing a clear understanding between coach and administration as to the nature of the coaching role, the expectations about how much time should be spent in various activities, and the importance of avoiding a supervisory role. The expectations for the roles of both the coach and the teacher must be clearly communicated among all involved, to promote relationships of trust and to clarify that the coach is not an evaluator (Toll, 2005).

Much of the previous discussion has highlighted the coach's work with individual teachers; however, a coach should also focus on working with groups of teachers, to foster professional learning communities centered on the teaching of reading. Coaches must recognize, however, that merely getting a group of teachers together to talk about their reading instruction does not necessarily foster a professional learning community. Rather, collaborative groups must be formed to explore specific questions and directions for reflection and growth, and coaches must work to recognize and respond to the different needs of teachers within a group and use their understanding of different individuals to facilitate productive conversation. One of the most effective ways in which coaches can support the implementation of best practices among a group of teachers is to provide opportunities for teachers to visit one another's classrooms to observe instruction. A coach may take a teacher's place in the classroom to provide release time for the observation visit, and the coach can facilitate the observation process by helping teachers determine who would be the best match for them to observe.

Getting Started with Coaching in a SEM-R Program

In a school that is planning to adopt the SEM-R across a diverse range of classrooms, a coach should be involved in the process from the beginning. As a group of teachers prepares to implement the SEM-R program, the coach can provide support and leadership while considering the following elements of professional development and logistical planning:

- **Understanding the SEM-R.** The coach must take the lead role in developing a thorough understanding of the SEM-R through such activities as careful reading of this guidebook, exploration of the SEM-R Web site (www.gifted .uconn.edu/semr), and participation in professional development activities.

- **Making linkages to the SEM-R.** Beyond understanding the model itself, the coach should also take the lead on aligning the SEM-R program with local expectations for reading instruction. This responsibility includes identifying elements in adopted textbooks or curricula that may transfer easily to the SEM-R classroom and recognizing how reading standards can be achieved within a SEM-R program through such elements as instruction during book hooks and Phase Two conferences.

- **Documenting how state and district standards will be addressed and integrated.** To clarify the connections between local expectations for reading instruction and the SEM-R program for all stakeholders, the coach may create written documentation that explains how reading standards will be addressed and assessed. Such a written document will help to alleviate any concerns of teachers, parents, or administrators about how the SEM-R framework fits within the larger picture of the school's reading goals.

- **Facilitating teachers' goal setting.** As teachers prepare to implement the SEM-R program, they should be purposeful and proactive about their own professional development by setting specific short-term and long-term goals for how they will enact the SEM-R framework in their own classroom. Careful goal setting helps to make a new program more manageable, and it also facilitates ongoing reflection on progress. An important responsibility of the literacy coach is facilitation of goal setting and reflection. Prior to beginning implementation of a SEM-R program, the coach should meet with teachers individually and in groups to review the framework, discuss questions, and develop goals. The coach should not dictate the teacher's goals. Rather, the coach may ask questions that help teachers to recognize their own areas of strength and interest and to determine what they will focus on as they begin implementation.

- **Collecting resources.** The coach should work collaboratively with administrators, media specialists, and classroom teachers to collect the resources needed to begin SEM-R implementation. This task includes helping teachers to assess their current classroom library in order to discover gaps in their book collection in terms of genres, topics, and levels of difficulty. The coach should also lead a discussion about the kinds of options that teachers would like to provide during Phase Three, to ensure that any necessary resources for Phase Three activities are available.

- **Communicating with parents.** Depending on the nature of a school's current reading program, a SEM-R program may represent a departure from the norm, and it is important that parents understand how the program works and how they can work in partnership with teachers to support their children's reading development at home. In a schoolwide implementation of a SEM-R program, coaches should take the lead in preparing letters to parents and, possibly, organizing parent meetings about the program and its implications for student learning in reading.

- **Developing relationships.** The effectiveness of the coaching model is grounded in collaborative, collegial relationships between coach and teachers. Before implementation even begins, coaches must be proactive about building those relationships and about establishing the routines to be followed during the SEM-R program.

Coaching During All SEM-R Phases

SEM-R coaches work with teachers throughout all aspects of implementation, and often their main areas of focus will be determined by what each teacher or group of teachers may identify as goals or areas of concern. However, there are some specific activities within each phase that coaches may wish to consider in planning their support role for a SEM-R program.

Coaching for Phase One

During Phase One, coaches may on occasion demonstrate how to lead a book hook by sharing one or more selections of their choice with students and providing some brief reading instruction as part of the process, as described in detail in Chapter Four. This process enables the coach to model book hooks for other teachers and also adds some variety to the students' listening experience and to their learning from the reading habits of others. If a teacher specifically requests that a coach watch his book hook and provide feedback, the coach may use this experience as a basis for a follow-up conversation with the teacher about Phase One activities, with a clear understanding that the observation will not take on an evaluative slant.

Another way that coaches can support teachers in Phase One is to talk about and model how best to incorporate targeted reading instruction in Phase One. Because coaches are often reading specialists or have a strong background in reading instruction, they can guide teachers in identifying their students' areas of need for strategy instruction and best practices to implement such instruction. For example, a coach may work with a teacher to select discussion questions to help assess students' predicting skills during a Phase One discussion. Or a coach and a teacher might work together to identify several reading selections that demonstrate the patterns that characterize a particular genre or tradition in literature. Further, because the coach works with teachers across a range of classrooms, she can facilitate sharing about what works in Phase One, including both instructional activities that are embedded in the read-alouds and particular book selections to make book hooks both educational and enjoyable.

Coaching for Phase Two

Phase Two is perhaps the most critical part of the SEM-R framework because it is the phase in which teachers provide differentiated and individualized instruction and foster one-on-one relationships with students that focus on reading. Coaches offer several kinds of support during this phase, including direct interaction with students, although it is critical for coaches to remain in a supporting role so that teachers can continue to learn their new role.

Coaches can hold conferences with students during Phase Two in order to model good practices as well as to assist teachers in instructing students of various levels of reading achievement and self-regulation. By conducting these conferences themselves, coaches can help adjust the teacher-student ratio more favorably and enable more students to participate in conferences on a regular schedule. This may prove particularly helpful in the first few weeks of implementation when SIR reading times may be short and both teacher and students are still adjusting to new instructional goals. As noted, though, coaches should primarily focus on supporting teachers in their professional development and appropriate implementation of the framework by modeling conferences and offering guidance to teachers on the conferencing process.

Several aspects of conferences that are more challenging and may require more coaching support include the length of conferences and the types of instruction provided, particularly to more advanced readers and other students with special needs. As discussed in Chapter Seven, conferences should be brief and efficient; yet our research has suggested that teachers are often tempted to conduct a longer conference with a given student, thereby reducing the total number of students who can have conferences, as well as the time certain students spend reading and developing their self-regulation skills. As coaches visit classrooms and notice the ways in which teachers interact with students, coaches should remain aware of issues, such as the length of conferences and which students are receiving more or less frequent conferences, so that they can help teachers to focus their attention on needed improvements. Our research suggests that direct observation of teachers' conferences followed by positive and constructive feedback is most beneficial in helping teachers improve their implementation of a SEM-R program.

A second area for coaches' attention during Phase Two is the guidance provided to readers with particular needs during conferences. Because the coach is likely to have a more comprehensive background in reading instruction, he should be able to guide teachers in recognizing the individual reading strategy needs among students, from students who struggle with fluency to students who have advanced fluency and comprehension in reading. Conferences are intended to provide a context for instruction in reading strategies and for encouraging and modeling critical thinking about the texts that students are reading. Often, teachers are well-prepared to provide individualized instruction in reading strategies and self-questioning for readers who tend to struggle. However, teachers may wrestle with how to provide appropriate levels of challenge for readers who are more advanced and do not seem to need specific guidance in standard decoding and comprehension strategies. Coaches can model conferences with advanced readers in order to encourage teachers to ask critical thinking questions and to challenge their advanced readers to take on books that are sufficiently difficult for them as well as to employ advanced skills in the use of reading strategies. Such modeling can help teachers in implementing similar conferencing strategies with other advanced students. Coaches can also work with teachers to use the SEM-R bookmarks to support critical thinking and to encourage the development of additional bookmarks that target specific skills for students.

One strategy for making coaching in Phase Two more effective is to ensure careful documentation of student progress during conferences. When teachers make notes in a student's reading log immediately following a conference, they provide both themselves and the coach with important information that can serve as a basis for discussion about individual students or about their class as a whole. Student logs can be used in later discussions to help teachers remind themselves of strategies that seemed particularly effective and questions that they raised in their own mind as they worked with students.

Coaching for Phase Three

Each phase of the SEM-R framework reflects the individual characteristics of teachers and the students in their classrooms, but none more so than Phase Three. The options provided by a teacher for choice and exploration during Phase Three mirror the particular interests of the teacher and of the students, as well as the teacher's management style and the classroom environment in general. Coaches can help teachers explore possibilities for Phase Three that will match their individual strengths and interests as well as those of the students. Coaches can also support implementation and facilitation of Phase Three options through modeling and goal-directed conversation that occurs during the other SEM-R phases. For example, if a student expressed an interest in a topic that was introduced in a book hook, the coach should be able to discuss options for pursuing that interest during Phase Three time. Coaches could also use modeling during conferences with students to discuss choices for follow-up activities and interests during Phase Three. In addition, a coach might support teachers' implementation of this phase by offering suggestions about how to organize classrooms for independent investigations.

Some SEM-R teachers, depending on their teaching background, may be less familiar than others with the idea of establishing investigation centers in the classroom and having multiple groups of students engaged in different kinds of activities at the same time. SEM-R coaches can assist teachers in developing ideas for Phase Three choices as well as managing those choices with students. This may involve finding resources online for students to access, organizing materials for a particular type of project or creative exploration, or even helping a teacher establish a system for selecting activities.

Depending on the size of a school, the interests of students, the scheduling of reading classes, and the organization of the SEM-R program within the overall schedule of the school day, teachers may wish to increase their Phase Three options by making all of their choices available simultaneously to students across multiple classrooms. This can be successful if all teachers implementing the SEM-R program decide to use at least an hour of SEM-R time on one day each week to offer Phase Three activities simultaneously. A group of teachers may choose to capitalize on their individual strengths by offering different options for students in different classrooms and allowing students to move among the classrooms to select their activities. Coaches can facilitate this scheme by organizing a time for teachers to meet and plan their range of Phase Three options and then by helping to coordinate the movement of students across classrooms. The coach may also bring particular interests of her own to share with students during Phase Three time and volunteer to work with a group of students who are pursuing a particular interest or activity. In this way, coaches can again help to reduce the teacher-to-student ratio and to provide students with different choices and perspectives on what they are learning.

Ongoing Professional Development and Classroom Support

Throughout the SEM-R implementation, coaches provide attention to organizational and material details, support and facilitate teachers' classroom practice and professional development, and guide collaborative efforts among teachers. It is recommended that coaches develop a consistent but flexible schedule that will allow them to interact with each SEM-R teacher during each phase on a regular basis but also to find regular times to respond to specific teachers' requests for in-class support or release time. In addition, coaches' work on a SEM-R program goes beyond their activities in specific classrooms. Within and beyond classrooms, our experiences suggest that SEM-R coaches' work usually involves some combination of the following activities:

- Direct instruction and interaction with students

- Modeling or co-teaching

- Supporting reflection and offering feedback to teachers

- Creating contexts for teacher interaction and collaboration

- Obtaining and developing support materials

- Serving as a primary liaison among teachers, administrators, and parents

This section will highlight some of the tasks that SEM-R coaches have been asked to do in addition to the time they spend working with specific teachers on the various SEM-R phases in particular classrooms.

Coaches serve as the primary contact persons for the SEM-R program, playing the role of liaison between teachers and administrators and between teachers and parents. They can communicate teachers' needs and concerns to the administration and request support in the form of planning time, materials, and so on. They provide ongoing information by communicating with parents about the SEM-R program and the school's progress in implementing it. Coaches can also work with both administrators and teachers to document the ways in which the SEM-R framework enables progress toward local goals for reading.

These efforts to promote communication reflect a larger central element in the work of a SEM-R coach: a focus on developing relationships. The first and most significant type of relationship consists of interactions between coaches and teachers. Coaches need to be proactive in their efforts to develop trusting relationships with teachers that focus on honest, open communication about classroom practice. Each teacher relationship will be different, and different teachers will want and need different kinds of support from the coach. The coach must consider carefully how to encourage, guide, and support each teacher, using each teacher's professional goals as a central focus of the relationship. Coaches must also actively explore how to foster collaborative relationships among teachers who are implementing the SEM-R framework.

Other important relationships that the coach can foster in order to facilitate SEM-R implementation include relationships with school librarians and media specialists as well as with local librarians, given that these individuals can provide invaluable support for implementation of the SEM-R program due to their knowledge of children's literature and access to books and other resources. Supporting students' needs in all phases of a SEM-R program also requires careful attention to students with special needs, so involvement of resource teachers in special education and gifted education is important to effective implementation. The coach can integrate these specialist teachers into the program to both support and work directly with students in all SEM-R phases. Finally, as noted earlier, coaches facilitate educators' relationships with parents and relationships between teachers and administrators as the SEM-R program is implemented.

Coaches also are scavengers of both books (of all types) and equipment (tape players, CD players, computers), always on the lookout for more resources that students can use. They also can support teachers by acquiring books in response to particular student needs; for example, if a certain genre or author inspires great interest in a given classroom, the coach can work to find additional books within that genre or by that author, within the school or in other schools in the district or by purchasing them with reserved funds that enable the school to invest in materials that will foster higher levels of student interest. Coaches can work to provide books at lower or higher levels of challenge as needed for individual students. Moreover, in cases in which individual students show a particular strength, interest, or need that is not met by the classroom library, coaches can seek out books that respond to these children's particular needs.

Assessment is a key element in any instructional program, and a SEM-R program integrates both formal assessment with instruments such as the Iowa Test of Basic Skills and Oral Reading Fluency tests, as well as the use of informal assessment conducted on an individualized level and on an ongoing basis. Coaches can assist with both formal and informal assessment in a number of ways. For example, a coach's assistance with fluency testing at the beginning and at the end of the SEM-R implementation eases the classroom teacher's burden of the time spent. More important, however, coaches can assist with ongoing assessment through the conferences they conduct with students and their subsequent discussions of these conferences with teachers. Coaches can assist teachers with the use of assessment information gleaned from conferences with students. Working collaboratively with groups of teachers, coaches can help with the interpretation of assessment data for instructional planning and with decision making about the ways in which student work in the SEM-R program can and should be used for grading purposes.

Finally, beyond their varied continuing efforts to support SEM-R implementation, coaches should also consider ways to celebrate and acknowledge the progress of teachers in implementing the SEM-R program. For example, increasing levels of student engagement and self-direction in reading might be highlighted. Good work can be acknowledged in several ways. For example, a teacher luncheon might be held during which teachers reflect on and celebrate progress toward goals. Progress might also be highlighted in a SEM-R newsletter sent to each classroom that features updates from individual teachers or articles about effective implementation of the SEM-R program. Several schoolwide reading events might be scheduled—for example, author visits or character costume days. Naturally, the teachers who are implementing the SEM-R program should also be involved in decisions about which combination of these events should be used to celebrate their success, but the coach can coordinate and facilitate these events and activities across classrooms and bring parents, students, and teachers together to celebrate the work that has been done.

Coaching in Action: Sample Situations

In the previous pages, we highlighted many roles and responsibilities of the SEM-R coach, including phase-specific activities as well as efforts related to more general support. In this section, a few concerns of teachers who are implementing a SEM-R program are highlighted, and each concern is followed by a discussion of how a SEM-R coach might respond.

Situation 1: *A group of teachers is interested in implementing a SEM-R program. The teachers are excited about the program, but they are concerned about the state standards in reading and whether their students will be prepared for the state tests if they participate in a SEM-R program. Teachers and administrators raise their concern with the coach both individually and in groups during meetings about planning a SEM-R implementation.*

To ease this concern and to facilitate communication and understanding among teachers, parents, and administrators, coaches can carefully review the existing expectations for reading and systematically align the SEM-R program with them. In most cases, many of the goals of a reading program can be met through use of the SEM-R framework, but the instruction will be different because of the individualized nature of the SEM-R format. For example, a SEM-R program does not incorporate formal guided reading in the same way that most other reading programs do, yet the individualized conferences provide a method that is intended to accomplish the same goals. Therefore, it is important for someone to review existing goals and objectives and demonstrate clearly how they will be met through SEM-R reading instruction. For example, one coach worked with teachers to develop bookmarks that specifically incorporated the types of questions that are on state tests; these bookmarks helped to demonstrate to teachers how they might incorporate the same skills within the SEM-R program that they used with other reading programs. As we have also discussed, the SEM-R program is not intended to be a complete language arts program; for example, spelling and writing activities are not an integral part of this approach to an enriched and differentiated experience in reading.

Some specific efforts that will enable a coach to respond to this situation are as follows:

- Carefully review SEM-R information and local or state reading standards to document alignment of goals and outcomes. Read the background information on the SEM-R that demonstrates evidence of student achievement in reading fluency and achievement (no difference or higher reading achievement in the SEM-R group when compared with a control group). Create a document that highlights the ways in which the SEM-R supports local expectations.

- Meet with administrators to clarify expectations about reading instruction and to document any specific expectations about time devoted to particular instructional activities and documentation of student progress. Provide administrators with materials that demonstrate the alignment of the SEM-R program with local reading goals.

- Meet with teachers (preferably with an administrator present) to assure teachers of administrative support for the SEM-R implementation. Clarify for all present the expectations for reading instruction within the school, and initiate a discussion of overall expectations and areas of flexibility.

- Meet with teachers to discuss in detail the alignment of the SEM-R program with other standards and expectations. Discuss scheduling and lesson planning at a macro level (that is, year or semester plans) and at a micro level. Consider developing a sample plan to cover one to two weeks of reading instruction, highlighting how other expectations are woven into the SEM-R program, as well as a sample course plan for a year or semester, demonstrating how to coordinate the SEM-R program with other reading and language emphases. Discuss how teachers might plan a continuum of assessment to chart and document student progress.

- Work with individuals or groups of teachers to develop materials that support local reading expectations within the SEM-R (e.g., bookmarks using specific types of questions, Phase Three writing or other creative activities that support specific objectives).

- Prepare a parent-friendly explanation of how the SEM-R program meets reading expectations and will support students with the types of skills needed for state testing.

Situation 2: *A coach senses, based on teacher comments and body language, that teachers are concerned that the coach is evaluating teachers' implementation of the SEM-R program. Some teachers appear to be uncomfortable while the coach is in the room.*

Teachers are often unaccustomed to observations that are not evaluative in nature, and they generally have had very limited opportunities to visit one another's classrooms. Therefore, a relationship that involves extensive time with another professional in the classroom may initially feel uncomfortable to teachers. For many teachers, it is not the norm to have someone in a resource role in the classroom who may also be available to give non-evaluative feedback about students' progress or lesson planning. In addition, because the SEM-R represents new learning that may be a departure from a teacher's previous practice, he or she may be uncomfortable having someone there to experience the initial trial and error process of a change in instruction and classroom organization and management. Therefore, a coach needs to be proactive, organized, and open about classroom visits and what they will involve, and the role of coach as non-evaluative support person must be consistently communicated by all who are involved.

When a coach enters a classroom, whether at the specific invitation of the teacher or through another arrangement such as a rotating visitation schedule, it is important for the coach to know why he is going into that classroom (Toll, 2005). In other words, purposeful classroom visits can help to clarify the coaching role and may lead to more productive interactions with teachers. Coaches and teachers together may develop important questions that will help to identify the purpose of a classroom visit, including an emphasis on how certain teaching practices will affect particular students or groups of students, the content and timing of the lesson, and how each of these interact with a variety of coaching strategies (Blachowicz, Obrochta, & Fogelberg, 2005). These questions or plans for classroom visits should be linked directly to the individual teacher's goals for professional growth related to SEM-R implementation, because these linkages help to give the teacher more control over the visit, creating greater comfort for the teacher. Following a classroom visit, purposeful debriefing is important, again with the emphasis on facilitating reflection through questioning.

The in-class portion of coaching might also include team teaching or leading small-group work, enabling the coach to gain a sense of what is happening in a classroom as a basis for facilitating feedback without specifically conducting an observation. During a classroom visit, a coach may also conduct a portion of the lesson while the classroom teacher observes (Joyce & Showers, 1995). Either way, observations should serve as a basis for reflection and conversation; feedback should be given in a way that encourages the teacher to reflect on her own practice with the coach as a facilitator of that reflection and a sounding board for asking further questions.

The following suggestions and considerations can help coaches make teachers feel more comfortable during SEM-R classroom visits.

- Reflect carefully, before discussing classroom visits with teachers, on what can be accomplished through spending time in the classroom and which coaching strategies you want to use as an individual coach. Also, prepare a flexible, general schedule for visiting all classrooms, with time and space for additional classroom visits as requested or needed.

- As part of a meeting or training session with teachers prior to implementation, include classroom visits on the agenda for discussion. Share what you consider to be the goals of these visits in general, including the critical issue of helping teachers reflect on progress and on their individual goals.

- Create and share a set of options for your role during classroom visits. These might include modeling a strategy within one of the phases, co-teaching, or making notes on a particular practice or activity identified by the teacher. Discuss the suggested schedule for classroom visits, emphasizing that even scheduled visits will be preceded by a conversation in which the teacher and the coach work together to identify the purpose for the visit and the format it will take. Explain that teachers may also request classroom visits.

- Share an additional option for teachers in which they can request to have their class covered while they go to observe another SEM-R teacher. Emphasize that these other observations should also be purposeful and goal-directed.

- Following the group meeting, plan individual meetings with each teacher to discuss goals and questions or concerns about classroom visits and the non-evaluative methods. Keep notes and reflect on each teacher's areas of concern, to facilitate appropriate responses on an individual level.

- When conducting initial classroom visits and follow-up discussions, encourage the teacher to take the lead in discussing and debriefing the time you spent in his classroom. Throughout the conversation, you should keep the focus on each teacher's goals and reflections on their implementation of the SEM-R program.

- Think about the ways you can provide specific feedback—for example, through questions and more direct comments over time. Be sure to offer praise as well as suggestions for growth.

- Make discussions about classroom visits a part of regular group meetings with the SEM-R teachers. Encourage teachers to talk about what they expect from classroom visits and to share their experiences with one another in ways that might be productive for group growth.

Situation 3: *A group of teachers consistently raises the concern with the coach that they do not have time to read all of the books that students are reading and that they are not sure how to conduct conferences without prior knowledge of the books.*

Many teachers are used to developing and using questions that are specifically tied to the whole-group novels or readings they have used in the past. The concern about conferences with unfamiliar books is particularly important because of a strong emphasis in reading instruction on having students refer specifically to the text in responding to questions. Without comprehensive knowledge of the book, teachers are often uncertain about how to conduct conferences and give differentiated instruction to their students. Prior to implementation of the SEM-R program, through informal conversations or in more formal workshops or meetings, coaches can try to ease this concern by discussing the types of general questions that can be asked about books. They can also offer a context and opportunity for practicing questioning skills with books that teachers have not read during professional development sessions. The bookmarks developed for the SEM-R program provide examples of the kinds of general questions that can be asked, and groups of teachers can work collaboratively to develop their own additional bookmarks. By encouraging teachers to work together and by facilitating contexts in which teachers can share their experiences after implementation begins, coaches can help to alleviate teachers' concern about questioning students about books that the teacher is not familiar with. Other suggestions for how to address this concern include the following:

- Incorporate practice conferences into initial SEM-R training sessions. Encourage teachers to bring children's books or other books they are reading to a training session, and have them role-play conferences with each other and debrief about how they selected questions to ask.

- Conduct a mini-workshop with teachers in which Phase Two questioning is the primary focus. Include time for teachers to identify types of questions to ask, to develop sample generic questions about books, and to discuss their concerns. Allow time for group problem solving or suggestions.

- Encourage all teachers to incorporate questioning in their individual SEM-R goals. As we noted previously, coaches should not set teachers' goals, but a general suggestion to the group to keep a focus on questioning would be appropriate.

- Build time for discussion about questioning into every group meeting of SEM-R teachers. Encourage teachers to discuss regularly what has worked and what has not and to pay attention to their questioning skills with unfamiliar books and with students with specific kinds of needs. Individual conferences are a core element of the SEM-R and should be an integral part of professional development throughout implementation.

Situation 4: *Several teachers in a school have raised concerns about how to implement Phase Three effectively, focusing their discussion on management issues. Teachers who generally have not had multiple activities occurring at once in a classroom are uncomfortable with getting Phase Three started and are uncertain about whether students will remain focused and engaged.*

The variety of activities that should occur during Phase Three can make a teacher uncomfortable if she has generally fostered a classroom environment that is centered more on teacher instruction and whole-group learning. Coaches can help teachers gain greater confidence in their Phase Three management by assisting them with planning and implementation. As a group, SEM-R teachers can review the Phase Three options suggested in this guidebook and brainstorm additional activities they want to offer, and individual teachers can subsequently select the ones that suit their particular style from this larger set of options. A coach may wish to create several sample Phase Three choices to share with teachers in a planning meeting or training. Or the coach may present a collection of options that range from easiest to implement to those that require greater amounts of planning or flexibility.

Coaches should work closely with the teachers who are most concerned about implementing Phase Three to classify different options based on the amount of supervision they would require and the space, materials, and preparation needed. After completing this classification, the teacher and coach can work together to plan a start-up set of options that involve minimal preparation, with perhaps only one option that requires extra supervision. Once these options have been implemented, a teacher can consider broadening the options or trying new ones that might be a little more ambitious in terms of preparation or student activity. Coaches should also encourage teachers who are concerned about Phase Three to select some aspect of Phase Three as a major goal for their own growth in SEM-R implementation.

Coaches can also facilitate discussion among teachers about Phase Three management strategies, including signals for quiet or for cleanup time, guidelines for students in selecting a Phase Three activity, methods of documenting student work in Phase Three, and classroom setup. Coaches should encourage teachers who have more experience with investigation centers and other strategies similar to those in Phase Three to share their experiences and perhaps some of their materials with teachers who are more uncertain.

Some specific strategies for discussing Phase Three concerns include the following:

- Encourage teachers to start small and remind them that the goal of Phase Three is to move gradually from teacher-directed, teacher-selected options to student-selected options as everyone gains the strategies and skills needed for independent learning. Identify a few Phase Three activities that teachers can implement with limited preparation and limited classroom busyness (for example, buddy reading, audio books, or Internet exploration). Encourage teachers to start their SEM-R implementation with just a few of these strategies and to build their bank of options for students over time.

- Identify and acquire ready-made materials and equipment that can support Phase Three, including listening centers for recorded books, bookmarked Web sites for student access, and resources such as plays for a readers' theater. Also, identify others in the school with specific interests and expertise who might be able to guide or work with teachers to plan a particular Phase Three exploration.

- Provide release time for teachers to observe one another's Phase Three activities, and follow up with discussion about effective management strategies and encouragement for engaging activities.

- Encourage teachers to work together to provide Phase Three options across classes that build on teachers' own strengths.

Summary

A SEM-R coach helps to ensure the success of the SEM-R program within a community of teachers by facilitating teachers' goal setting and professional growth, answering questions and serving as a resource in response to implementation challenges, and assisting with the logistics of implementation. The following key strategies for effective coaching summarize this chapter and can also serve as indicators of a high-quality SEM-R implementation:

- **Be supportive and encouraging, not evaluative.** The coach is not an evaluator but a facilitator of growth and reflection. Through a combination of affirming successful implementation efforts, working collaboratively to identify areas for growth, and pushing teachers to take on new challenges, coaches serve as a resource that supports teachers' professional progress.

- **Keep the focus on student learning and growth.** In conversations with teachers about their implementation of the SEM-R program, coaches should guide the discussion to focus on how and why students are reading and growing in their skills, and they should encourage teachers to explore evidence of that in the conferences they conduct and the conversations they have with students. In both group and individual meetings with teachers, coaches should use specific evidence of student work in reading as a basis for discussion about how the SEM-R is working in classrooms.

- **Help teachers to be goal-oriented about their work.** In addition to helping teachers examine evidence of student growth in relation to program objectives, coaches should facilitate discussion of how teachers' progress links to their own individually determined goals for growth. Coaches should not set teachers' goals for them; rather, they should facilitate the processes of goal setting and self-evaluation in regard to progress.

- **Provide opportunities for teachers to validate their own professional growth and judgment.** Teachers' concerns about whether they are implementing the framework appropriately may be alleviated by giving them opportunities to observe other teachers and to discuss what they are doing with one another. Coaches can provide these contexts by helping with release time and by organizing group meetings to discuss the progress of the SEM-R program. Furthermore, by reinforcing a clear focus on student learning, as described earlier, coaches can help teachers to recognize that their efforts are making a difference for students.

- **Define the role.** The coach's role should be clearly defined for the coach, as well as for administrators and teachers. The coach must engage in thoughtful reflection on the responsibilities of her role and communicate her own understanding of the role to teachers and to supervisors. Coaches should also encourage teachers to help in defining which support activities would be of greatest assistance to them.

- **Build trusting relationships.** The coach is a guide, a facilitator, and a liaison, all of which require emphasis on communication and trust. Coaches should actively promote purposeful communication among teachers about the program. In addition, coaches should work to be supportive, collaborative professionals whose arrival in the classroom is welcomed as an opportunity for interactive professional development and conversation.

- **Remember that the focus is on enjoying reading, taking on new challenges, and pursuing interests.** Coaches should help teachers to understand the connections between the goal of the SEM-R—to support enjoyment of challenging reading—and their own opportunities to enjoy professional growth and challenge.

In the next chapter, we introduce some ideas about how the SEM-R can be used in after-school settings, highlighting the creative ways in which this approach can be used in extensions of the regular school day.

The SEM-R Program in After-School and Other Settings

10

In this chapter, we review the many ways in which a SEM-R program can be implemented beyond the regular reading classroom. For example, many schools have implemented SEM-R after-school programs. For some schools, the after-school setting may be a practical option for SEM-R implementation because of conflicting curricular and administrative requirements during the school day. In some schools, the SEM-R program has been implemented as a separate literacy block for either struggling or talented readers to enhance the reading instruction already given in the school. Teachers in some schools that already use the SEM-R program during the school day might consider also offering it after school at a different time of year, for different grade levels, as an extension of the daily classroom practice, or with a different combination of students from the application of the framework during the school day. In this chapter, we also offer some final thoughts about the implementation of the SEM-R program in your school.

The SEM-R Program After School

The SEM-R program in the after-school setting follows the same basic structure as it does during the school day, with time allocated to each of the three phases and central emphases on reading for enjoyment, reading at challenging levels, and developing self-regulation. However, implementing a SEM-R program after school involves some logistical questions that differ somewhat from the school-day application, raising different kinds of challenges and opportunities. Also, because an after-school SEM-R program might meet less frequently than it would during the regular school day (that is, on fewer days per week), teachers must make instructional decisions about phase scheduling to ensure continuity for their students with the books they are reading.

Recruiting Students

Careful consideration and discussion must be given to the recruitment of students for an after-school SEM-R program. Although the framework is designed to support reading growth in any student who is capable of reading independently for at least a brief period, it is questionable whether an after-school SEM-R program is appropriate for a child who is a very reluctant reader or a child who may have difficulty continuing an academic program beyond the school day because of a need for physical movement or a change of activities. An after-school SEM-R program is probably best suited for students who already enjoy reading somewhat—at least, when they can choose what they read. The program is less effective if students do not want to be there. A SEM-R program after school is very appropriate for talented readers who may not be challenged by the reading instruction they receive during the day.

Schools have approached recruitment for SEM-R programs in a variety of ways. A school might choose to prepare an invitation letter to send home with all students at relevant grade levels, offering the option for students and parents to express interest in participating, and then have program staff select participants from the total group of respondents through a review or lottery process. In such a circumstance, the letter of invitation should clearly communicate that the program is not intended to be a remedial program or one for highly reluctant readers. A school also might choose to conduct a rolling recruitment strategy in which they begin by inviting students based on scores or inviting those who have been specifically recommended by their teacher and then broaden recruitment as space allows. Part of the determination of how recruitment should proceed is based on an understanding of the school community; in some schools, opening a program such as this might lead to a flood of interest and the need to establish a lottery or a waiting list. In other schools, a wide net might need to be cast in order to bring in enough students to make the program worthwhile to run.

Scheduling the Program

In planning an after-school SEM-R program, one of the first issues to be determined is program duration—the number of sessions per week, the length of each session, and the total number of weeks. Scheduling options for implementing a SEM-R program after school vary and depend largely on the resources available. Schools that have implemented a SEM-R program after school so far have generally scheduled sessions twice a week. A consideration in determining how many days per week to run the program is the issue of avoiding overload. Reading instruction is an expected part of every school day, so a five-day-a-week schedule for SEM-R programming works as part of regular reading time in school. However, a SEM-R program after school should have a greater feeling of something enjoyable, a treat, or a special enrichment experience that becomes more exciting if it is a little less frequent.

In our experience, after-school SEM-R programs generally run about seventy-five to ninety minutes per session. This length of time allows some flexibility in incorporating all three phases as well as key elements of an after-school program that might differ from those in a reading class, such as time for a snack or some movement activities. A ninety-minute session also allows Phase Two to be lengthy enough so that students can make good progress in their books each week, despite meeting on only two days.

The first pilot implementation of an after-school SEM-R program ran for six weeks, twice a week. This time frame allowed the students to become accustomed to the program, to begin to demonstrate some of the expected enjoyment and self-regulation, and to have opportunities for multiple reading conferences.

Some additional variables to consider in determining the schedule for an after-school SEM-R program are the following:

- Are other programs going to overlap with the SEM-R schedule in ways that will affect participation and attendance?

- What is the staffing budget, and how will compensation per session vary for different program lengths? Although volunteers can make significant contributions to an after-school SEM-R program, it is important to try to hire paid professional staff in order to ensure both consistency and strong instructional implementation.

- Will the program rely on volunteers from local colleges or high schools? If so, are there elements in the college or high school schedules that should be considered in scheduling dates for the SEM-R program?

Other scheduling issues may arise in the course of setting up and implementing the program. The box shows some possible scenarios and solutions.

Sample Program Scheduling Decisions

Scenario 1: The program will run on Mondays and Thursdays. One student interested in the program already has an after-school activity scheduled for Thursdays but could participate on Mondays. Can he participate one day a week instead of two?

Decision: No. Participation only one day a week is generally too inconsistent for the program to have any effect, and the student will have difficulty maintaining any continuity in what he is reading and in the relationships he is developing. (Note that this attendance decision for students differs from the guideline given for volunteers.)

Scenario 2: The program runs from 4:00 until 5:30 on Tuesdays and Thursdays. One student has a karate lesson on Thursdays at 5:30 and would have to leave at 5:15. Can he participate?

Decision: Yes. In this case, the staff decided to allow the student to participate because the program time missed would be relatively brief.

> **Scenario 3:** The program has been meeting for two weeks already, and one enrolled student has yet to attend. School records indicate that she has been out sick for those two weeks. Should she be removed and her spot given to another student?
>
> **Decision:** No. In general, the program was linked to the attendance policy of the school. If a child was in school on a given day, she should attend the after-school program; if a child was absent from school, the absence from the after-school program would not count against her.

Staffing

During the school day, teachers take primary responsibility for implementing the SEM-R program and use their expertise in reading instruction and instructional differentiation to support student growth. Because this expertise is necessary for an effective program, after-school SEM-R programs should also involve teachers as primary instructors and facilitators. Ideally, teachers would facilitate the program, and ideally, they would have some expertise in reading instruction; however, after-school programs also offer perfect opportunities to reduce the student-teacher ratio through the use of volunteers and support staff.

In addition to the teachers who facilitate the instructional portion of the program, larger programs that incorporate the SEM-R after school should also consider employing a coordinator to handle administrative and organizational tasks. A SEM-R after-school coordinator might be a teacher, administrator, or other employee of the district, or he might be someone hired from outside the district to administer the program. This person can be responsible for student recruitment, acquisition of materials, arrangements for snacks and transportation, and communication with parents. In addition, a coordinator can substitute for a teacher who might need to be away from the program on a given day, thereby preventing the program from having to be cancelled if the regular teacher is unavailable.

An after-school SEM-R program provides an ideal context for involving volunteers from the local community in a school-based activity. Volunteers help to reduce the child-adult ratio, which means that even though the program may only meet twice a week, each child can likely still have a conference every two to three sessions. Moreover, the reduced ratio and the involvement of multiple adults allows the program to have a focus on developing strong staff-student relationships, which is a key aspect of successful out-of-school-time programs (Hall, Yohalem, Tolman, & Wilson, 2003; Halpern, 2003). The two boxes show a simple ad for recruiting volunteers and a set of volunteer guidelines.

Sample Advertisement for Volunteers

Do you like working with kids? Do you love to read? Come volunteer in an after-school reading program for elementary and middle school students. Help classroom teachers in local schools work with kids to strengthen their enjoyment of reading and their understanding of what they read. We are looking for volunteers on Monday, Tuesday, and/or Thursday afternoons for about an hour and a half each visit, starting in mid-September and finishing in early December. We will provide training on the specific program activities before you begin, including tips on how to ask challenging questions about books and how to help kids choose books they might enjoy. Please contact Jane Doe at 415-555-5555 or janedoe@school.com if you are interested in volunteering.

Expectations for Volunteers

- Please be at the school when you say you will be there! The teachers and the kids are very excited that you are volunteering to help them, and they are depending on you to stick to your set schedule. If you cannot go to your school on your scheduled day, please e-mail or call Jane Doe as far in advance as possible so we can let your teacher know.
- If the school district has an early dismissal due to weather, the program is canceled for the day. Jane Doe will e-mail you to let you know of any closings, so please check your e-mail! You may also check the school districts' Web sites for information on school closings.
- Just a few reminders about visiting schools:
  - Please dress appropriately. You might be sitting on the floor, bending down, or otherwise moving around, and you don't want the kids to see more than your outer layer of clothes.
  - Make a conscious effort to watch your language while you are at the schools.
  - You are a pre-professional representing the university, so please remember to conduct yourself in a professional manner.
  - When you arrive at the school, please check in at the main office; checking in might involve signing in or wearing a name badge.
- Ideas *you* can contribute to our project:
  - If you have ideas for class activities, especially for Phase Three activities, please let us know!
  - The teacher you work with may ask you to do a book hook during Phase One. If you have a favorite book that you'd like to share, let your teacher know!

Implementing the Program

In general, the organization and presentation of the three SEM-R phases should follow the same pattern after school as during the school day. Sessions should begin with one or more book hooks and possibly some related discussion or instruction on a reading strategy, followed by time for supported independent reading, and conclude with choices of interest-based activities.

Planning for an after-school SEM-R program requires consideration of several resource questions. As we described in previous chapters, the program requires a large library of books as its primary resource and additional materials such as reading logs, CD players or tape players with headphones, computers with Internet access, and art supplies for some Phase Three activities. Schools may also want to consider providing a snack to begin the SEM-R session at the end of the school day.

Searching for Funding: Selected Resources

Afterschool Alliance: This advocacy organization works to raise awareness of the importance of after-school programming and to provide resources for programs. This site includes a page on funding and sustainability, with suggestions for how to search for funding and a database of funding sources.

http://www.afterschoolalliance.org

National After School Association: This organization accredits after-school programs and advertises itself as the leading professional association in the field. The Web site includes a resource page with links to information and funding sources.

http://www.naaweb.org

For information on local resources, refer to the lists of state affiliates on both of the Web sites in the above box. One of the recommendations from evaluations of after-school programs is to be sure that they are different from what kids experience during the school day (Hall, Yohalem, Tolman, & Wilson, 2003; Halpern, 2003). An after-school version of the SEM-R program should maintain the challenge and integrity of the framework but should be different from what students experience during their school-day reading class. After-school SEM-R programs also offer opportunities for flexible grouping, including cross-grade grouping, which allows students to share reading time with students from other grade levels and other classes with whom they may not normally interact during the school day.

Expanding the Vision

After-school settings represent a good context for implementing the SEM-R program in a way that thoroughly promotes enjoyment of reading and allows a little more flexibility than might be available during the school day, in terms of staffing, timing, and other aspects of implementation. After-school settings are by no means the only out-of-school-time options for SEM-R programming; schools also might consider whether a summer or Saturday SEM-R program might be feasible or whether a modified version of the program might be presented as a "lunch bunch" activity or an elective or enrichment class at the middle school level. The flexibility of the SEM-R framework allows it to be applied smoothly across a range of settings, and out-of-school time provides a special context for students' reading experiences to go beyond the school day. As Kathleen Norris wrote in *Hands Full of Living* (1931), "Just the knowledge that a good book is awaiting one at the end of a long day makes that day happier."

Appendix A
Sample SEM-R Bookmarks

Setting

In what way does the setting of this story relate to your life or to other books you have read?

Do you think the setting for this story was real or imaginary? Why?

How would the book change if the setting was 100 years in the future or 100 years in the past?

What details does the author provide about the setting that helps build the mood for the story?

Plot

Who is the antagonist of the book? How do you know?

What actions of one of the characters confused you?

How would the book be different if told from another character's point of view?

Does the protagonist force the antagonist to change? If so, why and how?

Describe the appearance of your favorite characters.

Character

Do any of the characters display the trait of honesty?

Were you surprised by the actions of any of the characters?

Describe a decision or choice made by one of the characters? Do you agree with this decision?

Who is the protagonist of the book? How do you know?

Illustrations

What media did the illustrator use? Did this help tell the story better?

Could the illustrations in the book tell the same story without the words? Why or why not?

What colors does the illustrator use to tell the story? Why might he or she have chosen these colors?

Biography

Why would an author write a biography about this individual?

What additional questions do you have about this person and his/her experience that this book did not answer?

How is this person's life different from your own? How is it similar?

What does the person about whom the biography is written value? Do you value similar things? Why or why not?

Theme: Power

Power can relate to personal/individual power, institutional power (in work or government), or spiritual power to believe in forces that are bigger than ourselves.

Do authors have power? What is the power of the pen?

Do you think that authors have responsibility to use their power to make positive changes? Why?

Does a person with personal or individual power have the right to use it for evil? Explain.

Does any character in this book use his/her power for good? Explain.

Fairy Tales

What other fairy tales does this story remind you of?

What is the problem in this fairy tale and how do you think it will be solved?

Are there characters in this fairy tale that remind you of characters in other stories? Who are they? What traits make them similar?

If you could play one of the characters in the movie version of this fairy tale, who would you be? Why?

Philosophy

Have you changed any of your ideas based on reading this book?

Does the author have a main point in this book? What is it?

Did the author try to persuade you to agree with his/her beliefs? If so, how?

What kind of support does the author give for his/her arguments?

How is the information the same or different from your own beliefs?

Nonfiction

Why might a nonfiction book have more than one author? Why is collaboration important in this type of writing?

What part of this book could the author have left out without changing your understanding of the topic?

Compare what you learned in this book with what you already knew or thought you knew about the topic.

What is one big question you still have after reading the book?

Make your own bookmark!

(Then leave it in the book to test your classmates.)

Book Title: _____

Author: _____

Easy Question: _____

_____

_____

Hard Question: _____

_____

_____

_____

Thought-Provoking Question: _____

_____

_____

_____

Make your own bookmark!

(Then leave it in the book to test your classmates.)

Book Title: _____

Author: _____

Easy Question: _____

_____

_____

Hard Question: _____

_____

_____

_____

Thought-Provoking Question: _____

_____

_____

_____

Make your own bookmark!

(Then leave it in the book to test your classmates.)

Book Title: _____

Author: _____

Easy Question: _____

_____

_____

Hard Question: _____

_____

_____

_____

Thought-Provoking Question: _____

_____

_____

_____

Appendix B
Reading Interest-a-Lyzer

READING INTEREST-A-LYZER

Based on the Interest-a-Lyzer by Joseph S. Renzulli

Name _____ Grade _____ Age _____

1. Are you currently reading a book for pleasure?   ❏ **Yes**   ❏ **No**

2. Do you ever read a book for pleasure?   ❏ **Yes**   ❏ **No**

3. When I read for pleasure, I pick the following (check all that apply):

❏ Novels or chapter books   ❏ History books   ❏ Picture books

❏ Newspapers   ❏ Sports books   ❏ Mystery books

❏ Poetry books   ❏ Fantasy books   ❏ Fiction books

❏ Cartoons or comic books   ❏ Science books   ❏ Biographies

❏ Humorous books   ❏ Scary books   ❏ Nonfiction books

❏ Magazines   ❏ Poetry books   Other:

4. **I am more likely to read a book for pleasure that**

❑ a teacher suggests   ❑ my friend suggests

❑ a librarian suggests   ❑ has won an award

❑ is by an author whose books I have   ❑ I just happened to see (hear about)
   read   in _____

5. **Three favorite books that I would take on a month-long trip are**

1. _____

2. _____

3. _____

6. **In the past week, I read for at least half an hour (30 minutes) on**

❑ No days   ❑ 1–2 days   ❑ 3–5 days   ❑ 6–7 days

7. **In the past month, I have read _____ for pleasure.**

❑ No books   ❑ 1 book   ❑ 2 books   ❑ 3 books   ❑ More than 3 books

8. **My favorite time to read for pleasure is:**

❑ Never   ❑ In the morning before school

❑ During school   ❑ During the midmorning

❑ Lunchtime   ❑ After school

❑ In the evening   ❑ Before falling asleep

❑ Whenever I can   ❑ _____

9. **When I read I like to** ❑ read one book ❑ read more than one book at a time

10. **I like to receive books as presents.**   ❑ **Yes**   ❑ **No**

11. **I have a <u>public</u> library card.**   ❑ **Yes**   ❑ **No**

12. **I borrow books from the <u>public</u> library:**

❑ Once a week   ❑ Twice a week   ❑ A couple of times a month

❑ Every few months   ❑ A few times a year   ❑ Hardly ever

❑ Never

13.   I borrow books from the <u>school</u> library:

❑ Once a week   ❑ Twice a week   ❑ A couple of times a month

❑ Every few months   ❑ A few times a year   ❑ Hardly ever

❑ Never

14.   The number of books I have at home is

❑ None   ❑ 0–9   ❑ 10–19

❑ 20–29   ❑ 30–50   ❑ More than 50

15.   If I could meet any literary character (for example, Hermione from *Harry Potter* or the dog from *Because of Winn-Dixie*), I would want to meet

_____

_____

16.   The last three books that I read are

1. _____
2. _____
3. _____

17.   I would like to read a book about

_____

Appendix C
Books for Young, Talented Readers

	Appropriate for Grades		Genre	Topic or Theme
	K–1	2–3		
**The Adventures of Sparrowboy* (Brian Pinkney, 1997) Sparrowboy takes on some of the characteristics of the superhero he admires by doing his own good deeds. The comic book features enhance the story.	●		Fiction, picture book	Bravery, heroes
The Best-Loved Doll (Rebecca Caudill, 1965, 1997) This sweet story of a girl's love for her doll is reminiscent of *The Velveteen Rabbit*. Both stories show readers the meaning of sacrifice in understandable terms.	●	●	Fiction, novel	Love, sacrifice
Clementine (Sara Pennypacker, 2006) The book is the first in a new series about Clementine, an amusing heroine reminiscent of Ramona Quimby who also gets into her fair share of trouble at school.	●	●	Fiction, novel	Humor, sense of identity
***Diary of a Spider* (Doreen Cronin, 2005) The reader gets a spider's eye view of the world from these journal entries. As in the 2003 book by Cronin, *Diary of a Worm*, the humorousness of the story may even convert nonreaders.	●		Fiction, picture book	Adventure, friendship
***Escape! The Story of the Great Houdini* (Sid Fleischman, 2006) This book is the biography of Houdini, a man of magic. It is set at the turn of the century, and readers will see how the life of this famous man coincided with important historical events.		●	Biography	Magic, science, history
Girl Wonder: A Baseball Story in Nine Innings (Deborah Hopkinson, 2003) This Parents' Choice Award winner tells the story of Alta Weiss, who proved that girls can play too. (Based on a true story)	●		Historical fiction, picture book	Equality, women's rights

The Hundred Dresses (Eleanor Estes, 1944) A class of girls learn compassion when they find out that their classmate did have a hundred dresses in her closet—each beautifully drawn.	●		Fiction, novel	Kindness, compassion, poverty
**I, Freddy* (Dietlof Reiche, 1998) Freddy, a golden hamster, writes the humorous autobiography of his brave life.		●	Fiction, novel	Fantasy, adventure
The Island of the Skog (Steven Kellogg, 1973) When mouse friends leave the city, they have to deal with the only island inhabitant—the skog! The mice must pull together to solve their problem and stay safe. Critical thinking and creative thinking are shown throughout this book.	●		Fiction	Cooperation, compromise
Joyful Noise: Poems for Two Voices (Paul Fleischman, 1989) This nature poetry was created for two readers. These poems are wonderful tools for introducing young students to the beauty of language and poetry. (Newbery Medal Winner, 1989)	●		Poetry	Nature
Magic Tree House Series (Mary Pope Osborne, 1992–present) Although the books in this series are repetitive, they are good for the younger reader because they encourage hypothetical thinking, which is usually not yet strongly developed in children of this age. The nonfiction series can be used to bridge the fantasy with informational reading about places, times, and cultures that Jack and Annie visit on their Magic Tree House adventures.	●		Fiction, nonfiction	Adventure, cooperation
The Mysterious Benedict Society (Trenton Lee Stewart, 2007) This story follows four gifted youngsters at the Learning Institute for the Very Enlightened as they face the ultimate test, one of bravery.		●	Fiction, novel	Friendship, giftedness, being different
The Mysterious Tadpole (Steven Kellogg, 1977) A gift gets out of hand when the tadpole that Louis's uncle sent him grows too big for Louis's bathtub, and he must really get creative if he wants to keep his pet.	●		Fiction, novel	Mystery, problem solving
The New Way Things Work (David Macaulay, 1998) This book is for the curious student. The author explains the workings of gadgets and technology, complete with rich descriptions, interesting comparisons, and clear illustrations.	●	●	Nonfiction	Engineering
Not One Damsel in Distress: World Folktales for Strong Girls (Jane Yolen, 2000) These fairy tales from around the world will inspire young readers.		●	Folktale, picture book	Equality, bravery
The Paper Bag Princess (Robert Munsch, 1980) In this fractured fairy tale, Elizabeth battles a dragon, rescues a prince, and learns her true worth.	●	●	Fiction, picture book	Bravery, equality

**Phineas Gage: A Gruesome But True Story About Brain Science (John Fleischman, 2002) This book tells the story of Phineas Gage, who was either a lucky or an unlucky man who didn't die when a railroad stake went through his skull. We continue to learn about the brain from Phineas, even though he has been gone for many years.		●	Nonfiction	Human body, amazing events
*Utterly Me, Clarice Bean (Lauren Child, 2002) First created for British readers, Clarice has traveled across the pond to delight a new audience. The author uses different-sized fonts and words swirled across the pages of this "diary" to illustrate Clarice's short attention span.		●	Fiction, novel	Humor, creativity

* These titles are especially appropriate for girls.
** These titles are especially appropriate for boys.

Appendix D
Template for
Sun/Cloud Card

Appendix E
Chart for Recording Growth in Reading Time

Watch Your Reading Time Grow!

Use the following chart to graph the number of minutes that you have read independently each day during SIR.

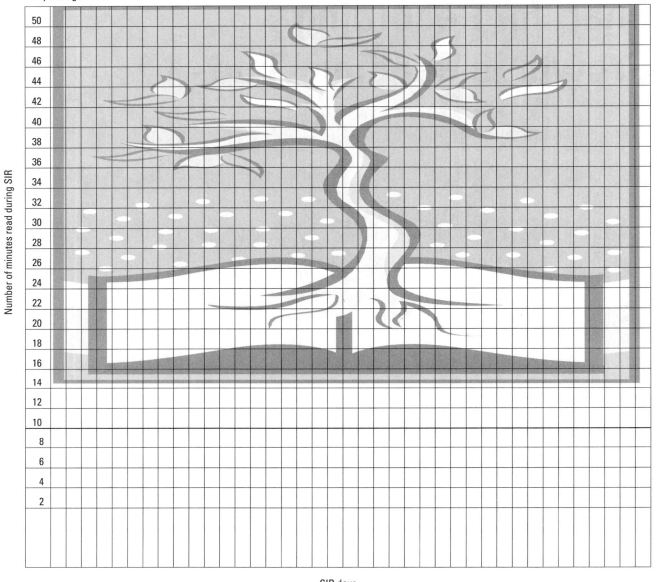

SIR days

Insert Date or Day of the Week in Last Row of Chart

Appendix F
Teacher Log: Sample and Template

Teacher: _Miss Shirley_   Dates: _Week One_

Weekly goal:
To develop a positive classroom climate and introduce SIR and the reading logs.

	PHASE ONE	PHASE TWO	PHASE THREE
MONDAY	Books: _Matilda_ Introduce other books by Roald Dahl	Student conferences with: Circulated to observe and encourage students	Choices offered: Entire class completed the Reading Interest-a-Lyzer
	No. of minutes = 20	No. of minutes = 15	No. of minutes = 15
TUESDAY	Books: _The Librarian of Basra_ Discussion of care and use of classroom library	Student conferences with: Worked with Carlos, Maria, and Jack to find books; circulated to observe and guide	Choices offered: Continue to read book Audio books Buddy read Renzulli Learning
	No. of minutes = 19	No. of minutes = 16	No. of minutes = 15
WEDNESDAY	Books: _It Looks Like Spilt Milk_ Discussion of metaphors & similes	Student conferences with: Yesica Milton	Choices offered: Creativity in Language Arts whole-class lesson followed by activity (Way Out Words)
	No. of minutes = 18	No. of minutes = 17	No. of minutes = 15
THURSDAY	Books: _Thank you, Mr. Falker_	Student conferences with: Pedro Julissa	Choices offered: Audio books Buddy read Renzulli Learning Creativity in Language Arts activity
	No. of minutes = 17	No. of minutes = 18	No. of minutes = 15
FRIDAY	Books: _Frindle_ Introduce other books by Andrew Clements	Student conferences with: Ami Tania Arman	Choices offered: Audio books Buddy read Renzulli Learning
	No. of minutes = 15	No. of minutes = 20	No. of minutes = 15

Weekly reflection:

I was surprised at how quickly my students got used to the idea of reading silently for an extended period of time. I expected that getting them settled would require much effort! When they started to lose interest on Thursday, I put a sticky note by the target stop time on the clock. It really helped to focus the most inattentive students.

What went well this week:

I am able to connect with students personally, and the bookmark questions are enabling me to ask conference questions even when I do not know the plot of the book.

What I will improve next week:

As I conference with individual students, I would like to bring their awareness to the text-to-self connections they are making, to improve their metacognitive skills.

Personal goal for next week:

Keeping conferences to five minutes

Goal for students for next week:

Get all students to understand a text-to-self connection and have my advanced readers understand the concept within the context of the conference

Teacher: _Miss Shirley_   Dates: _Week Six_

Weekly goal:
To increase student exposure to and comfort with the use of nonfiction materials

	PHASE ONE	PHASE TWO	PHASE THREE
MONDAY	Books: _The Rajah's Rice_ Guest reader: Principal Johnson No. of minutes = 10	Student conferences with: Arman Carmen Austin Jose Pedro No. of minutes = 30	Choices offered: Continue to read book Audio books Buddy read Renzulli Learning No. of minutes = 10
TUESDAY	Books: No. of minutes =	Student conferences with: _**Field trip to the Avonlea Public Library**_ _The librarian will provide a tour that focuses on nonfiction resources. Students may also get library cards._ No. of minutes =	Choices offered: No. of minutes =
WEDNESDAY	Books: _Good Queen Bess: The Story of Elizabeth I of England_ No. of minutes = 7	Student conferences with: Maria Juan Yesica Tamika Tyronne Ami No. of minutes = 33	Choices offered: Audio books Buddy read Renzulli Learning Readers' theater Investigation centers No. of minutes = 10
THURSDAY	Books: _Elephant Book: For the Elefriends Campaign_ No. of minutes = 10	Student conferences with: Carlos Milton Cheyann Emmanuel Marcus Tania No. of minutes = 34	Choices offered: Investigation centers Readers' theater Renzulli Learning Buddy read No. of minutes = 11
FRIDAY	Books: _The Cod's Tale_ No. of minutes = 5	Student conferences with: Julissa Mikayla Bobby Carlita Vanessa Jung No. of minutes = 35	Choices offered: Investigation centers Readers' theater Renzulli Learning Independent projects No. of minutes = 10

Weekly reflection:

Wow, what a busy and productive week! The kids seem re-energized by the principal's visit and the short trip to the library. Meeting the goal of exposing the students to nonfiction materials required a bit of work to collect interesting and challenging books, but I am pleased with the results. I think we'll continue the focus on nonfiction into next week.

What went well this week:

Providing students with choices in Phase Three. They really respond well to having interest-based choices.

What I will improve next week:

I want to be able to move more fluently between different Phase Three. options so that all students have some support from me.

Personal goal for next week:

I want to provide more freedom during Phase Three. and maintain a relaxed state of mind while students work independently.

Goal for students for next week:

Have all students be able to identify 3 to 5 questions for the current nonfiction book they are reading.

3 for readers who are below grade level

4 for readers who are on grade level

5 for advanced readers

Teacher: _Miss Shirley_ _____   Dates: _Week Twelve_

Weekly goal:

To provide more time for independent investigations

	PHASE ONE	PHASE TWO	PHASE THREE
MONDAY	Books: _Babe: The Gallant Pig_ _Introduce other Dick_ _King-Smith books_ No. of minutes = 10	Student conferences with: _Julissa Carmen_ _Arman Tyronne_ _Austin_ _Tamika_ _Pedro_ No. of minutes = 40	Choices offered: No. of minutes =
TUESDAY	Books: _1 story from More Stories to Solve_ No. of minutes = 5	Student conferences with: _Carlita Juan_ _Vanessa Maria_ _Tania_ _Emmanuel_ _Mikayla_ No. of minutes = 45	Choices offered: No. of minutes =
WEDNESDAY	Books: _The Great Brain_ _(student recommendation)_ No. of minutes = 5	Student conferences with: _Carlos Julissa_ _Jose Austin_ _Yesica_ _Milton_ _Jung_ _Ami_ No. of minutes = 45	Choices offered: No. of minutes =
THURSDAY	Books: _Chasing Vermeer_ No. of minutes = 10	Student conferences with: _Austin_ _Pedro_ _Tyronne_ _Carmen_ _Tamika_ _Carlita_ No. of minutes = 40	Choices offered: No. of minutes =
FRIDAY	Books: No. of minutes = 0	Student conferences with: No. of minutes = 0	Choices offered: _Investigation centers_ _Renzulli Learning_ _Independent projects_ _Buddy read_ _Independent reading_ No. of minutes = 50

Weekly reflection:

Everyone (including me) loved putting aside an entire day for Phase Three. I have been so impressed with Arman's research on important figures in African American history. After reading <u>Lives: Poems About Famous Americans,</u> he is planning to write a book of poetry, using the information that he has uncovered.

What went well this week:

My advanced readers are finally reading books that are challenging for them. This has been a process because they always wanted to read books that were too easy for them. This is a huge success!

What I will improve next week:

I want to continue to increase the complexity of student conferences by asking more open-ended questions and increasing student awareness of the strategies they utilize as readers.

Personal goal for next week:

I'm meeting with our librarian and the high school media specialist next week to try to find additional challenging interest-based books for my advanced readers.

Goal for students for next week:

Have all students identify the reading strategies they used as part of their conference—at least 2 strategies per student conference.

Teacher: _____   Dates: _____

Weekly goal:

	PHASE ONE	PHASE TWO	PHASE THREE
MONDAY	Books: No. of minutes =	Student conferences with: No. of minutes =	Choices offered: No. of minutes =
TUESDAY	Books: No. of minutes =	Student conferences with: No. of minutes =	Choices offered: No. of minutes =
WEDNESDAY	Books: No. of minutes =	Student conferences with: No. of minutes =	Choices offered: No. of minutes =
THURSDAY	Books: No. of minutes =	Student conferences with: No. of minutes =	Choices offered: No. of minutes =
FRIDAY	Books: No. of minutes =	Student conferences with: No. of minutes =	Choices offered: No. of minutes =

Weekly reflection:

What went well this week:

What I will improve next week:

Personal goal for next week:

Goal for students for next week:

Appendix G
Student Log: Sample and Template

Dates: ___September 18___ **through** ___September 22___

	Book Title		
MONDAY	*Surviving the Applewhites* *By Stephanie Tolan*	Pages read	166 – 186
		Minutes read	35
		Conf. Y/N	Y
TUESDAY	*Surviving the Applewhites* *By Stephanie Tolan*	Pages read	187 – 216
		Minutes read	35
		Conf. Y/N	N
WEDNESDAY	*City by David Macaulay*	Pages read	1 – 58
		Minutes read	40
		Conf. Y/N	N
THURSDAY	*City by David Macaulay*	Pages read	58 – 112
		Minutes read	40
		Conf. Y/N	N
FRIDAY	*Inkspell by Cornelia Funke*	Pages read	1 – 15
		Minutes read	20
		Conf. Y/N	Y

This week's writing prompt:

If you could change the behavior of any character, which one would you change? Why?

Reflection

At first when I started writing this, I thought that I would say that Jake in Surviving the Applewhites was the character whose behavior I would change. Now, however, I think his behavior was tied to the plot too much. After all, if he had never been as naughty as he was, like lighting fires and skipping school and stuff, then no one would have tried to help him. Instead, I wish that the father would have paid more attention to Jake because it really seemed like he needed a dad during lots of this story. He is the character that I would change to make him pay more attention to Jake. I think that if the author had done this Jake would have a better attitude for more of the story. This part of the story made me think about my relationship with my father. I am very grateful that my own father pays attention to me and I know how lucky I am. This book made me realize that all kids are not as fortunate as I am.

Conference Information

Date:	Book:	*Surviving the Applewhites*			
9/18	Did the student read aloud? Ⓨ/ N Is this book a good match? Ⓨ/ N				
	Conference focus: *Plot & character development*		Focus for next time: *Using inferences to describe aspects of the book*		
Length: *6 min*	Notes: *Alex will use sticky notes to mark areas of the book where he has questions about the plot.*				

Dates:_____ through _____

	Book Title		
MONDAY		Pages read	
		Minutes read	
		Conf. Y/N	
TUESDAY		Pages read	
		Minutes read	
		Conf. Y/N	
WEDNESDAY		Pages read	
		Minutes read	
		Conf. Y/N	
THURSDAY		Pages read	
		Minutes read	
		Conf. Y/N	
FRIDAY		Pages read	
		Minutes read	
		Conf. Y/N	
	This week's writing prompt:		

Reflection

_____

_____

_____

_____

_____

_____

_____

_____

_____

_____

_____

_____

_____

Conference Information

Date:	Book:	
	Did the student read aloud? Y / N	Is this book a good match? Y / N
	Conference focus:	Focus for next time:
Length:	Notes:	

Date:	Book:	
	Did the student read aloud? Y / N	Is this book a good match? Y / N
	Conference focus:	Focus for next time:
Length:	Notes:	

Date:	Book:	
	Did the student read aloud? Y / N	Is this book a good match? Y / N
	Conference focus:	Focus for next time:
Length:	Notes:	

References

ACT, Inc. (2006). *Reading between the lines: What the ACT reveals about college readiness in reading.* Iowa City, IA: Author.

Afflerbach, P., Pearson, P. D., & Paris, S. (2007). Skills and strategies: Their differences, their relationships, and why it matters. In K. Mokhtari & R. Sheorey (Eds.), *Reading strategies of first- and second-language learners* (pp. 11–24). Norwood, MA: Christopher-Gordon.

Afflerbach, P., Pearson, P. D., & Paris, S. (2008). Clarifying differences between reading skills and reading strategies. *The Reading Teacher, 61,* 364–373.

Anderson, R. C., Wilson, P. T., & Fielding, L. G. (1988). Growth in reading and how children spend their time outside of school. *Reading Research Quarterly, 23,* 285–305.

Biemiller, A. (2003). Vocabulary: Needed if more children are to read well. *Reading Psychology, 24,* 315–327.

Blachowicz, C. L. Z., Obrochta, C., & Fogelberg, E. (2005). Literacy coaching for change. *Educational Leadership, 62*(6), 55–58.

Burns, D. (1998). *The SEM directory of programs.* Storrs, CT: University of Connecticut, Neag Center for Gifted Education and Talent Development.

Chall, J. S., & Conard, S. S. (1991). *Should textbooks challenge students? The case for easier or harder textbooks.* New York: Teachers College Press.

Colangelo, N., Assouline, S. G., & Gross, M. U. M. (2004). *A nation deceived: How schools hold back America's brightest students* (Vol. 2). Iowa City, IA: Connie Belin & Jacqueline N. Blank International Center for Gifted Education and Talent Development.

Corbo, M. (1984). Research in learning style and reading: Implications for instruction. *Theory into Practice, 23,* 72–76.

Council for Exceptional Children. (2004). *Definition of a well-prepared special education teacher.* Retrieved February 23, 2008, from http://www.cec.sped.org/Content/NavigationMenu/PolicyAdvocacy/CECProfessionalPolicies/default.htm

Dole, J. A. (2004). The changing role of the reading specialist in school reform. *The Reading Teacher, 57,* 462–471.

Duke, N. K. (2000). For the rich it's richer: Print experiences offered to children in very low and very high-socioeconomic status first grade classrooms. *American Education Research Journal, 37,* 441–478.

Duke, N. K., & Pearson, P. D. (2002). Effective practices for developing reading comprehension. In A. E. Farstrup & S. J. Samuels (Eds.), *What research has to say about reading instruction* (3rd ed., pp. 205–242). Newark, DE: International Reading Association.

Education Trust. (2006a). *African American achievement in America.* Retrieved May 30, 2008, from http://www2.edtrust.org/NR/rdonlyres/9AB4AC88-7301-43FF-81A3-EB94807B917F/0/AfAmer_Achievement.pdf

Education Trust. (2006b). *Latino achievement in America.* Retrieved May 30, 2008, from http://www2.edtrust.org/NR/rdonlyres/7DC36C7E-EBBE-43BB-8392-CDC618E1F762/0/LatAchievEnglish.pdf

Fehrenbach, C. R. (1991). Gifted/average readers: Do they use the same reading strategies? *Gifted Child Quarterly, 35,* 125–127.

Field, G. (2007). *An experimental study using Renzulli Learning to investigate reading fluency and comprehension as well as social studies achievement.* Unpublished doctoral dissertation, University of Connecticut, Storrs.

Fogarty, E. A. (2006). *Teachers' use of differentiated reading strategy instruction for talented, average, and struggling readers in regular and SEM-R classrooms.* Unpublished doctoral dissertation, University of Connecticut, Storrs.

Forman, B. R., Francis, D. J., Fletcher, J. M., Schatschneider, C., & Mehta, P. (1998). The role of instruction in learning to read: Preventing reading failure in at-risk children. *Journal of Educational Psychology, 90,* 37–55.

Fountas, I., & Pinnell, G. S. (2001). *Guiding readers and writers grades 3–6: Teaching comprehension, genre, and content literacy.* Portsmouth, NH: Heinemann.

Fry, E. (2002). Readability versus leveling. *The Reading Teacher, 56,* 286–291.

Fuchs, L. S., Fuchs, D., Hosp, M. K., & Jenkins, J. R. (2001). Oral reading fluency as an indicator of reading competence: A theoretical, empirical, and historical analysis. *Scientific Studies of Reading, 5,* 239–256.

Gentry, M. L. (1999). *Promoting student achievement and exemplary classroom practices through cluster grouping: A research-based alternative to heterogeneous elementary classrooms* (RM99138). Storrs: The National Research Center on the Gifted and Talented, University of Connecticut.

Graves, M. F., Juel, C., & Graves, B. B. (2001). *Teaching reading in the 21st century* (4th ed.). Boston: Allyn & Bacon.

Greenberg, D., Gilbert, A., & Fredrick, L. (2006). Reading interest and behavior in middle school students in inner-city and rural settings. *Reading Horizons, 47,* 159–173.

Guthrie, J. T. (2004). Teaching for literacy engagement. *Journal of Literacy Research, 36,* 1–29.

Hall, G., Yohalem, N., Tolman, J., & Wilson, A. (2003). *How after-school programs can most effectively promote positive youth development as a support to academic achievement: A report commissioned by the Boston After-School for All Partnership.* Wellesley, MA: National Institute on Out-of-School Time.

Halpern, R. (2003). *Making play work: The promise of afterschool programs for low-income children.* New York: Teachers College Press.

Halsted, J. W. (1990). *Guiding the gifted reader.* Washington, DC: U.S. Department of Education, Office of Educational Research and Improvement. (ERIC Document Reproduction Service No. ED 321 486)

Halsted, J. W. (1994). *Some of my best friends are books: Guiding gifted readers from pre-school to high school.* Dayton, OH: Ohio Psychology Press.

Hart, B., & Risley, T. (2003). The early catastrophe. *American Educator, 27,* 6–9.

Harvey, S., & Goudvis, A. (2000). *Strategies that work: Teaching comprehension to enhance understanding.* Portland, ME: Stenhouse.

Hiebert, E. (1994). Reading Recovery in the United States: What difference does it make to an age cohort? *Educational Researcher, 23*(9), 15–25.

International Reading Association. (2004). *The role and qualifications of the reading coach in the United States: A position statement of the International Reading Association.* Newark, DE: Author. Retrieved November 15, 2006, from http://www.reading.org/downloads/positions/ps1065_reading_coach.pdf

International Reading Association & National Council of Teachers of English. (1996). *Standards for the English language arts.* Newark, DE: Author.

Joyce, B., & Showers, B. (1995). *Student achievement through staff development.* White Plains, NY: Longman.

Juel, C. (2005). The impact of early school experiences on initial reading. In D. Dickinson & S. Neuman (Eds.), *Handbook of early literacy research* (pp. 410–426). New York: Guilford Press.

Kaplan, S. (1999). Reading strategies for gifted readers. *Teaching for High Potential, 1*(2), 1–2.

Kaplan, S. (2001). An analysis of gifted education curriculum models. In F. A. Karnes & S. M. Beane (Eds.), *Methods and materials for teaching the gifted* (pp. 133–158). Waco, TX: Prufrock Press.

Keene, E., & Zimmerman, S. (1997). *Mosaic of thought.* Portsmouth, NH: Heinemann.

Kintsch, W., & Kintsch, E. (2005). Comprehension. In S. G. Paris and S. A. Stahl (Eds.), *Children's reading comprehension and assessment* (pp. 71–92). Mahwah, NJ: Lawrence Erlbaum Associates.

Kulik, J. A., & Kulik, C. L. C. (1991). Ability grouping and gifted students. In N. Colangelo & G. A. Davis (Eds.), *Handbook of gifted education* (pp. 179–196). Boston: Allyn & Bacon.

Learning Disabilities Association of America. (2001). Reading and Learning Disabilities: Position Paper of the Learning Disabilities Association of America. Retrieved December 8, 2008, from http://www.ldanatl.org/about/position/print_reading_learning.asp

Lewis, C. W., James, M., Hancock, S., & Hill-Jackson, V. (2008). Framing African American students' success and failure in urban settings. *Urban Education, 43,* 127–153.

McKenna, M. C., & Kear, D. J. (1990). Measuring attitude toward reading: A new tool for teachers. *Reading Teacher, 43*(9), 626–639.

McKenna, M., Kear, D., & Ellsworth, R. (1995). Children's attitudes toward reading: A national survey. *Reading Research Quarterly, 30,* 934–957.

MetaMetrics, Inc. (2004). *The Lexile Framework for Reading, FAQ.* Retrieved February 26, 2007, from http://www.lexile.com/DesktopDefault.aspx?view=ed&tabindex=6&tabid=18

National Assessment of Education Progress. (2002). *The 2002 nation's report card on reading.* Retrieved June 22, 2003, from the National Center for Education Statistics Web site at http://nces.ed.gov/nationsreportcard/reading/results2002/

National Association for Gifted Children. (1994). *Position paper: Differentiation of curriculum and instruction.* Retrieved February 23, 2008, from http://www.nagc.org/index.aspx?id=375

National Center for Education Statistics. (2007). *The nation's report card on reading 2007.* Retrieved May 29, 2008, from the National Center for Education Statistics Web site at http://nces.ed.gov/nationsreportcard/pdf/main2007/2007496.pdf

National Council of Teachers of English. (2004). *On reading, learning to read, and effective reading instruction: An overview of what we know and how we know it.* Urbana, IL: Author.

National Endowment for the Arts. (2004). *Reading at risk: A survey of literary reading in America* (Research Division Report No. 46). Washington, DC: Author.

National Endowment for the Arts. (2007). *To read or not to read: A question of national consequence* (Research Report No. 47). Washington, DC: Author.

National Institute of Child Health and Human Development. (2000). *Report of the National Reading Panel. Teaching children to read: An evidence-based assessment of the scientific research literature on reading and its implications for reading instruction* (NIHPublication No. 00-4769). Washington, DC: U.S. Government Printing Office.

National Reading Panel. (2000). *Teaching children to read: An evidence-based assessment of the scientific research literature on reading and its implications for reading instruction.* Washington, DC: Author.

Norris, K. T. (1931). *Hands full of living.* New York: Doubleday, Doran & Company, Inc.

Olenchak, F. R. (1988). The Schoolwide Enrichment Model in the elementary schools: A study of implementation stages and effects on educational excellence. In J. S. Renzulli (Ed.), *Technical report on research studies relating to the revolving door identification model* (2nd ed., pp. 201–247). Storrs: University of Connecticut, Bureau of Educational Research.

Olenchak, F. R., & Renzulli, J. S. (1989). The effectiveness of the Schoolwide Enrichment Model on selected aspects of elementary school change. *Gifted Child Quarterly, 33,* 36–46.

Paris, S. G. (2001). Developing readers. In R. F. Flippo (Ed.), *Reading researchers in search of common ground* (pp. 69–77). Newark, DE: International Reading Association.

Paris, S. G. (2004, July). *How to teach and assess reading comprehension.* Seminar conducted at the CIERA Summer Institute, Ann Arbor, MI.

Paris, S. G., & Jacobs, J. (1984). The benefits of informed instruction for children's reading awareness and comprehension skills. *Child Development, 55,* 2083–2093.

Perfetti, C. A. (1985). *Reading ability.* New York: Oxford University Press.

Pressley, M., El-Dinary, P. B., Gaskins, I., Schuder, T., Almasi, J., & Brown, R. (1992). Beyond direct explanation: Transactional instruction of reading comprehension strategies. *Elementary School Journal, 92,* 513–555.

RAND Labor and Population. (2005). *Children at risk: Consequences for school readiness and beyond.* Santa Monica, CA: Author.

The Reading Foundation. (2005). *Stages of language and reading development.* Retrieved March 7, 2007, from http://www.thereadingfoundation.com/stages.html

Reardon, S. F. (2008). *Differential growth in the Black-White achievement gap during elementary school among initially high- and low-scoring students.* Stanford, CA: Institute for Research on Education Policy and Practice at Stanford University.

Reis, S. M., & Boeve, H. (in press). How academically gifted elementary urban students respond to challenges in an enrichment reading program. *Journal for the Education of the Gifted.*

Reis, S. M., Burns, D. E., & Renzulli, J. S. (1992). *Curriculum compacting: The complete guide to modifying the regular curriculum for high ability students.* Mansfield Center, CT: Creative Learning Press.

Reis, S. M., Eckert, R. D., McCoach, D. B., Jacobs, J. K., & Coyne, M. (2008). Using enrichment reading to increase reading, fluency, comprehension, and attitudes. *Journal of Educational Research, 101,* 299–315.

Reis, S. M., Eckert, R. D., Schreiber, F. J., Jacobs, J., Briggs, C. J., Gubbins, E. J., Coyne, M., & Muller, L. (2005). *The Schoolwide Enrichment Model—Reading framework* (RM05214). Storrs: The National Research Center on the Gifted and Talented, University of Connecticut.

Reis, S. M., & Fogarty, E. A. (2006). Savoring reading, schoolwide. *Educational Leadership, 64*(2), 32–36.

Reis, S. M., Gubbins, E. J., Briggs, C. J., Schreiber, F. J., Richards, S., Jacobs, J., Eckert, R. D., & Renzulli, J. S. (2004). Reading instruction for talented readers: Case studies documenting few opportunities for continuous progress. *Gifted Child Quarterly, 48,* 309–338.

Reis, S. M., Hébert, T. P., Díaz, E. I., Maxfield, L. R., & Ratley, M. E. (1995). *Case studies of talented students who achieve and underachieve in an urban high school* (Research Monograph No. 95120). Storrs: University of Connecticut, National Research Center on the Gifted and Talented.

Reis, S. M., McCoach, D. B., Coyne, M., Schreiber, F. J., Eckert, R. D., & Gubbins, E. J. (2007). Using planned enrichment strategies with direct instruction to improve reading fluency and comprehension: An evidence-based study. *Elementary School Journal, 64,* 32–36.

Reis, S. M., Muller, L. M., Housand, A., Housand, B. C., Sweeny, S., & Fogarty, E. A. (2008). *The Schoolwide Enrichment Model–Reading project: Annual performance report.* Storrs: University of Connecticut, Neag Center for Gifted Education and Talent Development.

Reis, S. M., & Renzulli, J. S. (1989). Developing challenging programs for gifted readers. *Reading Instruction Journal, 32,* 44–57.

Reis, S. M., Westberg, K. L., Kulikowich, J., Caillard, F., Hébert, T., Plucker, J., Purcell, J. H., Rogers, J. B., & Smist, J. M. (1993). *Why not let high ability students start school in January?* (RM93106). Storrs, CT: The National Research Center on the Gifted and Talented, University of Connecticut.

Renzulli, J. S. (1977). The Enrichment Triad Model: A plan for developing defensible programs for the gifted and talented: II. *Gifted Child Quarterly, 21,* 227–233.

Renzulli, J. S. (1988). The multiple menu model for developing differentiated curriculum for the gifted and talented. *Gifted Child Quarterly, 32,* 298–309.

Renzulli, J. S., Callahan, C. M., Smith, L. S., Renzulli, M. J., & Ford, B. G. (2000). *New directions in creativity package.* Mansfield Center, CT: Creative Learning Press.

Renzulli, J. S., & Reis, S. M. (1985). *The Schoolwide Enrichment Model: A comprehensive plan for educational excellence.* Mansfield Center, CT: Creative Learning Press.

Renzulli, J. S., & Reis, S. M. (1994). Research related to the Schoolwide Enrichment Triad Model. *Gifted Child Quarterly, 38,* 7–20.

Renzulli, J. S., & Reis, S. M. (1997). *The Schoolwide Enrichment Model: A how-to guide for educational excellence* (2nd ed.). Mansfield Center, CT: Creative Learning Press.

Rogers, K. B. (1991). Grouping the gifted and talented: Questions and answers. *Roeper Review, 16*(1), 8–12.

Ross, P. O. (1993). *National excellence: A case for developing America's talent.* Washington, DC: U.S. Department of Education, Office of Educational Research and Improvement.

Scholastic, Inc. (2007). *Leveling resource guide.* Retrieved February 25, 2007, from http://content.scholastic.com/browse/article.jsp?id=4476

Siegle, D., & Reis, S. M. (1998). Gender differences in teacher and student perceptions of gifted students' ability and effort. *Gifted Child Quarterly, 42,* 39–47.

Slavin, R. E., & Madden, N. A. (1999). *Success for All: Roots and wings. Summary of research on achievement outcomes.* Baltimore: Center for Research on the Education of Students Placed at Risk.

Snow, C. E., Burns, S. M., & Griffin, P. (Eds.). (1998). *Preventing reading difficulties in young children.* Washington, DC: National Academy Press.

Stanovich, K. (1986). Matthew effects in reading: Some consequences of individual differences in the acquisition of literacy. *Reading Research Quarterly, 24,* 7–26.

Stanovich, K. E. (2000). *Progress in understanding reading: Scientific foundations and new frontiers.* New York: Guilford Press.

Stevenson, H. W., Lee, S., Chen, C., Stigler, J. W., Hsu, C., Kitamura, S., & Hatano, G. (1990). Contexts of achievement: A study of American, Chinese, and Japanese children. *Monographs of the Society for Research in Child Development, 55,* 1–116.

Suskind, R. (1995). *A hope in the unseen: An American odyssey from the inner city to the Ivy League.* New York: Random House.

Sweeny, S. M. (2008). *Successful implementation of differentiated reading conferences: Case studies of Schoolwide Enrichment Model–Reading classrooms.* Unpublished doctoral dissertation, University of Connecticut, Storrs.

Taylor, B., Frye, B., & Maruyama, G. (1990). Time spent reading and reading growth. *American Educational Research Journal, 27,* 351–362.

Toll, C. A. (2005). *The literacy coach's survival guide: Essential questions and practical answers.* Newark, DE: International Reading Association.

Tomlinson, C. A. (1995). *How to differentiate instruction in mixed-ability classrooms.* Alexandria, VA: Association for Supervision and Curriculum Development.

Tomlinson, C. A. (2000). Reconcilable differences? Standards-based teaching and differentiation. *Educational Leadership, 58*(1), 6–11.

Topping, K. J. (1995). *Paired reading, spelling and writing: The handbook for teachers and parents.* New York: Cassell.

Vygotsky, L. S. (1962). *Thought and language.* Cambridge, MA: MIT Press.

Walker, B. J. (1996). *Diagnostic teaching of reading: Techniques for instruction and assessment* (3rd ed.). Englewood Cliffs, NJ: Merrill.

Walker, B. J. (2000). *Diagnostic teaching of reading* (4th ed.). Columbus, OH: Merrill.

Walker, B. J. (2005). *Techniques for reading assessment and instruction.* Upper Saddle River, NJ: Pearson/Merrill Prentice Hall.

Wigfield, A. (1997). Children's motivations for reading and reading engagement. In J. T. Guthrie & A. Wigfield (Eds.), *Reading engagement: Motivating readers through integrated instruction* (pp. 14–33). Newark, DE: International Reading Association.

Wolf, M. (2007). *Proust and the squid: How the brain learns to read and the different brains that don't.* New York: HarperCollins.

Wyner, J. S., Bridgeland, J. M., & DiIulio, J. J. (2007). *Achievement trap: How America is failing millions of high-achieving students from lower-income families.* Washington, DC: Jack Kent Cooke Foundation.

Young, A. R., Bowers, P. G., & MacKinnon, G. E. (1996). Effects of prosodic modeling and repeated reading on poor readers' fluency and comprehension. *Applied Psycholinguistics, 17*(1), 59–84.

Zimmerman, B. J. (1989). A social cognitive view of self-regulated academic learning. *Journal of Educational Psychology, 81*(3), 329–339.

Zimmerman, B. J. (1990). Self-regulated learning and academic achievement: An overview. *Educational Psychology, 25,* 3–17.

Zimmerman, B. J. (2008). Investigating self-regulation and motivation: Historical background, methodological developments, and future prospects. *American Educational Research Journal, 45*(1), 166–183.

Index

A

Ability: effort and, 27–28; need for self-regulation and, 34–35

Academic background. *See* Prior knowledge

Academic success, 153

Acceleration, 37, 165

Access to books, 143

Accountability, 153

Accuracy, of reading, 50

Achievement gap, 153, 154

ACT college-entrance test, 22–23

Advanced readers: demographic changes and, 22; differences in, 24; effort-ability interaction in, 27–28

Adventures of Sparrowboy (Pinkney), 209

Affect, 27

Afflerbach, P., 40, 43

African American students, 22, 23, 25

Afterschool Alliance, 198

After-school programs, 193–198

Age-appropriate books, 93–94

Aliki, 73

Aliteracy, 157, 163

Almasi, J., 40

Alphabet, 48, 49, 67

American Library Association (ALA), 86

Anderson, R. C., 90

Anne of Green Gables (Montgomery), 55

Aptitudes, 24–25

Artistic modifications, 16

Artistic talents, 25; investigation centers and, 125; as product style, 31

Arts: book hook matches in, 73; personal interest in, 28, 29

Assessments: for book hook matches, 73; coaches' role in, 183; for comprehension, 51; in curriculum compacting, 37; of enjoyment for reading, 101–102; of fluency, 98–99; of personal interests, 39, 128–130; of Phase Three products, 128; of Phase Two conferences, 112; reading interest and, 20; of reading problems, 168; types of, 5

Assouline, S. G., 37

Athletics, 29

Attitude, toward reading: decline in, 5; non-differentiated classrooms and, 156; SEM-R research on, 18–19

Audience, 127

Audio books, 74, 83, 122, 157

Audiovisual products, 31

Auditory learning style, 30

Auditory processing, 168

Authors: as book hook resources, 83, 84; voice of, in writing, 76

Average readers, 155–157

Award-winning books: book hook resources for, 83, 85; in classroom libraries, 136

B

Balanced instruction, 47

Basal readers, 5, 9, 39, 46

Bathroom procedures, 106

Behavior management. *See* Classroom management

Behavioral self-regulation strategies, 33, 103

Best-Loved Doll (Caudill), 209

Biemiller , A., 49

Bilingual students, 7–8, 156

Biographies, 201

Birchbark House (Erdrich), 58

Blachowicz, C.L.Z., 186

Blume, J., 84

Book bins, 143, 147

Book chats, 71–72

Book clubs, 56, 165

Book hooks: choosing books for, 11, 70–71, 82–84; creating environment for, 70; definition of, vi; description of, 10; goals of, 69; for high-achieving students, 167; importance of, 65–66; integrating reading strategies in, 77; literacy advantages and, 66–68; making inferences in, 58; matching books to students in, 73–77, 137–142; planning for, 71–73; purpose of, 10–11; quality indicators for, 84–87; reading strategies in, 77; resources for, 82–84; student jobs related to, 149; transitions from, 147, 148; using themes in, 78–80; visualizing in, 57. *See also* Phase One, of SEM-R

Book introductions, 71–72

Book series, 136

Book shopping, 106

Book Wizard tool (Scholastic), 140

Bookmarks: benefits of, 77; description of, 11; examples of, 200–203; in Phase One of SEM-R, 77–78; for Phase Three activities, 123; in Phase Two of SEM-R, 100, 104; to promote self-regulation, 104; for questioning, 56; reading strategies in, 80–82; student jobs related to, 149; templates for, 78, 203

Bowers, P. G., 169

Brainstorming, 126

Bridgeland, J. M., 22, 23

Briggs, C. J., vi, 3, 8, 17, 22, 45, 138, 155, 156, 161, 164, 165, 166, 167

Brown, R., 40

Bud, Not Buddy (Curtis), 58–59

Buddy reading, 104, 122, 169

Bulletin of the Center for Children's Books, 86

Burns, D., 14

Burns, D. E., 37, 165

Burns, S. M., 46, 153, 156

Business, interest in, 29, 31

C

Caillard, F., 37, 38

Caldecott Medal, 83, 85

Callahan, C. M., 124

Caudill, R., 209

CD players, 122

Center for the Improvement of Early Reading Achievement (CIERA), 142

Centers, learning, 124–125

Chall, J. S., 16, 39, 161, 164

Chapter books, 136

Characters, in books: bookmark strategies for, 80–82, 200; visualizing of, 57–58

Chen, C., 34

Child, L., 211

Children's Book Council, 86

Choice, student. *See* Self-selected activities; Self-selected books

Chunking, 33, 169

CIERA (Center for the Improvement of Early Reading Achievement), 142

Classic books, 70–71, 136

Classroom libraries: for book hooks, 70; coaches' role in, 178, 183; creation of, 135–137, 157–161; organization of, 137–142; physical setup of, 142–144; student jobs in, 149

Classroom management: for book hooks, 70; coaches' help with, 188–190; to develop self-regulation, 104–112; differentiation of, 16; for student conferences, 145–147; of transitions, 147–150

Classroom visits, 176–177, 186, 187

Cleary, B., 84

Clementine (Pennypacker), 209

Cloze instruction, 169

Cluster groups, 36

Coaches. *See* Literacy coaches

Colangelo, N., 37

Collaboration: to develop self-regulation, 104, 108; in Phase Three activities, 122–123, 126–128

Color coding books, 138–141

Committee on the Prevention of Reading Difficulties in Young Children, 156

Complexity of content, 92–93

Comprehension, reading: assessment of, 51; benefits of, 99; definition of, 51; fluency's link to, 50–51, 98; importance of, 153; levels of, 51–52; during Phase One of SEM-R, 77–82; versus phonics, 45–46; in phonics approach, 46; requisites of, 50; signs of problems in, 168; strategies for, 51, 52–61, 98–101; in whole-language approach, 47

Conard, S. S., 16, 39, 161, 164

Concrete learning style, 30

Conferences. *See* Student conferences

Confusion, while reading, 107

Constructive criticism, 127

Content: book matches and, 157–161; of classroom library books, 138; complexity of, 92–93; differentiation of, 15, 41

Content areas: book hook choices in, 71; in Phase Three activities, 124–128; in themed book hooks, 79

Content-level acceleration, 37

Control, 41–43

Conversations, about reading: in book hook planning, 71–72; to match books to students, 160; need for, 43; in Phase Three activities, 122–123; during student conferences, 99–100

Cooney, B., 74

Corbo, M., 30

Coretta Scott King Award, 83, 85

Costumes, 76

Council for Exceptional Children, 41

Coyne, M., 3, 17, 138, 155, 165, 166

Creativity, 13, 123–124

Cronin, D., 209

Cultural differences: classroom libraries and, 136–137; implications of, 26–27; self-regulation and, 34

Curriculum: differentiation of, 35–42; pacing of, 42; role of SEM-R in, 8–9

Curriculum compacting: description of, 37–38; high-achieving readers and, 165

Curtis, C. P., 55, 58–59

D

Dahl, R., 71

Dark-Thirty: Southern Tales of the Supernatural (McKissack), 6

DEAR (Drop Everything and Read) program, 89

Decoding level of comprehension, 51, 60

Demographics, of students, 21–22

Desks, 143, 148

Determining importance, 55–56

Developmental Reading Assessment (DRA), 138–140

Developmentally appropriate practice, 47–52

Diary of a Spider (Cronin), 209

Díaz, E. I., 40, 164

Differentiated instruction: attitude toward reading and, 156; challenges of, 154; definition of, 15; dimensions of, 15–16; for high-achieving students, 163–167; instructional approaches to, 35–41; learning process in, 16; during Phase Two, 12, 95–102; professional support for, 41; purpose of, 15, 35; rationale for, 21–35, 36; for self-regulation, 35; in SEM-R program, 41–43; teachers' tasks in, 16–17

DiIulio, J. J., 22, 23

Directed reading-thinking activity, 170

Discipline. *See* Self-regulation

Discussion groups, 165

Distractions, 33, 34, 105–107

District standards, 177

Diversity, in classrooms: book matches and, 159–160; and classroom libraries, 136–137; demographic changes related to, 22; implications of, 26–27; teaching practices for, 154–155

DK Publishing, 83, 84

Dole, J. A., 176

DRA (Developmental Reading Assessment), 138–140

Drop Everything and Read (DEAR) program, 89

Duke, N. K., 40, 156

Dyslexia, 49

E

Early Childhood Longitudinal Study of Kindergarten Cohort, 25

Echo reading, 168–169

Eckert, R. D., 3, 8, 17, 22, 45, 138, 155, 156, 161, 164, 165, 166, 167

Education Trust, 23

Effort, student: ability and, 27–28; in curriculum compacting, 37–38

El-Dinary, P. B., 40

Elementary Reading Attitude Survey, 17

Elementary school students: appropriate subject matter for, 93; book recommendations for, 209–211; coding reading levels for, 138–140; current achievement of, 25; decreased reading engagement in, 5; emergence of phonics in, 48–49; phonics instruction for, 50; physical classroom arrangement for, 143; popular book hooks for, 74–75; SEM-R implementation in classrooms of, 150; SEM-R research on, 17

Ellsworth, R., 5

Emergent literacy, 67, 155

Encouragement, 127, 171, 190

Engagement, in reading: in book hook planning, 72–73; case studies on, 6–8; decline in, 5; definition of, 4; development of, 12; as function of Phase Three, 12–13; as goal of SEM-R, 20; importance of, 5; in Phase Two, 102; tips for increasing, 4–5

English proficiency, 156

Enrichment approach, to reading: classroom diversity and, 154; versus remedial model, 4; in Schoolwide Enrichment Model, 13–15

Enrichment Triad Model, 9–10, 13–15

Enthusiasm, for reading: in book hooks, 72–73; importance of, 27; Phase One book choices for, 70–71

Environment, classroom: to aid transitions, 145–147; for book hooks, 70; to develop self-regulation, 104–108; physical setup in, 142–144; student jobs related to, 149

Environmental self-regulation strategies: definition of, 103; description of, 33; in home, 34–35

Erdrich, L., 58

Escape! The Story of the Great Houdini (Fleischman), 209

Esperanza Rising (Ryan), 8

Estes, E., 210

Expectations, of students, 105

Explorations: description of, 124–128; in Phase Three activities, 117

Exposure, to books: book matches and, 159; in Enrichment Triad Model, 14; Phase One goals for, 10–11, 65–69, 73

Expression, reading with, 50

Expression styles, 31

External resources, 33

F

Fairy tales, 202

Favorite books, 137

Feedback, from coaches, 187

Fehrenbach, C. R., 156

Field, G., 129

Fielding, L. G., 90

Fine arts, 29

Fleischman, J., 211

Fleischman, P., 8, 210

Fleischman, S., 209

Fletcher, J. M., 23

Flexibility, in thinking, 123–124

Fluency: assessment of, 98–99; audio books for, 122; comprehension's link to, 50–51, 98; definition of, 50; effects of SEM-R on, 17–18; in high-achieving versus struggling readers, 45, 50; importance of, 50; instructional methods in, 50; metacognition and, 60, 99; need for, 45; in Phase Three activities, 122, 123; in Phase Two book selection, 92, 93; strategies to increase, 98–99, 169

Fogarty, E. A., 8, 17, 56

Fogelberg, E., 186

Ford, B. G., 124

Forethought, 110–111

Forman, B. R., 23

Fountas and Pinnell reading levels, 138–140

Fountas, I., 136, 138–140

Francis, D. J., 23

Fredrick, L., 5

Frustration, 111

Fry, E., 137

Frye, B., 90

Fuchs, D., 51

Fuchs, L. S., 51

Furniture, 143, 148

G

Gaskins, I., 40

Genre, of literature: book matches and, 157–161; in classroom libraries, 136; exposing students to, 73–74

Gentry, M. L., 36–37, 163, 164

Gifted and talented students. *See* High-achieving students

Gilbert, A., 5

Gioia, D., 23

Girl Wonder: A Baseball Story in Nine Innings (Hopkinson), 209

Goal setting/planning: coaches' facilitation of, 177; in curriculum compacting, 37; of high achievers, 35; to increase reading time, 109; to reduce distractions while reading, 108; in self-regulation phases, 111; as self-regulation strategies, 32, 34

Goudvis, A., 40, 51, 53

Grammatical markers, 46

Graves, B. B., 138

Graves, M. F., 138

Greenberg, D., 5

Griffin, P., 46, 153, 156

Gross, M.U.M., 37

Group roles, 123

Grouping students: to differentiate instruction, 36–37, 42; who are struggling, 171; who are talented readers, 163–164

Gubbins, E. J., 3, 8, 17, 22, 45, 138, 155, 156, 161, 164, 165, 166, 167

Guest readers, 76

Guided practice, 16

Guided reading, 50, 140

Guthrie, J. T., 4

H

Hall, G., 196, 198

Halpern, R., 198

Halsted, J. W., 45, 155

Hancock, S., 25

Hands Full of Living (Norris), 198

Hands-on/tactile learning style, 30, 31

Hart, B., 49, 67

Harvey, S., 40, 51, 53

Hatano, G., 34

Hébert, T., 37, 38, 40, 164

Hiebert, E., 23

High-achieving students: aliteracy and, 163; benefits of differentiation for, 39, 40, 154–155, 163–167; book selections for, 209–211; case study of, 161–163; characteristics of, 35; developmentally appropriate instruction for, 48–52; fluency of, 45, 50; grouping options for, 36; inference making by, 58; instructional needs of, 163–164; need for conversations with, 43; needs and characteristics of, 155–157; Phase Two book selection of, 91–95; questioning by, 56–57; traditional methods of teaching for, 161; word calling of, 60–61

The Higher Power of Lucky (Patron & Phelan), 100–101

High-interest books, 10–11

Hillary, E., 83

Hill-Jackson, V., 25

Historical fiction, 73, 85, 86

History, 29, 79

Holt, K. W., 59–60

Home environment, 66–68

Homework, 33, 34, 111

Hope in the Unseen (Suskind), 26

Hopkinson, D., 209

Horrible Joe series (Kline), 161

Hosp, M. K., 51

Housand, A., 17

Housand, B. C., 17

Hsu, C., 34

Humiliation, 39

The Hundred Dresses (Estes), 210

Hurst, C., 80, 86

I

I, Freddy (Reiche), 210

Illustrations: award for, 83, 85; book hook choices and, 71; book matches and, 160–161; bookmarks for, 201; importance of, 66

Independent activities. *See* Reading activities

Inferences, making: in bookmarks, 80–82; description of, 58–59

Inferential level of comprehension, 51–52

Instructional methods: in book hooks, 77; developmentally appropriate, 47–52; for different learning styles, 30; differentiation of, 35–43; for diverse classrooms, 154–155; for fluency development, 50; for high-achieving students, 163–164; during Phase One, 10–11; during Phase Two, 27–28, 96–105; quality indicators in, 51; role of SEM-R in, 8–9; for struggling readers, 167–171; student demographics and, 22; types of, 46–47; use of personal interests in, 28–29. *See also specific methods*

Interest, in reading. *See* Engagement, in reading

Interest-a-Lyzer assessment, 12, 73

International Reading Association, 41, 86, 89

Internet resources: for after-school programs, 198; to assess personal interests, 128–130; for book hooks, 83, 84, 86–87; for book leveling, 140, 142

Interruptions, 105–107

Investigations. *See* Explorations

Iowa Test of Basic Skills (ITBS), 17

Island of the Skog (Kellogg), 210

J

Jack Kent Cooke Foundation, 23

Jacobs, J., vi, 3, 8, 17, 22, 40, 45, 138, 155, 156, 161, 164, 165, 166, 167

Jacobs, J. K., 17

James, M., 25

Jenkins, J. R., 51

Jennings, C., 26

Jobs, classroom, 149

Journalism, 28

Journals, 56

Joyce, B., 175, 176, 186

Joyful Noise: Poetry for Two Voices (Fleischman), 8, 210

Joyful Reading Resource Kit, 124, 128

Juel, C., 49, 138

K

Kaplan, S., 45, 164, 167

Kear, D., 5, 17

Keene, E., 40, 51

Kellogg, S., 210

Kintsch, E., 51

Kintsch, W., 51

Kitamura, S., 34

Kline, S., 161

Kulik, C.L.C., 36, 164

Kulik, J. A., 36, 164

Kulikowich, J., 37, 38

K-W-L-H technique, 170

L

Language-rich environment, 66–68

Latino students, 22, 23

Learning: areas of difference in, 24–31; coaches' focus on, 190; communities of, 176–177; differentiation in, 16, 24; to read, 48–49; styles of, 29–30, 47

Learning Disabilities Association of America, 24

Learning disabled students: book selection by, 39; coaches' role with, 182–183; emergence of phonics in, 48–49; feelings of, 39; number of, 23–24

Lee, S., 34

Legislation, 22, 153

Lewis, C. W., 25

Lexile leveling system, 138–140, 142

Libraries: for after-school programs, 197; as book hook resources, 83; for Phase Three activities, 127

Listening skills: audio books for, 122; during book hook sessions, 10–11, 65, 66, 76

Literacy: balanced approach to, 47; home-school connections and, 66–68; learning to read as part of, 48–49

Literacy coaches: benefits of, 174; characteristics and skills of, 174–175; description of, 173; importance of, 175–176; ongoing support from, 181–184; versus reading specialists, 174; responsibilities of, 173–174; role of, 176–177, 190–191; during SEM-R phases, 178–181; as supervisors, 175

Literacy coaching: examples of, 184–189; implementation of, 177–178; quality indicators of, 190–191

Literature: in book hook planning, 73–74; book hook resources for, 82–84; for Phase Three activities, 122–123; in Phase Two book selection, 91–95; quality indicators of, 84–87; for talented readers, 164–165; versus basal readers, 46; in whole-language approach, 47

Literature circles, 122–123

Logos, 48

Low-achieving students. See Struggling readers

Low-income students, 22–23, 49

Low-level books, 57

M

MacKinnon, G. E., 169

Madden, N. A., 22

Magic Tree House Series (Osborne), 210

Main idea, 170

Making connections: bookmark questions for, 80–82; description of, 53–55

Maruyama, G., 90

Mathematics, 28

Maxfield, L. R., 40, 164

McCoach, D. B., 17

McKenna, M., 5, 17

McKissack, P., 6

Meaning processing, 168, 169–171

Media specialists, 182

Meetings, with teachers, 186, 187

Mehta, P., 23

Melville, H., 6

Memorizing information, 32

Metacognition: bookmarks for, 77–78; definition of, 53; description of, 60–61; in fluency, 60, 99; making connections and, 55; and Phase Two distractions, 107–108; as self-regulation strategy, 32

Mick Harte Was Here (Park), 102

Middle school students: adapting SEM-R for use with, 150–152; coding reading levels for, 138–140; decreased reading engagement in, 5; popular book hooks for, 74–75

Minority students, 22–23, 136. See also specific minority groups

Miss Rumphius (Cooney), 74

Moby Dick (Melville), 6

Monitoring learning. See Metacognition

Monster (Myers), 102

Montgomery, L. M., 55

Motivation to read: achievement and, 25; in after-school programs, 194; self-regulation strategies and, 33; of struggling readers, 171; sublevel books and, 164

Muller, L., 3, 17, 138, 155, 165, 166

Mummies Made in Egypt (Aliki), 73

Munsch, R., 210

Myers, W. D., 102

Mysterious Benedict Society (Stewart), 210

Mysterious Tadpole (Kellogg), 210

N

A Nation Deceived (Colangelo, Assouline, & Gross), 37

National After School Association, 198

National Assessment of Educational Progress (NAEP), 4, 23, 25

National Association for Gifted Children, 41

National Center for Education Statistics, 4

National Council for the Social Studies, 87

National Council of Teachers of English, 41, 46, 86–87

National Endowment for the Arts, 23, 40

National Excellence: A Case for Developing America's Talent (Ross), 154

National Institute of Child Health and Human Development (NICH), 24
National Reading Panel, 40, 50, 51, 68, 89–90, 153
National Science Teachers Association, 87
New Directions in Creativity Package (Renzulli, Callahan, Smith, Renzulli, & Ford), 124
The New Way Things Work (Macaulay), 210
Newbery Medal, 83, 85
No Child Left Behind (NCLB) legislation, 22
Norris, K. T., 198
Not One Damsel in Distress: World Folktales for Strong Girls (Yolen), 210
Notable Tradebooks for Young People, 87
Note taking, 145–146
Novel studies, 151

O

Objectives, in curriculum compacting, 37
Obrochta, C., 186
Off-task behavior, 104–112
Olenchak, F. R., 14
Optimal matches, 39–40
Optimal texts, 16
Oral projects, 31, 68
Oral reading analysis, 168
Organizing/transforming information, 32, 127
Originality, 123–124
Osborne, M. P., 210
Outstanding Science Trade Books for Children, 87

P

Pacing, 42
Paired reading, 169
Paper Bag Princess (Munsch), 210
Parents: and age-appropriate reading material, 93; benefits of reading aloud by, 65–66; coaches' communication with, 178; as guest readers, 76; literacy advantages and, 66–68; reading for enjoyment by, 68; self-regulation and, 34
Paris, S., 40, 43, 46, 51, 53, 165
Park, B., 102
Patron, S., 100–101
Paulsen, G., 84
Pearson, P. D., 40, 43
Pennypacker, S., 209
Perfetti, C. A., 50
Performance control, 111
Performing arts, 28
Personal interests: book hook resources and, 82; book hook selections and, 71; for book

matches, 73, 138, 157–161; coaches' role in, 180–181; development of, 73–74; for differentiated instruction, 38–40; Internet resources for, 128–130; in Phase Three activities, 116, 124–125; Phase Three significance of, 12–13; in Phase Two book selection, 94; in Phase Two enjoyment of reading, 102; of reluctant readers, 157; of struggling readers, 171; in Triad Enrichment Model, 15; use of, in instruction, 28–29
Personal self-regulation strategies, 32, 103
Phase One, of SEM-R: benefits of read-alouds in, 65–66; bookmarks in, 77–82; coaching in, 178–179; differentiated instruction in, 42–43; goals of, 68; grouping in, 42; home-school connection and, 66–68; implementation of, 69–80; literacy advantages and, 66–68; making inferences in, 58; processes in, 42–43; reading for enjoyment in, 69; for talented readers, 165; teachers' tasks in, 68–69; time allotment for, 150, 151; visualizing in, 57. *See also* Book hooks
Phase Three, of SEM-R: coaching in, 180–181; continuum of services in, 119–121; differentiated instruction in, 42–43; examples of, 117–119; grouping in, 42; implementation of, 119, 120, 188–189; processes in, 43; quality indicators of, 130; rationale for, 115–117; for talented readers, 166; teacher-directed activities in, 123–124; time allotment for, 150, 151; transition to, 149–150. *See also* Self-selected activities
Phase Two, of SEM-R: assessing reading enjoyment in, 101–102; book matches in, 91–95, 137–142, 158–159; coaching in, 179–180; description of, 90; differentiated instruction in, 42–43; goal of, 90; grouping in, 42; instructional methods in, 96–105; mini-lesson in, 90–91, 94–95, 109; processes in, 43; products in, 43; quality indicators in, 113; self-regulation in, 102–112; for struggling readers, 171; for talented readers, 165; time allotment for, 150, 151; transition to, 148–149. *See also* Student conferences
Phases, of SEM-R: overview of, 5, 9–13; transitions between, 147–150
Phelan, M., 100–101
Philosophy, 202
Phineas Gage: A Gruesome But True Story About Brain Science (Fleischman), 211
Phonemes, 46, 50
Phonemic awareness, 49, 50, 67–68

Phonics: age of emergence of, 48–49; versus comprehension, 45–46; in early language experiences, 68; importance of, 46, 50; instructional methods in, 46, 47; in Phase Two conferences, 97

Photography, 29

Picture books: in book hook matches, 74–75; in classroom libraries, 136; reading aloud from, 66

Pinkney, B., 209

Pinnell , G. S., 136, 138–140

Plot bookmarks, 78, 80–82, 200

Plucker, J., 37, 38

Poetry, 8

Polacco, P., 161

Poverty. *See* Low-income students

Praise, 127

Precocious readers, 166–167

Prediction skills, 170

Pre-reading activities, 122

Pressley, M., 40

Pretests, 37

Print processing, 168–169

Prior knowledge: book hook choices and, 71; book hook planning and, 72; book matches and, 138, 159; connecting text to, 53–55; description of, 26; literacy advantages and, 67; in Phase Three activities, 128; in reading comprehension levels, 52; in reading development, 155; strategies for struggling readers regarding, 170

Processes, 15, 42–43

Product styles, 31

Products: definition of, 43; differentiation of, 15–16; of Phase Three activities, 126–128; types of, 43. *See also* Reading activities

Professional development. *See* Literacy coaches

Professional learning communities, 176–177

Proximity to students, 104, 105

Publishers, 83, 84, 138

Pura Belpréacutee Award, 84, 85

Purcell, J. H., 37, 38

Purpose, for reading, 90–91

Q

Questioning: to clear confusion while reading, 107; for performance control, 111; during Phase One, 11, 77–82; in Phase Two book selection, 93, 99–100; in Phase Two conferences, 96–97, 100; Phase Two overview and, 12; as reading strategy, 56–57; for self-reflection, 111–112; use of bookmarks for, 77, 80–82

Questionnaires, 116

Questions, research, 126

Quiet study time, 34

R

RAND Labor and Population, 49

Random House, 83, 84

Ratley, M. E., 40, 164

Readability: assessment of, 98; book selection based on, 92–93; of classroom library books, 137–142; description of, 92

Read-alouds: to aid scaffolding, 69; benefits of, 65–66; to hook students, 10–11, 72; to identify reading problems, 168; during Phase Two conferences, 98, 99–100; in Type I enrichment, 14

Readers' theater, 169

Reading: definition of, 46; development of, 155–157; developmentally appropriate practices for teaching, 47–52; skills needed for, 46–47

Reading achievement: academic background and, 26; in curriculum compacting, 37–38; differences in, 24–26; differentiated instruction for, 35–41; and early literacy experiences, 67; importance of vocabulary to, 49; of low-income students, 22–23, 49; of minority students, 22–23; remedial programs and, 4; research on, 17–18; role of differentiation in, 21; school success's link to, 45; since NCLB legislation, 22

Reading activities: Phase Three function and, 12–13; Phrase Three options for, 121–130; self-selected types of, 12–13; in Triad Enrichment Model, 15. *See also* Products; Self-selected activities

Reading at Risk: A Survey of Literary Reading in America (National Endowment for the Arts), 23

Reading conferences. *See* Student conferences

Reading disability, 24

Reading folders, 149

Reading, for enjoyment: coaches' role in, 191; decrease in, 23; effect of basal readers on, 46; in high-achievers versus struggling readers, 45; importance of read-alouds in, 65–66; in parents, 68; in Phase One of SEM-R, 69; Phase Two assessment of, 101–102

Reading Interest-a-Lyzer form: blank copy of, 205–207; for book hook matches, 73; book hook resources and, 82; in Phase Three activity selection, 116; in Phase Two book selection, 94; purpose of, 12

Reading levels: assessment of, 98; book matches and, 157–161; of classroom library books, 137–142; in curriculum clumping, 37–38; grouping for, 36–37; questioning and, 57; for reading buddies, 122; selection of, 16–17; teachers' beliefs about, 47–48; in tiered reading instruction, 38

Reading specialists, 168, 171, 174

Reading time: in after-school program, 195–196; chart for tracking, 214–215; conference management tips regarding, 144–145, 147; development of self-regulation and, 103–104, 108–109; in elementary versus middle school classrooms, 150–151; in Phase One, 11

Reardon, S. F., 25

Recognition, of teachers, 183–184

Record keeping: reading time tracker for, 214–215; as self-regulation strategy, 32; of student conferences, 145–146, 180

Recruitment, for after-school programs, 194

Reiche, D., 210

Reis, S. M., 3, 4, 8, 13, 14, 15, 17, 22, 27, 37, 38, 40, 45, 116, 128, 138, 155, 156, 161, 164, 165, 166, 167

Relationship development, 178, 182–183, 191

Reluctant readers, 156–157

Remedial education, 4

Renzulli, J. S., 4, 8, 12, 13, 14, 15, 16, 22, 35, 37, 45, 69, 116, 124, 128, 156, 161, 164, 165, 166, 167

Renzulli Learning, 116, 128–130

Renzulli, M. J., 124

Repeated reading, 169

Repetition, 50

Research projects, 126–128

Rewards, self-regulation, 33

Richards, S., 8, 22, 45, 156, 161, 164, 166, 167

Risley, T., 49, 67

Rogers, J. B., 37, 38

Rogers, K. B., 36, 164

Role models: coaches as, 174–175, 180; during Phase Two book conferences, 100–101; for self-regulation, 33, 34; for visualizing, 57–58

Ross, P. O., 154

Routines, 105

Rowling, J. K., 84

Rubrics, 112

Ryan, P. M., 8

S

Sachar, L., 6

Scaffolding: in book hooks, 69; in phases of SEM-R, 12, 13, 90

Schatschneider, C., 23

Schedule, for after-school program, 194–196

Scholastic, 84, 140

Schoolwide Enrichment Model for Reading (SEM-R): background on, 13–17; case studies of, 6–8; components of, 9–10; description of, vi–vii, 3, 8–9; focus of, 4, 5, 116; foundation for, 4; goals of, 9–13, 20; implementation variety in, 21; overview of phases in, vi, 5, 9–13; positive effects of, 3–4, 5, 17–20; purpose of, v, 8; research on, 17–18; teachers' perceptions of, 18–20

Schoolwide Enrichment Model (SEM): definition of, 4; description of, 13–14, 116; development of, 13; effectiveness of, 14; research on, 14

Schreiber, F. J., 3, 8, 17, 22, 45, 138, 155, 156, 161, 164, 165, 166, 167

Schreiber, R., vi

Schuder, T., 40

Science: book hook matches in, 73; book hook resources for, 87; personal interest in, 29; themed book hooks for, 79–80

Scieszka, J., 65–66, 71–72, 73

Scott O'Dell Award, 85

Self-correcting, 98–99

Self-judgment, 112

Self-monitoring. *See* Metacognition

Self-observation, 112

Self-reaction, 112

Self-reflection, 111–112

Self-regulation: case study in, 110; categories of, 32–35; conference management tips regarding, 145; definition of, 31, 103; development of, 103–105; differentiation of, 35; importance of, 31, 32; methods of acquiring, 31, 32, 33–35; mini-lesson in, 109; Phase Two and, 28, 102–112; types of, 103

Self-selected activities: benefits of, 39; coaches' help with, 188–190; as component of Phase Three, 12–13, 117; for differentiated instruction, 38–39; implementation of Phase Three and, 119; Phase Three options for, 119–130; transition to, 149–150; in Triad Enrichment Model, 15. *See also* Phase Three, of SEM-R; Reading activities; *specific activities*

Self-selected books: book shopping and, 106; classroom library for, 70, 157–161; coaches' help with, 187–188; for differentiated learning, 37, 38–40; Phase One and, 9–10; Phase Three and, 12–13, 122–123; Phase Two and, 11–12, 91–95; readability of

Self-selected books (*continued*)
classroom library books and, 137–142;
recommendations for, 209–211; for
talented readers, 167; in Triad Enrichment
Model, 14

SEM. *See* Schoolwide Enrichment Model

Semantics, 46

SEM-R. *See* Schoolwide Enrichment Model
for Reading

SEM-Xplorations, 128

Setting bookmarks, 80–82, 200

SFA (Success for All) program, 22

Shanahan, T., 89

Showers, B., 175, 176, 186

Sideways Stories from Wayside School (Sachar),
6

Siegle, D., 27

Sight words, 46

Sign-out logs, 106

Silent reading: evidence of benefit from,
89–90; for fluency instruction, 50; to
identify reading problems, 168; as Phase
Three activity choice, 121–122; popular
books for, 74–75; popular programs for, 89;
self-regulation and, 103–112

Silverstein, S., 71

Skill-based instruction, 22

Slavin, R. E., 22

Smist, J. M., 37, 38

Smith, L., 71–72, 73

Smith, L. S., 124

Snippets, 11

Snow, C. E., 46, 153, 156

Social action, 29

Social issues: book matches for, 160; self-
regulation and, 35; in themed book
hooks, 79

Sound awareness. *See* Phonemic awareness

Spoken language, 67–68

Sports activities, 29

SQ3R strategy, 170

Squids Will Be Squids (Scieszka & Smith),
71–72

SSR (Sustained Silent Reading), 89

Staffing, of after-school programs, 196–197

Stamina, reading, 144–145

Standards, for learning, 177

Stanovich, K., 50, 156

State standards, 177

Stereotypes, in literature, 136

Stevenson, H. W., 34

Stewart, T. L., 210

Sticky notes, 56, 104, 107

Stigler, J. W., 34

*Stinky Cheese Man and Other Fairly Stupid
Tales* (Scieszka), 65–66

Storytelling, 72–73, 76

Strategies, reading: in book hooks, 77; of
high-achieving versus struggling readers,
156; in Phase Two book selection, 93; in
Phase Two conferences, 97–105. *See also
specific strategies*

Stretch breaks, 144

Struggling readers: adult outcomes for, 23;
audio books for, 122; benefits of SEM-R to,
154–155; common problems of, 167–171;
conference time allotment for, 146–147;
demographic changes and, 22; developmentally appropriate instruction for, 48–52;
effort-ability interaction in, 28; emergence
of phonics in, 49; emotions of, 39; fluency of, 45, 50; inference making by, 58;
instructional methods for, 167–171; lack
of challenge for, 39–40; lack of questioning
by, 56, 57; metacognition and, 60; needs
and characteristics of, 155–157; Phase Two
book selection of, 91–95; Phase Two enjoyment of reading for, 102; typical strategies
taught to, 40–41, 43

Student conferences: assessment of, 112;
benefits of, 40; coaches' help with,
187–188; coaches' role in, 179–180, 183;
description of, 28; to help with book
selection, 11–12, 157–161; implementation of, 95–102; importance of, 90; interruptions during, 106; management tips for,
144–147; questioning during, 56–57; with
struggling readers, 171; and student-text
readability match, 137–142; summarizing
during, 59–60; for talented students, 165.
See also Phase Two, of SEM-R

Student logs: management of, 145; for Phase
Two conferences, 95–96, 97; template and
sample of, 227–223; in transitions, 149

Students. *See specific types*

Study skills, 32–35

Success for All (SFA) program, 22

Summarizing, 59–60

Sun/cloud cards, 104–105, 213–214

Supported independent reading (SIR): basis
of, 91; book selection for, 91–95; classroom library book matches for, 137–142;
coaches' role in, 179–180; conference management tips for, 144–147; description of,
11–12; goal of, 99; as Phase Three activity
choice, 121–122; planning for, 102–103;
quality indicators in, 113; research evidence
in support of, 89–90; self-regulation and,

103–112; time allotment for, 151; transition to, 148–149
Supported struggle, 155
Suskind, R., 26
Sustained Silent Reading (SSR), 89
Sweeny, S., 17, 41
Symbols, 48, 67
Synthesizing: bookmarks for, 78, 80–82; description of, 59–60

T
Talented readers. *See* High-achieving students
Talents, 25
Tally systems, 108
Taylor, B., 90
Teacher logs, 145, 217–225
Teacher-directed activities, 123–124
Teachers: in after-school programs, 196; beliefs of, about reading levels, 47–48; central tasks of, 16–17; coaches as supervisors of, 175; coaches' support of, 181–182; common questions of, 173; differentiation of, 16, 42; goals of, 177, 190; influence of prior teaching experiences on, 47; in learning of self-regulation, 33–34; location in classroom environment, 142–143, 145; perceptions of SEM-R by, 18–20; Phase One tasks of, 68–69; Phase Three quality indicators of, 130; recognition of, 183–184; role of, in explorations, 127–128; as think-aloud models, 100–101
Technology: for high-achieving students, 167; as product style, 31; student interest in, 29
Television viewing, 23
Text-to-self connections: bookmark questions for, 80–82; description of, 53–54
Text-to-text connections, 54–55
Text-to-world connections, 55, 80–82
Theme: in book hooks, 78–80; bookmarks for, 201; determining, 56
Think alouds, 100–101
Thinking skills: book hook planning and, 76–77; bookmarks for, 77–78; in Phase Two book selection, 93; in Phase Two conferences, 100; in reading development, 155; in Type II enrichment, 14
Tiered reading instruction, 38
Time Warp Trio series (Scieszka), 65
To Read or Not to Read (National Endowment for the Arts), 23
Toll, C. A., 174, 175, 176, 186
Tolman, J., 196, 198
Tomlinson, C. A., 15, 35
Topping, K. J., 169

Transitions, between phases, 147–150
Triple read outline, 170
Tut, Tut (Scieszka & Smith), 73
Type I–III enrichment, 14, 69

U
Urban schools, 25, 26
U.S. Department of Education, 23–24
Utterly Me, Clarice Bean (Child), 211

V
Visual errors, 168
Visual learning style, 30
Visualizing, 57–58
Vocabulary: importance of, 46, 49; in process of learning to read, 49; questioning and, 57; as requisite for comprehension, 50; of students with literacy advantages, 67
Volunteers, 195–197
Voting, 23
Vygotsky, L. S., 16, 155

W
Walker, B. J., 155, 168, 169
The Watsons Go to Birmingham—1963 (Curtis), 55
Westberg, K. L., 37, 38
When Zachary Beaver Came to Town (Holt), 59–90
Whole-language approach, 47
Wigfield, A., 5
Wilson, A., 196, 198
Wilson, P. T., 90
Wizard Project Maker (Renzulli Learning), 130
Wolf, M., 46, 50
Word callers, 60–61
Word walls, 169
Word-reading level. *See* Readability
Worksheets, 46–47
World knowledge, 55
Writing: in middle school SEM-R, 151–152; personal interest in, 28; as product style, 31
Written/verbal rehearsing, 32
Wyner, J. S., 22, 23

Y
Yohalem, N., 196, 198
Yolen, J., 210
Young, A. R., 169
Young Adult Library Services Association, 86

Z
Zimmerman, B. J., 31, 32, 33, 53, 103, 110
Zimmerman, S., 40, 51
Zone of proximal development, 16–17, 155

About the DVD

Joyful Reading for All Children

The DVD *Joyful Reading for All Children* describes the three phases of the Schoolwide Enrichment Model for Reading (SEM-R) and gives examples of how the SEM-R program can be implemented in a regular classroom.

The DVD presents a fifteen-minute overview of the SEM-R program and includes the following parts:

Introduction

Phase One: Book Hooks

Phase Two: Supported Independent Reading

Phase Three: Student Self-Choice Activities

How to Use the DVD

System Requirements

PC with Microsoft Windows 98 or later

Mac with Apple OS version 10 or later

You will also need:

Quicktime 7.0 or later (available at www.apple.com)

Adobe Acrobat Reader 8.0 or later (available at www.adobe.com)

Using the DVD

1. Insert the DVD into your computer's DVD drive. (Note: this DVD is NOT designed to work in a DVD player, such as the one that hooks up to your television.)

2. If you are using a PC, the DVD should automatically begin to run and give you the option of viewing the videos. You MUST have Quicktime to view the videos. If the DVD does immediately begin to run, go to "My Computer" and double-click on your computer's DVD drive. The DVD should begin to run.

3. If you are working on a Mac, click the DVD icon that appears on your desktop. Then click the "JB" icon that appears in the window that opens. The DVD should begin to run and give you the option of viewing the videos.

In Case of Trouble

If you experience difficulty using the DVD, please follow these steps:

1. Make sure your hardware and systems configurations conform to the systems requirements noted under "System Requirements" above.

2. Review the installation procedure for your type of hardware and operating system.

To speak with someone in Product Technical Support, call 800-762-2974 or 317-572-3994 M–F 8:30 A.M.–5:00 P.M. EST. You can also get support and contact Product Technical Support through our Web site at www.wiley.com/techsupport.

Before calling or writing, please have the following information available:

- Type of computer and operating system
- Any error messages displayed
- Complete description of the problem.

It is best if you are sitting at your computer when making the call.